A-Z SOUTHAMPTON

C000261201

Key to Map Pages	2-3
Large Scale City Centre	4-5
Map Pages	6-55

REFERENCE

Motorway	M27
A Road	A33
B Road	B3033
Dual Carriageway	
One-way Street Traffic flow on A Roads is also indicated by a heavy line on the driver's left.	
Road Under Construction Opening dates are correct at the time of publication.	
Proposed Road	
Restricted Access	
Pedestrianized Road	
Track / Footpath	
Residential Walkway	
Railway	Level Crossing Station Tunnel
Built-up Area	MILL ST.
Local Authority Boundary	
National Park Boundary	
Post Town Boundary	
Postcode Boundary (within Post Town)	
Map Continuation	40 Large Scale City Centre 4

Airport	✈
Berth Number	102
Car Park (selected)	P
Church or Chapel	†
Cycleway (selected)	
Dock Gate Number	⑤
Fire Station	■
Hospital	H
House Numbers (A & B Roads only)	37 44
Information Centre	𝒊
National Grid Reference	445
Police Station	▲
Post Office	★
Safety Camera with Speed Limit Fixed cameras and long term road works cameras. Symbols do not indicate camera direction.	30
Toilet	▽
Educational Establishment	■
Hospital or Healthcare Building	■
Industrial Building	■
Leisure or Recreational Facility	■
Place of Interest	■
Public Building	■
Shopping Centre or Market	■
Other Selected Buildings	■

SCALE

Large Scale Pages 4-5 1:7,920

8 inches (20.32cm) to 1 Mile 12.63cm to 1km

Map Pages 6-55 1:15,840

4 inches (10.16cm) to 1 Mile 6.31cm to 1km

A-Z AZ AtoZ
registered trade marks of
Geographers' A-Z Map Company Ltd

www./az.co.uk

EDITION 8 2018

Copyright © Geographers' A-Z Map Co. Ltd.

© Crown copyright and database rights 2018 OS 100017302.

Safety camera information supplied by www.PocketGPSWorld.com
Speed Camera Location Database Copyright 2018 © PocketGPSWorld.com

Every possible care has been taken to ensure that, to the best of our knowledge, the information contained in this atlas is accurate at the date of publication. However, we cannot warrant that our work is entirely error free and whilst we would be grateful to learn of any inaccuracies, we do not accept responsibility for loss or damage resulting from reliance on information contained within this publication.

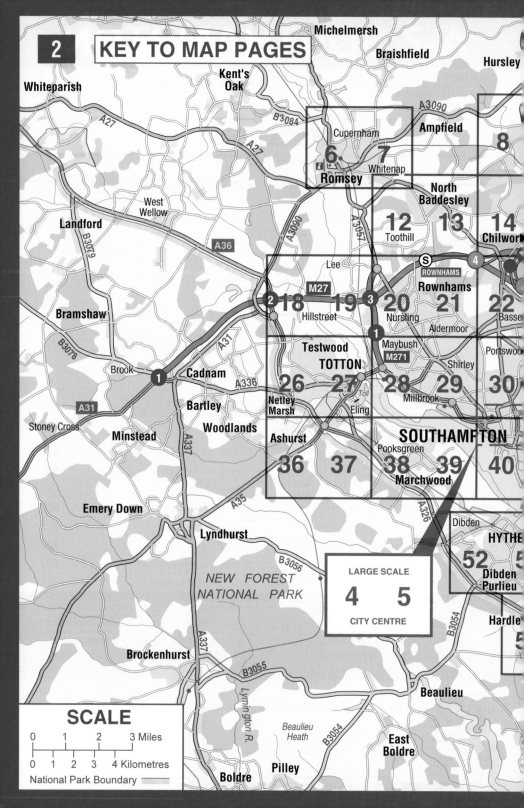

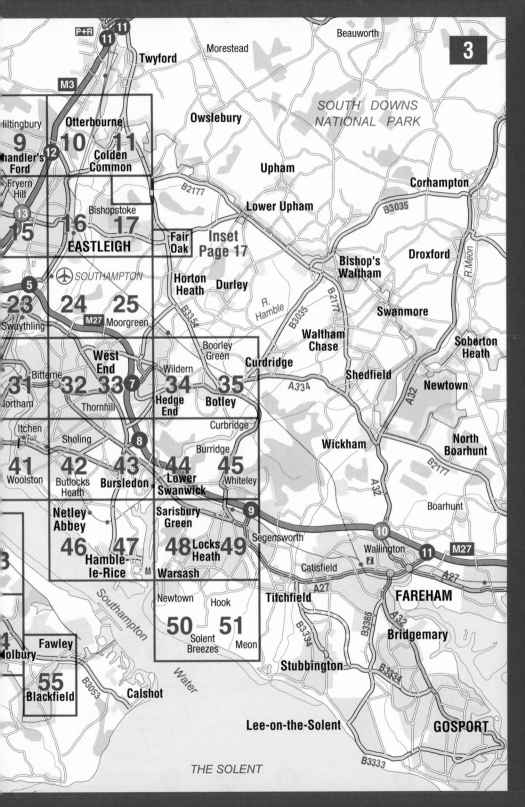

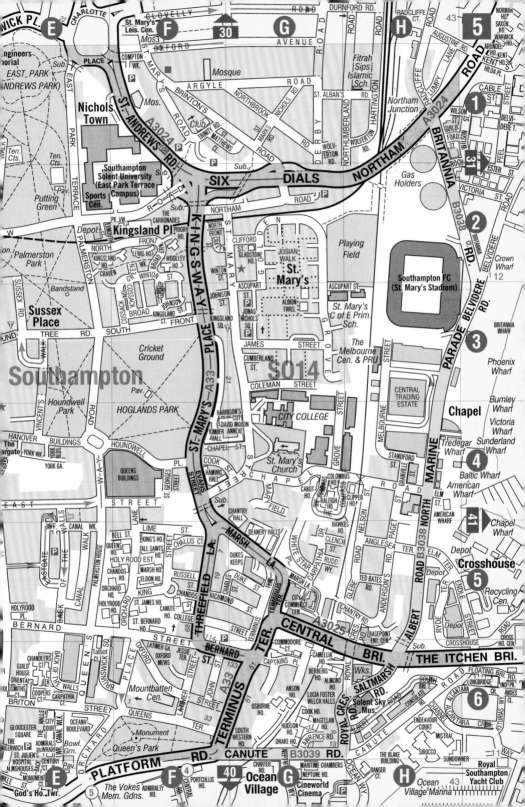

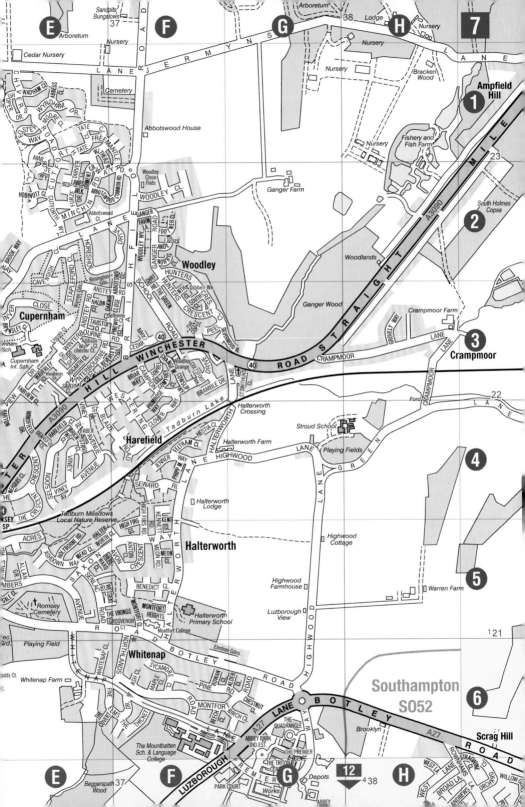

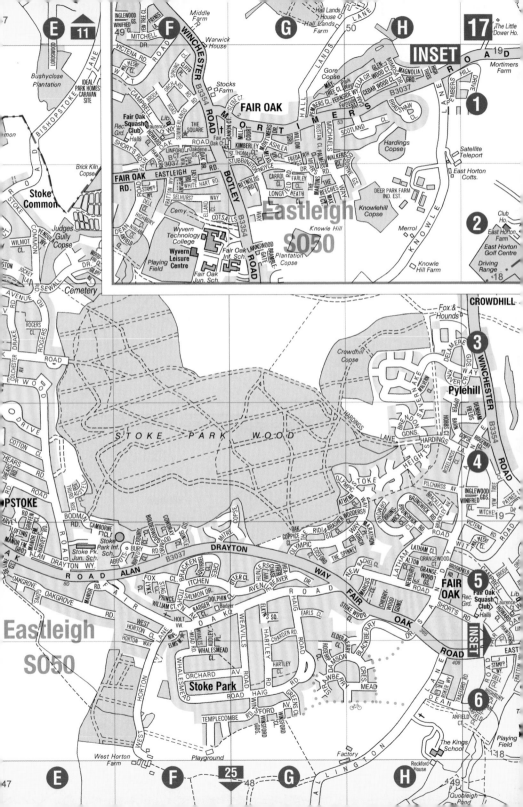

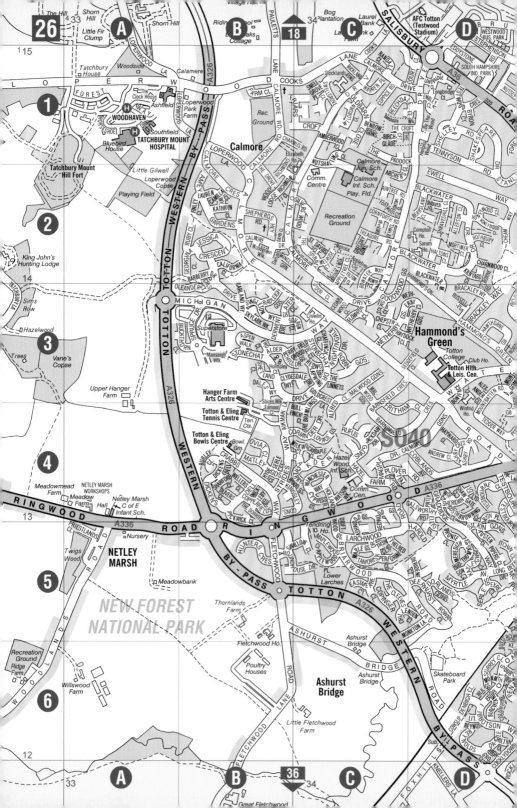

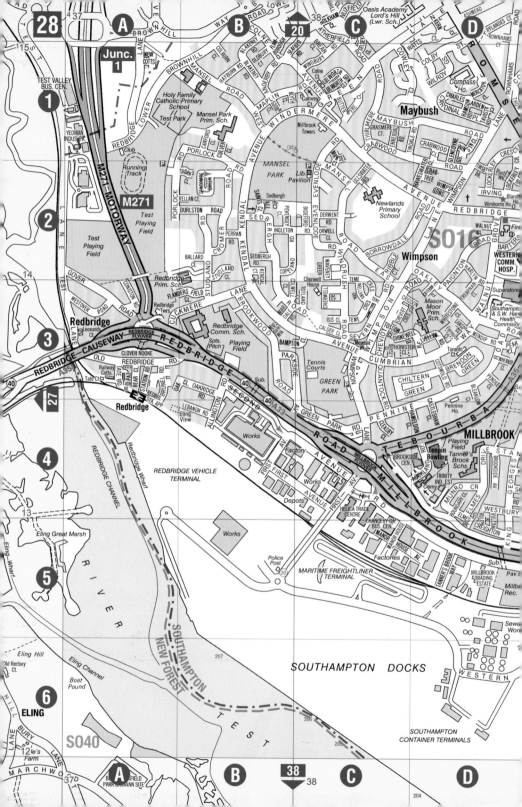

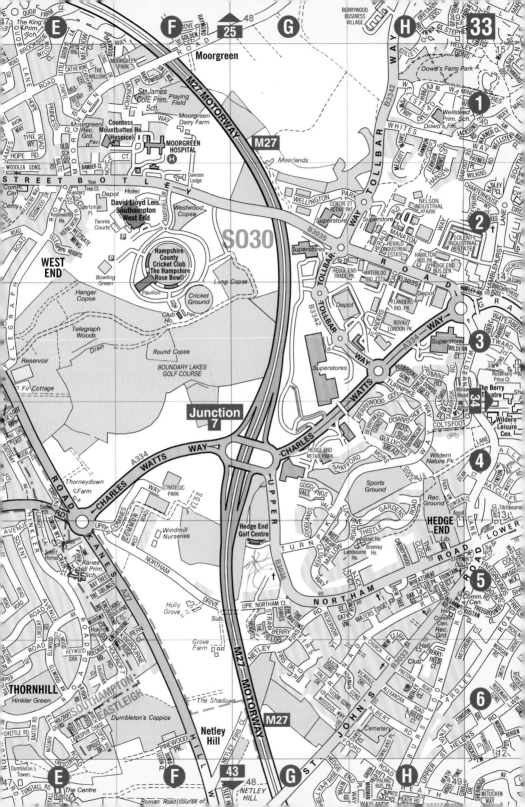

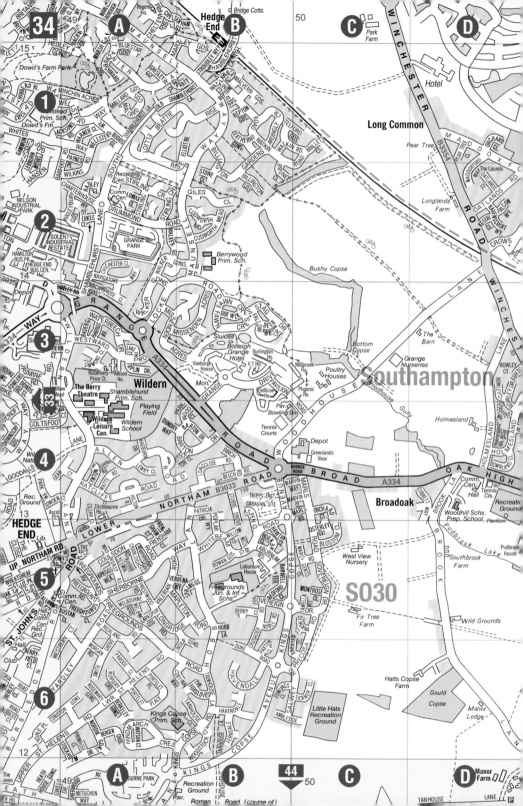

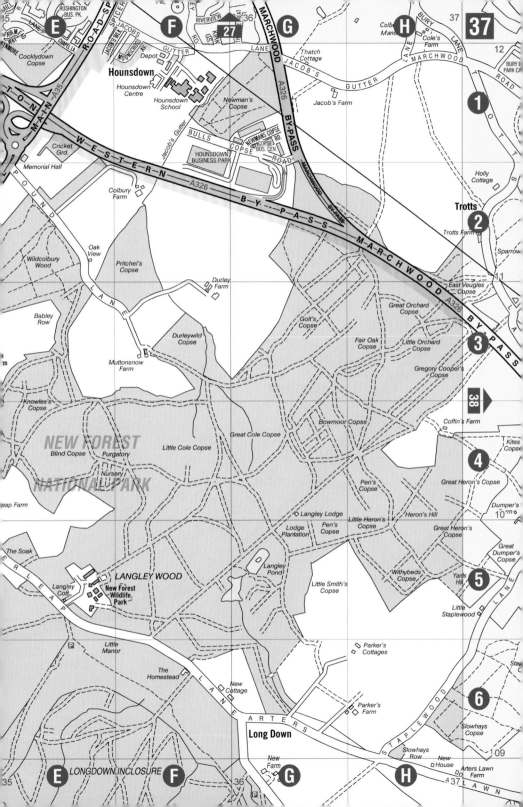

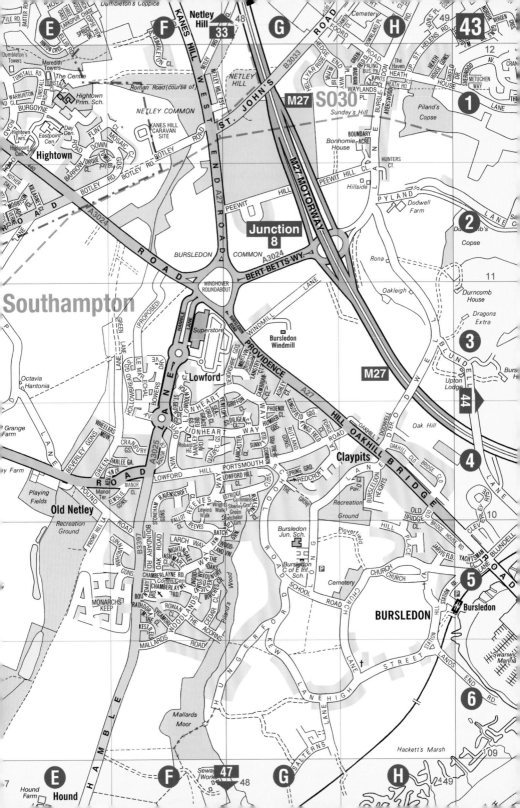

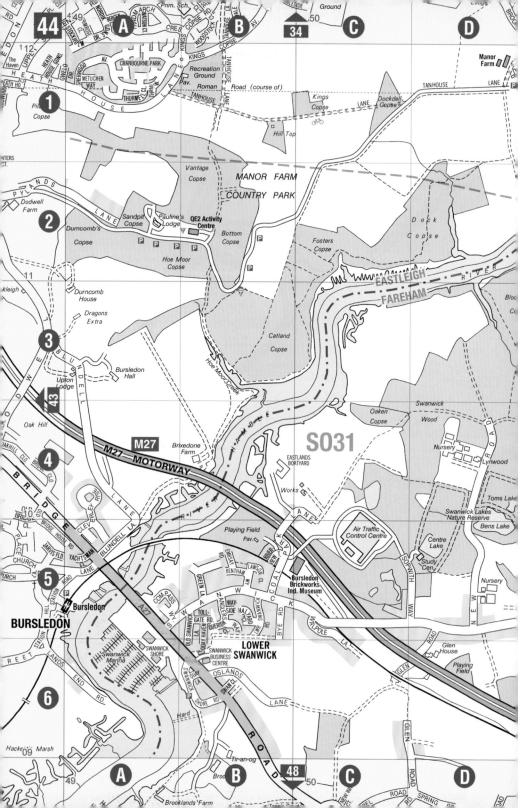

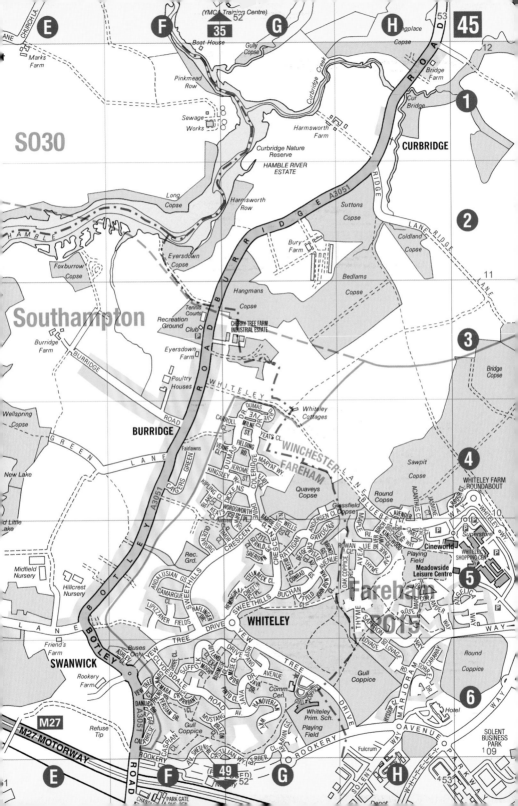

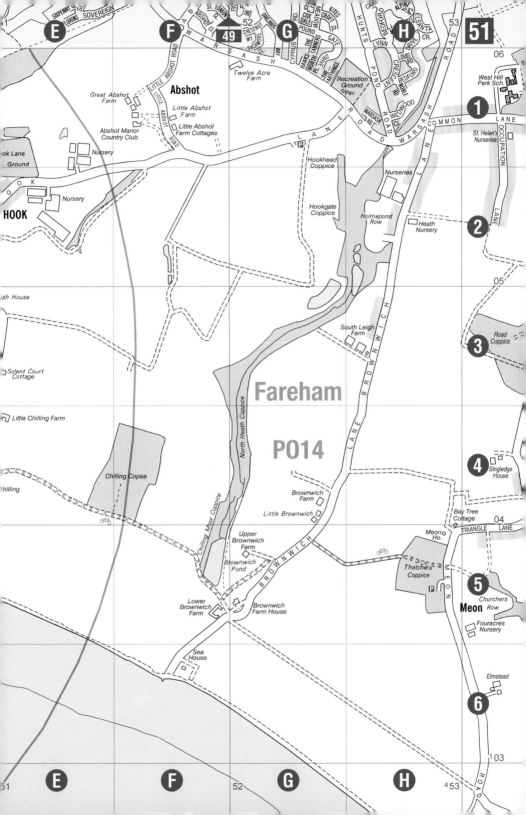

INDEX

Including Streets, Places & Areas, Hospitals etc., Industrial Estates,
Selected Flats & Walkways, Service Areas, Stations and Selected Places of Interest.

HOW TO USE THIS INDEX

1. Each street name is followed by its Postcode District, then by its Locality abbreviation(s) and then by its map reference;
e.g. **Abbey Hill** SO31: Net A . . . .6H **41** is in the SO31 Postcode District and the Netley Abbey Locality and is to be found in square 6H on page **41**.
The page number is shown in bold type.

2. A strict alphabetical order is followed in which Av., Rd., St., etc. (though abbreviated) are read in full and as part of the street name;
e.g. **Broad La.** appears after **Broadlands Rd.** but before **Broadleaf Cl.**

3. Streets and a selection of flats and walkways that cannot be shown on the mapping, appear in the index with the thoroughfare to which they are connected
shown in brackets; e.g. **Abbey Wlk.** *SO51: Rom . . . .5B* **6** (off Church St.)

4. Addresses that are in more than one part are referred to as not continuous.

5. Places and areas are shown in the index in BLUE TYPE and the map reference is to the actual map square in which the town centre or area is located and
not to the place name shown on the map; e.g. BISHOPSTOKE 4D 16

6. An example of a selected place of interest is Eastleigh Mus. 5A 16

7. Examples of stations are:
Ashurst New Forest Station (Rail) . . . .4A 36;   Romsey Bus Station 5B 6

8. Junction Names and Service Areas are shown in the index in BOLD CAPITAL TYPE; e.g. **OWER SERVICE AREA 1A 18**

9. An example of a Hospital, Hospice or selected Healthcare facility is FAREHAM COMMUNITY HOSPITAL 2E 49

10. Map references for entries that appear on large scale pages **4** & **5** are shown first, with small scale map references shown in brackets;
e.g. **Albert Rd. Nth.** SO14: South 5H **5** (2D **40**)

GENERAL ABBREVIATIONS

All. : Alley	**Ct.** : Court	**La.** : Lane	**Rdbt.** : Roundabout
App. : Approach	**Cres.** : Crescent	**Lit.** : Little	**Shop.** : Shopping
Arc. : Arcade	**Cft.** : Croft	**Lwr.** : Lower	**Sth.** : South
Av. : Avenue	**Dr.** : Drive	**Mnr.** : Manor	**Sq.** : Square
Blvd. : Boulevard	**E.** : East	**Mans.** : Mansions	**Sta.** : Station
Bri. : Bridge	**Ent.** : Enterprise	**Mkt.** : Market	**St.** : Street
B'way. : Broadway	**Est.** : Estate	**Mdw.** : Meadow	**Ter.** : Terrace
Bldg. : Building	**Fld.** : Field	**Mdws.** : Meadows	**Twr.** : Tower
Bldgs. : Buildings	**Flds.** : Fields	**M.** : Mews	**Trad.** : Trading
Bus. : Business	**Gdns.** : Gardens	**Mt.** : Mount	**Up.** : Upper
Cvn. : Caravan	**Ga.** : Gate	**Mus.** : Museum	**Va.** : Vale
C'way. : Causeway	**Gt.** : Great	**Nth.** : North	**Vw.** : View
Cen. : Centre	**Grn.** : Green	**Pde.** : Parade	**Vs.** : Villas
Circ. : Circle	**Gro.** : Grove	**Pk.** : Park	**Vis.** : Visitors
Cl. : Close	**Hgts.** : Heights	**Pl.** : Place	**Wlk.** : Walk
Comn. : Common	**Ho.** : House	**Res.** : Residential	**W.** : West
Cnr. : Corner	**Ind.** : Industrial	**Ri.** : Rise	**Yd.** : Yard
Cotts. : Cottages	**Info.** : Information	**Rd.** : Road	

POSTTOWN AND POSTAL LOCALITY ABBREVIATIONS

Abshot: PO14 . . . . .Abs	**Colden Common:** SO21 . . . . .Col C	**Hursley:** SO21 . . . . .Hurs	**Shawford:** SO21 . . . . .Shaw
Ampfield: SO51 . . . . .Ampf	**Compton:** SO21 . . . . .Comp	**Hythe:** SO45 . . . . .Hythe	**Shootash:** SO51 . . . . .Shoo
Ashfield: SO51 . . . . .A'field	**Crampmoor:** SO51 . . . . .Cram	**Lee:** SO51 . . . . .Lee	**Southampton:** SO14-15,SO16,SO17,
Ashurst: SO40 . . . . .A'hst	**Curdridge:** SO30,SO32 . . . . .Curd	**Lepe:** SO45 . . . . .Lepe	SO18-19 . . . . .South
Awbridge: SO51 . . . . .Awb	**Dibden:** SO45 . . . . .Dib	**Locks Heath:** SO31 . . . . .Loc H	**Southampton Airport:**
Bartley: SO40 . . . . .Bart	**Dibden Purlieu:** SO45 . . . . . . .Dib P	**Lower Swanwick:** SO31 . . . . .Lwr Swan	SO18 . . . . .S'ton A
Bassett: SO16,SO17 . . . . .Bass	**Eastleigh:** SO50 . . . . .E'leigh	**Marchwood:** SO40 . . . . .March	**Swanwick:** SO31 . . . . .Swanw
Beaulieu: SO42 . . . . .Beau	**Eling:** SO40 . . . . .Elin	**Netley Abbey:** SO31 . . . . .Net A	**Swaythling:** SO16,SO17,SO18 . . .S'ling
Bishopstoke: SO50 . . . . .B'stke	**Fair Oak:** SO50 . . . . .Fair O	**Netley Marsh:** SO40 . . . . .Net M	**Timsbury:** SO51 . . . . .Tims
Bishop's Waltham: SO32 . . . . .Bis W	**Fawley:** SO45 . . . . .F'ley	**North Baddesley:** SO52 . . . . . .N Bad	**Titchfield:** PO14,PO15 . . . . .Titch
Blackfield: SO45 . . . . .Blac	**Fisher's Pond:** SO50 . . . . .Fis P	**Nursling:** SO16 . . . . .Nur	**Titchfield Common:**
Botley: SO30,SO32 . . . . .Botl	**Hamble-le-Rice:** SO31 . . . . . . .Hamb	**Old Netley:** SO31 . . . . .Old N	PO14,SO31 . . . . .Titch C
Braishfield: SO51 . . . . .Brai	**Hardley:** SO45 . . . . .Hard	**Otterbourne:** SO21 . . . . .Ott	**Toothill:** SO51 . . . . .Toot
Brambridge: SO50 . . . . .B'dge	**Hedge End:** SO30,SO32 . . . . . .Hed E	**Ower:** SO51 . . . . .Ower	**Totton:** SO40 . . . . .Tott
Burridge: SO31 . . . . .Burr	**Hensting:** SO50 . . . . .Hens	**Park Gate:** SO31 . . . . .P Ga	**Twyford:** SO21 . . . . .Twy
Bursledon: SO31 . . . . .Burs	**Highbridge:** SO50 . . . . .Highb	**Romsey:** SO51 . . . . .Rom	**Warsash:** SO31 . . . . .Wars
Calmore: SO40 . . . . .Calm	**Holbury:** SO45 . . . . .Holb	**Rownhams:** SO16 . . . . .Rown	**West End:** SO18,SO30 . . . . . . .W End
Chandler's Ford: SO52-53 . . . .Cha F	**Horton Heath:** SO50 . . . . .Hor H	**Sarisbury Green:** SO31 . . . . . .Sar G	**Whiteley:** PO15 . . . . .White
Chilworth: SO16 . . . . .Chil	**Hound:** SO31 . . . . .Hou	**Segensworth:** PO15 . . . . .Seg	**Winsor:** SO40 . . . . .Wins
			Woodlands: SO40 . . . . .Woodl

	9th Street SO45: F'ley 4D **54**	**The Abbey** SO51: Rom 5B **6**
	10th Street SO45: F'ley 4D **54**	**Abbey Cl.** SO45: Hythe 3E **53**
	11th Street SO45: F'ley 3D **54**	**Abbey Ct.** SO15: South 4B **30**
	(not continuous)	**Abbey Enterprise Cen.**
1st Street SO45: F'ley 2G **55**	**12th Street** SO45: F'ley 3D **54**	SO51: Rom 2B **12**
2nd Street SO45: F'ley 2F **55**	(not continuous)	**Abbeyfield Cl.** SO31: Loc H 5E **49**
3d Health & Fitness 2D **14**	**13th Street** SO45: F'ley 3D **54**	**Abbeyfield Ho.** SO18: South 3G **31**
3rd Street SO45: F'ley 2F **55**	**14th Street** SO45: F'ley 3C **54**	**Abbeyfields Cl.** SO31: Net A 1D **46**
4th Street SO45: F'ley 2F **55**		**Abbey Fruit Pk. Ind. Est.**
(not continuous)		SO31: Net A 6B **42**
5th Street SO45: F'ley 2E **55**	# A	**Abbey Hill** SO31: Net A 6H **41**
(not continuous)		**Abbey M.** SO31: Net A 1B **46**
6th Street SO45: F'ley 1E **55**		**Abbey Pk. Ind. Est.**
(not continuous)	**Aaron Ct.** SO40: March 3D **38**	SO51: Rom 6G **7**
7th Street SO45: F'ley 2E **55**	**A Avenue** SO45: F'ley 3C **54**	**Abbey Wlk.** *SO51: Rom 5B* **6**
(not continuous)	(not continuous)	(off Church St.)
8th Street SO45: F'ley 1E **55**	**Abbess Cl.** SO51: Rom 1E **7**	

Abbey Water SO51: Rom 5B **6**	
Abbotsbury Rd. SO50: B'stke . . .5F **17**	
Abbotsfield SO40: Tott 4E **27**	
Abbotsfield Cl. SO16: South . . .4G **21**	
Abbots Way SO31: Net A 1D **46**	
ABBOTSWOOD 1E **7**	
Abbotswood Cl. SO51: Rom 3F **7**	
Abbotswood Comn. Rd.	
SO51: Rom 2E **7**	
Abbotswood Ct. SO51: Rom 2E **7**	
Abbotts Ho. SO17: South 2C **30**	
Abbotts Rd. SO50: E'leigh 6G **15**	
Abbotts Way SO17: South 2D **30**	
Abercrombie Gdns.	
SO16: South 5E **21**	
Aberdeen Rd. SO17: South 2E **31**	

Aberdour Cl.—Avonborne Way

Aberdour Cl. SO18: South 3B 32
Abingdon Gdns. SO16: Bass 6A 22
Above Bar St.
SO14: South 1D 4 (6B 30)
(not continuous)
Abraham Cl. SO30: Botl 6C 34
ABSHOT 1F 51
Abshot Cl. PO14: Titch C 6F 49
Abshot Rd. PO14: Titch C 6F 49
Acacia Rd. SO19: South 6H 31
Acanthus Ct. PO15: White 4H 45
Acastra Ho. *SO19: South 3F 41*
(off John Thornycroft Rd.)
Acorn Cl. SO40: March 4E 39
Acorn Ct. SO31: Hamb 4F 47
Acorn Dr. SO16: Rown 2C 20
SO53: Cha F 5E 9
Acorn Gro. SO53: Cha F 3B 14
Acorn Ind. Est. SO16: South 1F 29
The Acorns SO31: Burs 5F 43
Acorn Workshops
SO14: South 4D 30
Adams Cl. SO30: Hed E 6H 25
Adamson Cl. SO53: Cha F 5F 9
Adams Rd. SO45: Hythe 4E 53
Adams Way PO15: Seg 2G 49
Adams Wood Dr.
SO40: March 4D 38
Adanac Dr. SO16: Nur 5A 20
Adanac Pk. SO16: Nur 5A 20
Adcock Ct. SO16: Rown 2C 20
Addison Cl. SO51: Rom 3E 7
Addison Ct. SO31: P Ga 1F 49
Addison Rd. SO31: Sar G 1D 48
SO50: E'leigh 2B 16
Addis Sq. SO17: South 2D 30
(not continuous)
Adelaide Rd. SO17: South 3E 31
Adela Verne Cl. SO19: South ...2E 43
Adey Cl. SO19: South 3B 42
Admirals Cl. SO45: F'ley 2H 55
Admirals Ct. SO31: Hamb 5G 47
Admiral's Rd. SO31: Loc H 3F 49
Admirals Way SO45: Hythe 1E 53
Admirals Wharf SO14: South 6E 5
Admiralty Ho.
SO14: South 6F 5 (3C 40)
Admiralty Way SO40: March ...2D 38
Adur Cl. SO18: W End 2B 32
AFC Totton 6D 18
Africa Dr. SO40: March 4D 38
Agincourt Dr. SO31: Sar G 2D 48
(not continuous)
Agitator Rd. SO45: F'ley 1H 55
Agwi Rd. SO45: F'ley 1H 55
Aikman La. SO40: Tott 4B 26
Ailsa La. SO19: South 1F 41
Ainsley Gdns. SO50: E'leigh 2A 16
Aintree Ct. PO15: White 5F 45
Aintree Rd. SO40: Calm 2C 26
Airways Distribution Pk.
SO18: S'ing 3H 23
Alan Chun Ho. SO31: Net A 6C 42
Alandale Rd. SO19: South 1D 42
Alan Drayton Way
SO50: B'stke 5E 17
(not continuous)
Albacore Av. SO31: Wars 6C 48
Albany Pk. Ct. SO17: South 3B 30
Albany Rd. SO15: South 5G 29
SO45: Holb 4C 54
SO51: Rom 5C 6
Albemarle Ct. SO17: South 6E 23
Albert Cl. SO31: Net A 2C 46
(not continuous)
Albert Rd. SO30: Hed E 6H 33
SO50: E'leigh 2B 16
Albert Rd. Nth.
SO14: South 5H 5 (2D 40)
Albert Rd. Sth.
SO14: South 6H 5 (2D 40)
Albion Pl.
SO14: South 4D 4 (1B 40)
(not continuous)
Albion Towers
SO14: South 3G 5 (1D 40)
Albury Pl. SO53: Cha F 4D 8
Alcantara Cres.
SO14: South 6H 5 (2E 41)
Alder Cl. SO21: Col C 5G 11
SO40: March 3D 38
SO45: Dib P 3A 52
SO51: Rom 6G 7
Alder Hill Dr. SO40: Tott 3B 26
ALDERMOOR 6D 20
Aldermoor Av. SO16: South 5E 21
Aldermoor Cl. SO16: South 5G 21
Aldermoor Rd. SO16: South 5E 21
Alderney Cl. SO16: South 5C 20
Alder Rd. SO16: South 5D 20
Alderwood Av. SO53: Cha F 1C 14
Alexander Cl. SO40: Tott 3D 26
Alexander Ct. SO15: South 5H 29
Alexander Sq. SO50: E'leigh 3B 16
Alexandra Cl. SO45: Hythe 2E 53
Alexandra Rd. SO15: South 5H 29
SO30: Hed E 6H 33
SO45: Hythe 2E 53
SO53: Cha F 5G 9
Alexandra Way SO30: Botl 4E 35
Alfred Cl. SO40: Tott 4C 26
Alfred Rose Ct. SO18: S'ing 5G 23
Alfred St. SO14: South 5D 30
Alfriston Gdns. SO19: South ...1B 42
Allan Gro. SO51: Rom 5E 7
ALLBROOK 6B 10
Allbrook Hill SO50: E'leigh 6B 10
Allbrook Knoll SO50: E'leigh 6A 10
Allbrook Way SO50: E'leigh 5A 10
Allen Rd. SO30: Hed E 4A 34
Allerton Cl. SO40: Tott 2D 26
Allington La. SO30: W End 6B 24
SO50: Fair O 2G 25
Allington Mnr. Farm Bus. Cen.
SO50: Fair O 2E 25
Allington Rd. SO15: South 4B 28
Allison Ho. SO30: Hed E 3A 34
Allotment Rd. SO30: Hed E 5H 33
SO31: Sar G 2C 48
All Saints Cl. SO16: South 2B 28
All Saints Ho. SO14: South 5F 5
Allyn Ct. SO50: E'leigh 2B 16
Alma Rd. SO14: South 3C 30
SO51: Rom 5C 6
Almatade Rd. SO18: South 4A 32
Almond Ct. SO15: South 5G 29
Almond Ho. SO14: South 6G 5
Almond Rd. SO15: South 5G 29
Alpha Bus. Pk. SO14: South ...4D 30
Alpha Ho. SO16: Chil 6G 13
Alpine Cl. SO18: South 3B 32
Alpine Cres. PO14: Titch C 6H 49
Alpine Snowsports
Southampton 4A 22
Alton Cl. SO50: Fair O 5H 17
Alum Cl. SO45: Holb 5D 54
Alum Way SO18: South 4B 32
Alyne Ho. SO15: South 3B 30
Ambassador Wlk.
SO50: E'leigh 1H 23
Amberley Cl. SO30: Botl 4E 35
SO52: N Bad 2C 12
Amberley Ct. SO40: Tott 5E 27
Amberslade Wlk.
SO45: Dib P 5D 52
Amberwood Cl. SO40: Calm 1C 26
Ambledale SO31: Sar G 3C 48
Ambleside SO30: Botl 6B 34
Ambleside Gdns.
SO19: South 2A 42
Ambrose Way SO51: Rom 1E 7
American Wharf
SO14: South 4H 5 (1E 41)
Amey Gdns. SO40: Calm 2B 26
Amoy St. SO15: South 5B 30
AMPFIELD HILL 1H 7
Ampthill Rd. SO15: South 4F 29
Ancasta Rd. SO14: South 4D 30
Anchor Bus. Cen.
SO53: Cha F 2D 14
Andalusian Gdns.
PO15: White 5F 45
Anderby Rd. SO16: South 1B 28
Andersen Cl. PO15: White 5G 45
Anderson Cl. SO51: Rom 2F 7
Anderson's Rd.
SO14: South 5H 5 (2D 40)
Andes Cl.
SO14: South 6H 5 (2E 41)
Andes Rd. SO16: Nur 6H 19
Andover Rd. SO15: South 5H 29
Andrew Cl. SO40: Tott 4D 26
SO45: Dib P 5E 53
Andromeda Rd. SO16: South ...5C 20
Anfield Cl. SO50: Fair O 2F 17
Anfield Ct. SO50: Fair O 6H 17
Angel Cres. SO18: South 4A 32
Angelica Way PO15: White 5H 45
Anglers Way
SO31: Lwr Swan 5B 44
Anglesea Ct. SO15: South 2F 29
Anglesea Rd. SO15: South 2F 29
Anglesea Ter.
SO14: South 5H 5 (2D 40)
Annealilng Cl. SO50: E'leigh ...4H 15
Anson Dr. SO19: South 1C 42
Anson Ho. SO14: South 6G 5
Anson Pl. SO19: South 3E 41
Anstey Rd. SO51: Rom 3E 7
Antelope Pk. SO19: South 6D 32
Anton Cl. SO51: Rom 5F 7
Anvil Cl. SO30: W End 1C 32
Apollo Pl. SO18: South 3A 32
Apollo Rd. SO53: Cha F 6H 9
Apple Ind. Est. PO15: Seg 2G 49
APPLEMORE 3A 52
Applemore Health & Leisure Cen.
.......................3A 52
Appleton Rd. SO18: South 2G 31
Appletree Cl. SO40: Calm 2C 26
Appletree Ct. SO30: Botl 4E 35
Applewood SO31: P Ga 2E 49
Applewood Gdns.
SO19: South 2A 42
Applewood Pl. SO40: Tott 5C 26
April Cl. SO18: South 4B 32
April Gdns. SO45: Blac 4E 55
April Gro. SO31: Sar G 4C 48
Apsley Pl. SO53: Cha F 4D 8
Aquila Way SO31: Hamb 5F 47
Aquitania Ho. SO14: South 6E 31
Arabian Gdns. PO15: White 6G 45
Arakan Cres. SO40: March 4D 38
Arbour Ct. PO15: White 4H 45
Arcadia Cl. SO16: South 6G 21
Arcadia Pl. SO17: South 2F 31
Archers SO15: South 5A 30
Archers Cl. SO40: Calm 2C 26
Archers Rd. SO15: South 4A 30
SO50: E'leigh 3A 16
Archery Gdns. SO19: South 3H 41
Archery Gro. SO19: South 4G 41
Archery Rd. SO19: South 4G 41
Arden Cl. SO18: South 2B 32
Ardingly Cres. SO30: Hed E 1B 34
Ardnave Cres. SO16: Bass 4B 22
Argosy Cl. SO31: Wars 6D 48
Argosy Cres. SO50: E'leigh 1H 23
Argyle Rd.
SO14: South 1F 5 (6D 30)
Arliss Rd. SO16: South 2E 29
Arlott Ct. SO15: South 3A 30
Arlowe Dr. SO16: South 1H 29
Armada Cl. SO16: Rown 2C 20
Armada Dr. SO45: Hythe 4D 52
Armadale Ho. *SO14: South 5E 31*
(off Kent St.)
Armfield Ho. *SO17: South 2C 30*
(off Winn Rd.)
Armitage Av. SO45: Dib P 5D 52
The Armoury SO40: March 2E 39
Armstrong Ct. SO16: South 4D 20
Arnheim Cl. SO16: South 5G 21
Arnheim Rd. SO16: South 5H 21
Arnold Rd. SO17: South 1E 31
SO50: E'leigh 1A 24
Arnwood Av. SO45: Dib P 6D 52
Arreton SO31: Net A 1C 46
Arrow Cl. SO19: South 4F 41
SO50: E'leigh 2A 16
Arters Lawn SO40: March 6G 37
Arthur Rd. SO15: South 4H 29
SO50: E'leigh 3A 16
Arthurs Gdns. SO30: Hed E 6H 25
Arts Cen.
Southampton 2D 4 (6B 30)
Arundel Ho.
SO14: South 1H 5 (5E 31)
SO15: South 3B 30
Arundel Rd. SO40: Tott 3G 27
SO50: E'leigh 1A 16
Arun Rd. SO18: W End 6B 24
Ascot Cl. PO14: Titch C 5G 49
Ascot Pl. SO30: Hed E 4H 33
Ascupart Ho. SO17: South 3D 30
Ascupart St.
SO14: South 3G 5 (1D 40)
(not continuous)
Asford Gro. SO50: B'stke 3C 16
Ashbridge Ri. SO53: Cha F 4C 8
Ashburnham Cl. SO19: South ...6F 31
Ashburton Cl. SO45: Dib 3B 52
Ashby Cres. SO40: Tott 4D 26
Ashby Rd. SO19: South 2B 42
SO40: Tott 4D 26
Ash Cl. SO19: South 5C 32
SO21: Col C 4F 11
SO31: Burs 5F 43
SO45: Hythe 6E 53
SO51: Rom 6F 7
SO52: N Bad 2D 12
Ashcombe Ho. *off Meridian Way 5E 31*
(off Meridian Way)
Ash Ct. SO19: South 2H 41
Ashcroft Ct. SO53: Cha F 1F 15
Ashdene SO15: South 3F 29
Ashdene Rd. SO40: A'hst 3B 36
Ashdown SO45: F'ley 2F 55
Ashdown Cl. SO53: Cha F 3E 9
Ashdown Dr. SO53: Cha F 3E 9
Ashdown Rd. SO45: F'ley 3F 55
SO53: Cha F..............3E 9
Ashdown Way SO51: Rom 5E 7
Ashen Cl. SO53: Cha F 5E 9
ASHFIELD 3A 12
Ashfield Vw. SO52: N Bad 2E 13
Ashford Cres. SO45: Hythe 3F 53
Ash Gro. SO40: A'hst 2C 36
Ashlea Cl. SO50: Fair O 1G 17
Ashleigh Cl. SO45: Hythe 6E 53
Ashlett Cl. SO45: F'ley 2H 55
Ashlett M. SO45: F'ley 2H 55
Ashlett Rd. SO45: F'ley 2H 55
Ashley Cl. SO31: Swanw 6F 45
Ashley Ct. SO31: Burs 3G 43
Ashley Cres. SO19: South 3C 42
Ashley Cross Cl. SO45: Holb ...5D 54
Ashley Gdns. SO53: Cha F 2G 15
Ashley Ho. SO51: Rom 6B 6
Ashley Mdws. SO51: Rom 4D 6
Ashmead Rd. SO16: South 6D 20
Ashridge Cl. SO15: South 3B 30
Ash Rd. SO40: A'hst 3B 36
Ashton Gdns. SO50: E'leigh 3B 16
Ashton Pl. SO53: Cha F 4D 8
Ashtree Ct. SO53: Cha F 4E 15
Ash Tree Rd. SO18: South 2G 31
ASHURST 3B 36
ASHURST BRIDGE 6C 26
Ashurst Bri. Rd. SO40: Tott 5C 26
Ashurst Campsite 5A 36
Ashurst Cl. SO19: South 4A 42
SO40: A'hst 3B 36
Ashurst New Forest Station
(Rail) 4A 36
Ash Way PO15: White 5H 45
Ashwood PO15: White 2H 49
SO31: Loc H 5G 49
Ashwood Gdns. SO16: South ...6A 22
SO40: Tott 5C 26
Aspen Av. SO31: Wars 1B 50
Aspen Cl. SO21: Col C 5G 11
SO30: Hed E 4B 34
Aspen Holt SO16: Bass 4C 22
Aspen Wlk. SO40: Tott 3B 26
Aster Rd. SO16: S'ing 5E 23
Astra Ct. SO45: Hythe 1E 53
Astral Gdns. SO31: Hamb 4F 47
Asturias Way
SO14: South 6H 5 (2E 41)
Asylum Rd. SO15: South 5C 30
Atheling Rd. SO45: Hythe 2E 53
Athelstan Rd. SO19: South 4G 31
Athena Cl. SO50: Fair O 4G 17
Atherfield Rd. SO16: South 6C 20
Atherley Bowling Club 3A 30
Atherley Ct. SO15: South 3A 30
Atherley Rd. SO15: South 5H 29
Atlantic Cl. SO14: South 3D 40
Atlantic Pk. Vw.
SO18: W End 6A 24
Atlantic Way SO14: South 3C 40
Auckland Rd. SO15: South 4D 28
Audley Pl. SO50: B'stke 5F 17
Augustine Rd.
SO14: South 1H 5 (5D 30)
Augustus Cl. SO53: Cha F 6G 9
Augustus Way SO53: Cha F 6G 9
Austen Cl. SO40: Tott 5D 26
Austen Gdns. PO15: White 5G 45
Austen Hgts. *SO19: South 3F 41*
(off Capstan Rd.)
Authie Grn. SO52: N Bad 3E 13
Autumn Pl. SO17: South 2C 30
Autumn Rd. SO40: March 4E 39
Avebury Gdns. SO53: Cha F 4C 8
Avenger Cl. SO53: Cha F 2D 14
The Avenue SO14: South 4C 30
SO17: South 6B 22
Avenue C SO45: Hard 6H 53
Avenue Ct. SO17: South 3B 30
Avenue D SO45: Hard 6H 53
Avenue E SO45: Hard 6H 53
Avenue Rd. SO14: South 3C 30
Avery Flds. SO50: E'leigh 6B 10
Avington Cl. SO50: B'stke 2E 17
Avington Ct. SO16: Bass 5B 22
Avonborne Way SO53: Cha F 5D 8

A-Z Southampton 57

Avon Ct. SO31: Net A 2B 46
Avon Cres. SO51: Rom 5F 7
Avondale Ct. SO17: South 1D 30
Avondale Mobile Home Pk.
  SO21: Col C 4G 11
Avon Grn. SO53: Cha F 2F 15
Avon Ho. SO14: South 5E 31
Avon Rd. SO18: South 2H 31
Avon Way SO30: W End 1E 33
Avro Cl. SO15: South 4E 29
Avro Ct. SO31: Hamb 5F 47
Ayerswood SO30: Hed E 1H 43
Aynsley Ct. SO15: South 4H 29

B

Back of the Walls
  SO14: South 6E 5 (2C 40)
            (not continuous)
Bacon Cl. SO19: South 4H 41
Baddesley Cl. SO52: N Bad 2D 12
Baddesley Pk. Ind. Est.
  SO52: N Bad 3F 13
Baddesley Rd. SO52: N Bad 5C 8
  SO53: Cha F 5C 8
Baden Powell Ho. SO51: Rom . .5C 6
      (off Baden Powell Way)
Baden Powell Way
  SO51: Rom 5C 6
Bader Cl. SO30: Hed E 3A 34
Badger Cl. SO50: B'stke 5F 17
Badger Ct. SO50: B'stke 5F 17
The Badgers SO31: Net A 1C 46
Badgers Copse SO31: P Ga 2F 49
Badgers Run SO31: Sar G 1C 48
Badgers Wlk. SO45: Dib P 4D 52
Badger Wood Pl.
  SO18: South 2H 31
Badminston La. SO45: F'ley 4H 55
Bagber Rd. SO40: Tott 4F 27
Bagshot M. SO19: South 2H 41
Bailey Cl. SO30: Botl 5E 35
Bailey Grn. SO18: South 1A 32
Bakers Cres. SO50: E'leigh 4A 16
Bakers Drove SO16: Rown 4C 20
Bakers Wharf SO14: South 6E 31
Balaclava Rd. SO18: South 4A 32
Balfour Rd. SO19: South 6C 32
Ballard Cl. SO16: South 2B 28
Balliol Cl. PO14: Titch C 6G 49
Balmoral Cl. SO16: South 4G 21
  SO53: Cha F 5D 8
Balmoral Ct. SO15: South 5E 29
Balmoral Way SO16: Rown 3B 20
Baltic Rd. SO30: W End 2E 33
Bamber Cl. SO30: W End 2E 33
Bampton Cl. SO16: South 3B 28
Bampton Ct. SO53: Cha F 1E 15
Banbury Av. SO19: South 1C 42
Bangor Rd. SO15: South 5F 29
Banister Gdns. SO15: South 4B 30
Banister Grange
  SO15: South 4B 30
Banister M. SO15: South 4B 30
BANISTER PARK 4A 30
Banister Pk. Bowling Club 2E 23
Banister Rd. SO15: South 4B 30
Bankside SO18: S'ing 5G 23
Banning St. SO51: Rom 6B 6
Bannister Ct. SO40: Tott 4G 27
Barbe Baker Av.
  SO30: W End 1C 32
Barberry Dr. SO40: Tott 2B 26
Barclay M. SO45: Hythe 6E 53
Barfoot Rd. SO30: Hed E 2H 33
Barford Cl. SO53: Cha F 5D 8
Bargain Cl. SO16: Nur 6B 20
The Bargate 4E 5
Bargate St.
  SO14: South 4D 4 (1B 40)
Barker Mill Cl. SO16: Rown 3C 20
Bark Mill M. SO51: Rom 6B 6
Barle Cl. SO18: W End 1B 32
Barnbrook Rd. SO31: Sar G 3C 48
Barnes Cl. SO18: South 5C 32
  SO31: Sar G 3B 48
Barnes La. SO31: Sar G 1C 48
Barnes Rd. SO19: South 5C 32
Barnes Wallis Rd.
  PO15: Seg 3H 49
Barnfield Cl. SO19: South 4G 41
Barnfield Ct. SO19: South 4H 41
Barnfield Flats SO19: South 4H 41
Barnfield Rd. SO19: South 4H 41
Barnfield Way SO19: South 4H 41
Barn Piece SO53: Cha F 1B 14

Barnsfield Cres. SO40: Tott 4C 26
Barnsland SO30: W End 6C 24
Baron Rd. SO31: Hamb 4F 47
Barons Mead SO16: South 6C 20
Barratt Ind. Pk. PO15: Seg 2G 49
Barrie Cl. PO15: White 5G 45
Barrington Cl. SO50: E'leigh . . .2H 15
Barrow Down Gdns.
  SO19: South 2E 43
Barrowfields Cl.
  SO30: W End 1F 33
Barry Rd. SO19: South 5B 32
Barters Cl. SO16: South 2D 28
The Bartletts SO31: Hamb 5G 47
Bartley Av. SO40: Tott 5E 27
Barton Cl. SO51: Rom 4E 7
Barton Cres. SO18: South 2H 31
Barton Dr. SO30: Hed E 4B 34
  SO31: Hamb 4F 47
Barton Pk. Ind. Est.
  SO50: E'leigh 5B 16
Barton Rd. SO50: E'leigh 4C 16
The Bartons SO30: Hed E 5G 33
Bartram Rd. SO40: Elin, Tott . . .5G 27
Barwell Ter. SO30: Hed E 5B 34
Basepoint Ent. Cen.
  SO14: South 5H 5 (2D 40)
Basing Ho. SO15: South 4G 29
Basing Way SO53: Cha F 3C 14
BASSETT 4C 22
Bassett Av. SO16: Bass 6B 22
Bassett Cl. SO16: Bass 5B 22
Bassett Ct. SO16: Bass 5B 22
Bassett Cres. E. SO16: Bass 5B 22
Bassett Cres. W. SO16: Bass . . .6B 22
Bassett Dale SO16: Bass 3B 22
Bassett Gdns. SO16: Bass 5B 22
BASSETT GREEN 4D 22
Bassett Grn. Cl. SO16: Bass 4C 22
Bassett Grn. Ct. SO16: Bass 4D 22
Bassett Grn. Dr. SO16: Bass 3C 22
Bassett Grn. Rd.
  SO16: Bass, S'ing 2C 22
Bassett Grn. Village
  SO16: Bass 4D 22
Bassett Heath Av.
  SO16: Bass 2B 22
Bassett Lodge SO16: Bass 5B 22
Bassett Mdw. SO16: Bass 5B 22
Bassett M. SO16: Bass 4B 22
Bassett Row SO16: Bass 3B 22
Bassett Wood Dr.
  SO16: Bass 3B 22
Bassett Wood M.
  SO16: Bass 5B 22
Bassett Wood Rd.
  SO16: Bass 3B 22
Bastins Cl. SO31: P Ga 1F 49
Batchelor Grn. SO31: Burs 5F 43
Bath Cl. SO19: South 5B 32
Bath Rd. SO19: South 5B 32
Bath St. SO14: South 4C 30
Batten Way SO18: S'ing 5G 23
Battle Cl. SO31: Sar G 3E 49
B Avenue SO45: F'ley 1E 55
          (8th Street, not continuous)
  SO45: F'ley 3C 54
          (14th Street)
Baxter Rd. SO19: South 6E 33
Bay Cl. SO19: South 2A 42
Bay Rd. SO19: South 2A 42
Baytree Gdns. SO40: March 4D 38
Bay Trees SO19: South 5E 33
Beach La. SO31: Net A 1A 46
Beacon Bottom SO31: P Ga 1E 49
Beacon Cl. SO16: Rown 3B 20
  SO31: P Ga 1E 49
Beacon M. SO30: W End 3D 32
Beacon Mt. SO31: P Ga 1E 49
Beacon Rd. SO30: W End 2D 32
Beacon Way SO31: P Ga 1E 49
Beale Cres. SO50: E'leigh 6C 10
Bealing Cl. SO16: Bass 5D 22
Bearslane Cl. SO40: Tott 2D 26
Beatrice Rd. SO15: South 4G 29
Beattie Ri. SO30: Hed E 1A 34
Beatty Cl. SO31: Loc H 3F 49
Beatty Ct. SO19: South 6C 32
Beaulieu Cl. SO16: South 4F 21
Beaulieu Ct. SO17: South 2C 30
Beaulieu Rd. SO31: Hamb 4F 47
  SO42: Beau 6B 52
  SO45: Dib P, Hythe 6C 52
  SO50: E'leigh 3A 16
Beaumaris Cl. SO53: Cha F 3C 14
Beaumaris Gdns.
  SO45: Hythe 1D 52

Beaumont Cl. SO16: Bass 6A 22
Beaumont Rd. SO40: Tott 4G 27
Beauworth Av. SO18: South 3C 32
Beauworth Cl. SO50: E'leigh . . .6A 16
Beaver Dr. SO50: B'stke 5G 17
Beck Cl. SO31: Sar G 4C 48
Bedford Av. SO19: South 3G 41
Bedford Cl. SO30: Hed E 5B 34
Bedford Dr. PO14: Titch C 6H 49
BEDFORD PLACE 5B 30
Bedford Pl.
  SO15: South 1D 4 (5B 30)
Bedwell Cl. SO16: Rown 3D 20
Beech Av. SO18: South 4G 31
Beech Cl. SO31: Hamb 5E 47
  SO51: Rom 6F 7
  SO53: Cha F 4F 9
Beech Copse SO30: W End 2D 32
Beech Cres. SO45: Hythe 6E 53
Beechcroft Cl. SO53: Cha F 1F 15
Beechcroft Way SO53: Cha F . . .1F 15
Beechdale Cl. SO40: Calm 1C 26
Beechdale Wlk. SO40: Calm 1C 26
Beechfield Ct. SO15: South 3E 29
Beech Gdns. SO31: Hamb 5E 47
Beechmount Ho. SO16: Bass . . .4B 22
Beechmount Rd. SO16: Bass . . .4B 22
Beech Rd. SO15: South 5F 29
  SO30: Hed E 4B 34
  SO40: A'hst 3B 36
  SO53: Cha F 5F 9
Beechwood Cl. SO31: Wars 1B 50
  SO53: Cha F 4C 8
Beechwood Cres. SO53: Cha F . .4C 8
Beechwood Gdns.
  SO18: South 3H 31
Beechwood Ri. SO18: W End . . .2C 32
Beechwood Rd. SO45: Holb 5C 54
Beechwood Way
  SO45: Dib P 4A 52
Begonia Rd. SO16: Bass 5D 22
Belbins SO51: Rom 1C 6
Belbins Bus. Pk. SO51: Rom . . .1D 6
Belfry Wlk. PO14: Titch C 5G 49
            (not continuous)
Belgrave Ind. Est.
  SO14: South 5F 31
  SO17: South 1E 31
Belgrave Rd. SO17: South 1E 31
Bellamy Ct. SO17: South 3F 31
Bell Cl. SO45: F'ley 3F 55
Bell Ct. SO51: Rom 5B 6
Bellemoor Rd. SO15: South 2G 29
Bellevue Rd. SO15: South 5C 30
  SO50: E'leigh 4A 16
Bellevue Ter. SO14: South 5C 30
Bellflower Way SO53: Cha F 6B 8
Bell La. SO45: Blac 6C 54
Bell St. SO14: South . . .5F 5 (2C 40)
  SO51: Rom 5B 6
Belmont Cl. SO45: Dib P 4E 53
Belmont Rd. SO17: South 3D 30
  SO53: Cha F 4E 15
Belstone Rd. SO40: Tott 4E 27
Belvedere Rd. SO45: Dib P 4E 53
BELVIDERE 6E 31
Belvidere Ho. SO14: South 5E 31
Belvidere Rd.
  SO14: South 3H 5 (1E 41)
Belvidere Ter. SO14: South 6E 31
Bembridge SO31: Net A 1C 46
Bembridge Cl. SO16: S'ing 4E 23
Benbow Gdns. SO40: Calm 1C 26
Bencraft Ct. SO16: Bass 4D 22
Benedict Cl. SO51: Rom 5F 7
Benham Rd. SO16: Chil 6F 13
Benhams Farm Cl.
  SO18: South 2A 32
Benhams Rd. SO18: South 1A 32
Benjamin Cl. SO31: Net A 1C 46
Benmore Gdns. SO53: Cha F . . .5D 8
Bennett Wlk. SO45: F'ley 3F 55
Benny Hill Cl. SO50: E'leigh 4H 15
Benson Rd. SO15: South 3F 29
Bentham Ct. SO16: Bass 5C 22
Bentham Way
  SO31: Lwr Swan 5B 44
Bentley Cl. SO17: South 2C 30
Bentley Grn. SO18: South 3C 32
Berber Cl. PO15: White 1G 49
Berberis Ho. SO14: South 6G 5
Bere Cl. SO53: Cha F 5C 8
Beresford Cl. SO53: Cha F 2G 15

Beresford Gdns.
  SO53: Cha F 2G 15
Beresford Rd. SO53: Cha F 2G 15
Bergen Cres. SO30: Hed E 6A 34
Berkeley Cl. SO15: South 4A 30
Berkeley Gdns. SO30: Hed E . . .4A 34
Berkeley Rd. SO15: South 5B 30
Bernard St.
  SO14: South 5E 5 (2C 40)
Bernie Tunstall Pl.
  SO50: E'leigh 4B 16
            (off Romsey Rd.)
Bernwood Gro. SO45: Blac 6E 55
Berry Cl. SO30: Hed E 5B 34
Berryfield Cl. SO30: Hed E 6H 33
The Berry Theatre 4A 34
Berrywood Bus. Village
  SO30: Hed E 6H 25
Berrywood Gdns.
  SO30: Hed E 4H 33
Bert Betts Way SO31: Burs 2G 43
Berthon Ho. SO51: Rom 6B 6
Berwick Cl. SO16: South 4E 21
Beta Ho. SO16: Chil 6G 13
Betteridge Dr. SO16: Rown 3B 20
Beulah Rd. SO16: South 2E 29
Bevan Cl. SO19: South 4G 41
Beverley Cl. SO31: P Ga 4E 49
Beverley Gdns. SO31: Old N . . .4E 43
  SO51: Rom 3E 7
Beverley Hgts. SO18: South 6H 23
Beverley Rd. SO45: Dib P 6D 52
Bevis Cl. SO31: Wars 1B 50
  SO45: F'ley 3F 55
Bevois Gdns. SO14: South 4C 30
Bevois Hill SO14: South 3D 30
Bevois Mans. SO14: South 3D 30
            (off Bevios Hill)
Bevois M. SO14: South 4C 30
BEVOIS MOUNT 3C 30
BEVOIS TOWN 4C 30
BEVOIS VALLEY 4D 30
Bevois Valley Rd.
  SO14: South 4D 30
Biddlesgate Ct.
  SO14: South 5D 4 (2B 40)
Bideford Cl. SO16: South 2C 28
Bilberry Cl. SO31: Loc H 5D 48
Bilberry Dr. SO40: March 3C 38
Billington Gdns.
  SO30: Hed E 1B 34
Bill Luffman Way
  SO50: E'leigh 4H 15
Bindon Cl. SO15: South 1E 29
Bindon Ct. SO18: South 3G 31
Bindon Rd. SO15: South 1E 29
Binsey Cl. SO16: South 3C 28
Binstead Cl. SO16: S'ing 4E 23
Birch Cl. SO16: South 1E 29
  SO21: Col C 5F 11
  SO51: Rom 6G 7
Birchdale Cl. SO45: Hythe 4F 53
Birchdale Cl. SO31: Wars 1B 50
Birchen Cl. SO31: P Ga 3G 49
Birchen Rd. SO31: P Ga 3G 49
The Birches SO18: South 3B 32
  SO21: Col C 4F 11
The Birches Close
  SO52: N Bad 2D 12
Birchglade SO40: Calm 1C 26
Birch Gro. SO50: E'leigh 1H 15
Birchlands SO40: Tott 6D 26
Birch Lawn Cl. SO19: South 2C 42
Birch Rd. SO16: Chil 1B 22
  SO16: South 6E 21
  SO30: Hed E 4B 34
Birch Wood SO19: South 6E 33
Birchwood Gdns.
  SO30: Hed E 3A 34
Bird Fld. SO53: Cha F 6A 8
Bishops Cl. SO40: Tott 3E 27
Bishops Ct. SO50: B'stke 2D 16
Bishops Ga. PO14: Titch C 4G 49
Bishops Rd. SO19: South 2G 41
BISHOPSTOKE 4D 16
Bishopstoke La. SO50: B'dge . . .1E 17
Bishopstoke Mnr.
  SO50: E'leigh 4C 16
Bishopstoke Rd.
  SO50: E'leigh 4B 16
Bisley Ct. SO19: South 2B 42
BITTERNE 4A 32
Bitterne Cres. SO19: South 5A 32
Bitterne Leisure Cen. 4A 32
Bitterne Mnr. Ho.
  SO18: South 4E 31

Bitterne Park—Buchanan Rd.

BITTERNE PARK 2G 31
Bitterne Rd. SO18: South 5C 32
(Keats Rd.)
SO18: South 4H 31
(Maybray King Way, not continuous)
SO18: South 5A 32
(Milbury Cres.)
Bitterne Rd. E. SO18: South . . .4A 32
Bitterne Rd. W. SO18: South . . .4E 31
Bitterne Station (Rail) 4F 31
Bitterne Village SO18: South . . .4A 32
Bitterne Way SO19: South 5G 31
Bitumen Rd. SO45: F'ley 1H 55
Blackberry Dr. SO50: Fair O 6H 17
Blackberry Ter. SO14: South . . .4D 30
Blackbird Rd. SO50: E'leigh 6F 15
Blackbushe Cl. SO16: South . . .4D 20
Blackdown Cl. SO45: Dib P 4B 52
BLACKFIELD 4E 55
Blackfield Rd.
SO45: Blac, F'ley 4E 55
Blackthorn Cl. SO19: South 6H 31
Blackthorn Grn. SO21: Col C . . .5G 11
Blackthorn Rd. SO19: South . . .6G 31
Blackwater Dr. SO40: Tott 2D 26
Blackwater M. SO40: Tott 2D 26
Bladon Rd. SO16: South 1G 29
The Blake Bldg.
SO14: South 6H 5 (3D 40)
Blake Cl. PO15: White 4F 45
SO16: Nur 4B 20
Blake Gdns. SO19: South 2B 42
Blakeney Rd. SO16: South 1B 28
Blandford Ho. SO16: South 2D 28
Blann Cl. SO16: Nur 4A 20
Bleaklow Cl. SO16: South 3D 28
BLECHYNDEN 2B 4 (6A 30)
Blechynden Ter.
SO15: South 2B 4 (6A 30)
Blencowe Dr. SO53: Cha F 2A 14
Blendworth La. SO18: South . . .4C 32
Blenheim Av. SO17: South 2C 30
Blenheim Cl. SO40: Tott 5D 26
SO53: Cha F 3B 14
Blenheim Ct. SO17: South 2C 30
Blenheim Gdns.
SO17: South 1D 30
SO45: Dib P 4B 52
Blenheim Ho. SO50: E'leigh 5B 16
SO51: Rom 5E 7
(off Chambers Av.)
Blenheim Rd. SO50: E'leigh 5A 16
Blighmont Av. SO15: South 5F 29
Blighmont Cres.
SO15: South 5F 29
Blind La. SO30: W End 4H 25
SO32: Curd 1H 35
Bloomsbury Wlk.
SO19: South 3G 41
Blossom Cl. SO30: Botl 5C 34
Blue Anchor La.
SO14: South 5D 4 (2B 40)
Bluebell Cl. SO31: Loc H 5D 48
Bluebell Ct. PO15: White 5H 45
Bluebell Gdns. SO45: Hythe 4F 53
Bluebell Rd.
SO16: Bass, S'ing 5D 22
Bluebell Way PO15: White 4H 45
Bluestar Gdns. SO30: Hed E 1A 34
Blundell La. SO31: Burs 3H 43
Blyth Cl. SO16: South 1B 28
Blythe Gdns. SO30: Hed E 1G 43
Boakes Pl. SO40: A'hst 3C 36
Boardwalk Way SO40: March . . .2E 39
Bodding Av. SO16: Nur 5B 20
Bodmin Rd. SO50: B'stke 4E 17
Bodycoats Rd. SO53: Cha F 1F 15
Bolderwood Cl. SO50: B'stke . . .5F 17
Boldrewood Rd. SO16: Bass 5A 22
Bolhinton Av. SO40: March 4B 38
Bonchurch Cl. SO16: S'ing 4E 23
Bond Rd. SO18: South 2G 31
Bond St. SO14: South 5E 31
Boniface Cl. SO40: Tott 3D 26
Boniface Cres. SO16: South 6B 20
BOORLEY GREEN 2D 34
Boorley Grn. Development
SO32: Botl 1E 35
Boothby Cl. SO40: Elin 5G 27
Borden Way SO52: N Bad 3E 13
Borrowdale Rd. SO16: South . . .2C 28
Bossington Cl. SO16: Rown 4C 20
Boston Cl. PO14: Titch 5H 49
Boston Ct. SO53: Cha F 6F 9
Bosville SO50: E'leigh 1H 15
Boswell Cl. SO19: South 5C 32
SO30: Botl 4E 35
BOTANY BAY 3A 42
Botany Bay Rd. SO19: South . . .2B 42
BOTLEY 4E 35
Botley Gdns. SO19: South 2E 43
Botley Hill SO30: Botl 5F 35
Botley Mills Craft & Bus. Cen.
SO30: Botl 4E 35
Botley Rd. SO16: Chil 2E 13
SO19: South 3C 42
SO30: Hed E, W End 2E 33
SO31: Burr, Swanw 5E 45
SO32: Curd 4G 35
SO50: Fair O, Hor H 2G 17
SO51: Rom 5D 6
SO52: N Bad 2E 13
Botley Station (Rail) 4G 35
Bottings Ind. Est.
SO30: Curd 4G 35
Boundary Acre SO31: Burs 1H 43
Boundary Cl. SO15: South 4D 28
Boundary Lakes Golf Course . . .3F 33
Boundary Rd. SO31: Burs 5F 43
(not continuous)
Boundstone SO45: Hythe 3D 52
Bourne Av. SO15: South 2G 29
Bourne Cl. SO21: Ott 1C 10
Bournemouth Rd.
SO53: Cha F 5D 14
Bourne Rd.
SO15: South 1A 4 (6H 29)
Bowater Cl. SO40: Calm 2C 26
Bowater Way SO40: Calm 2C 26
Bowcombe SO31: Net A 6C 42
Bowden Ho. SO17: South 1E 31
Bowden La. SO17: South 1E 31
Bower Cl. SO19: South 4H 41
SO45: Holb 5C 54
Bowers Dr. SO31: Burs 3F 43
Bow Lake Gdns.
SO50: B'stke 2D 16
Bow Lake Wlk. SO50: B'stke . . .2D 16
Bowland Ri. SO53: Cha F 6C 8
Bowland Way SO45: Blac 6E 55
Bowman Ct. SO19: South 2F 41
(Florence Rd.)
SO19: South 2B 42
(Range Gdns.)
Boyatt Cres. SO50: E'leigh 5A 10
Boyatt La. SO21: Ott 4A 10
SO50: E'leigh 5A 10
BOYATT WOOD 2A 16
Boyatt Wood Shop. Cen. 2A 16
Boyes La. SO21: Col C 4G 11
(not continuous)
Boynton Cl. SO53: Cha F 5D 8
Boyton Mead SO50: E'leigh 6C 10
Brabant Cl. PO15: White 6F 45
Brabazon Rd. PO15: Seg 2H 49
Bracken Cl. SO52: N Bad 4E 13
Bracken Cres. SO50: B'stke 5F 17
Bracken Hall SO16: Chil 1D 22
Bracken La. SO16: South 2E 29
Bracken Pl. SO16: Chil 2C 22
Bracken Rd. SO52: N Bad 4E 13
The Brackens SO31: Loc H 5F 49
SO45: Dib P 3B 52
Brackenway Rd. SO53: Cha F 5E 9
Bracklesham Cl.
SO19: South 2H 41
Brackley Av. SO50: Fair O 4H 17
Brackley Way SO40: Tott 3D 26
Brading Cl. SO16: S'ing 4E 23
Bradley Grn. SO16: South 5F 21
Bradshaw Cl. SO50: Fair O 1H 17
Braehead SO45: Hythe 4D 52
Braeside Cl. SO19: South 6G 31
Braeside Cres. SO19: South 6G 31
Braeside Rd. SO19: South 6G 31
Braishfield Cl. SO16: South 2D 28
Braishfield Rd.
SO51: Brai, Rom 3F 7
Bramble Cl. SO45: Holb 5C 54
SO50: E'leigh 2B 16
Bramble Dr. SO51: Rom 3F 7
Bramblegate SO50: Fair O 2G 17
Bramble Hill SO53: Cha F 1D 14
Bramble La. SO31: Sar G 2C 48
Bramble M. SO18: South 3A 32
The Brambles SO40: Tott 1E 27
Brambles Cl. SO21: Col C 5G 11
Brambling Cl. SO16: South 3F 21
The Bramblings SO40: Tott 4C 26
BRAMBRIDGE 5F 11
Brambridge SO50: B'dge 5E 11
Brambridge Park 4E 11
Bramdean M. SO19: South 6G 31
Bramdean Rd. SO18: South 3D 32
Bramley Cres. SO19: South 3B 42
Bramley Ho. SO30: Hed E 5H 33
Brampton Mnr. SO16: Bass 4B 22
Brampton Twr. SO16: Bass 4B 22
Bramshott Rd. SO19: South 5H 41
Bramston Rd. SO15: South 3G 29
Bramtoco Way SO40: Tott 4E 27
Bramwell Ct. SO19: South 5B 32
Branewick Cl. PO15: Seg 4H 49
Branksome Av. SO15: South 2G 29
Bransbury Cl. SO16: South 5G 21
Bransley Cl. SO51: Rom 3E 7
Brasenose Cl.
PO14: Titch C 6G 49
Brasher Cl. SO50: B'stke 5G 17
Breach La. SO50: B'stke 2D 16
Breamore Cl. SO50: E'leigh 1A 16
Breamore Rd. SO18: South 4D 32
Brean Cl. SO16: South 1C 28
Brecon Cl. SO45: Dib P 3C 52
SO53: Cha F 4D 14
Brecon Ho. SO19: South 3F 41
Brecon Rd. SO19: South 6C 32
Brendon Cl. SO45: Dib P 4B 52
Brendon Gdns. SO50: Fair O . . .4H 17
Brendon Grn. SO16: South 3D 28
Brentwood Cres.
SO18: South 2A 32
Breton Cl. PO15: White 6F 45
Brewer Cl. SO31: Loc H 3F 49
Brewery La. SO51: Rom 4B 6
Briardene Ct. SO40: Tott 4E 27
Briarswood SO16: South 2F 29
Briarswood Ri. SO45: Dib P 4B 52
Briar Way SO51: Rom 3F 7
Briarwood Rd. SO40: Tott 5C 26
Brickfield La. SO53: Cha F 2D 14
Brickfield Rd. SO17: South 1E 31
Brickfield Trad. Est.
SO53: Cha F 2E 15
Brick La. SO51: Rom 5C 6
Brickmakers Rd.
SO21: Col C 5F 11
Brickwoods Cl. SO51: Rom 4E 7
Bridge Cl. SO31: Burs 4H 43
Bridge Ct. SO51: Rom 6B 6
Bridge Rd. SO19: South 2F 41
SO31: Burs 4H 43
SO31: Lwr Swan, P Ga, Sar G
. . . . .1C 48
SO51: Rom 5D 6
Bridgers Cl. SO16: Rown 4C 20
Bridges Cl. SO50: E'leigh 4H 15
Bridge Ter.
SO14: South 6H 5 (2D 40)
Bridgwater Ct. SO15: South 5G 29
Bridlington Av. SO15: South 3H 29
Bridport Ct. SO15: South 6G 29
Brigantine Rd. SO31: Wars 6C 48
Brighstone Cl. SO16: S'ing 4E 23
Brighton Rd. SO15: South 4B 30
Brightside Rd. SO16: South 1D 28
Bright Wire Cres.
SO50: E'leigh 5H 15
Brindle Cl. SO16: Bass 4C 22
Brinsley Cl. SO19: South 6C 32
Brinton La. SO45: Hythe 1E 53
Brinton's Rd.
SO14: South 1F 5 (6C 30)
Brinton's Ter. SO14: South 5C 30
Britannia Ct.
SO14: South 2H 5 (6E 31)
Britannia Gdns. SO30: Hed E . . .6H 25
Britannia Rd.
SO14: South 1H 5 (6D 30)
Britannia Wharf
SO14: South 3H 5 (1E 41)
Britannic Ho. *SO14: South 6E 31*
(off Kent St.)
Briton St.
SO14: South 6E 5 (2C 40)
Brittany Cl. SO40: March 4D 38
Broadbent Cl. SO16: Rown 3B 20
Broad Grn.
SO14: South 3F 5 (1C 40)
Broadlands *6B 6*
(off Romsey By-Pass)
Broadlands Av. SO50: E'leigh . . .1A 16
Broadlands Lake 4E 19
Broadlands Rd. SO17: South . . .5D 22
Broad La. SO52: N Bad 2C 12
Broadleaf Cl. SO45: Dib P 5C 52
Broadley Cl. SO45: Holb 4C 54
Broadmeadow Cl. SO40: Tott . . .4E 27
Broadmead Rd. SO16: Nur 3B 20
BROADOAK 4D 34
Broad Oak SO30: Botl 4C 34
Broadoak Cl. SO45: Holb 5C 54
Broadwater Rd.
SO18: South 6H 23
SO51: Rom 6B 6
Broadway SO31: Hamb 2E 47
The Broadway SO17: South 2D 30
SO18: South 4D 32
Brocks Cl. SO45: Dib P 4B 52
BROKENFORD 4D 26
Brokenford Av. SO40: Tott 4G 27
Brokenford Bus. Cen.
SO40: Tott 4F 27
Brokenford La. SO40: Tott 4F 27
Bromley Rd. SO18: South 2H 31
Bronte Cl. SO40: Tott 5D 26
Bronte Gdns. PO15: White 5G 45
Bronte Way SO19: South 5G 31
Brook Av. SO31: Wars 4A 48
Brook Cl. SO31: Sar G 4B 48
SO52: N Bad 4E 13
SO53: Cha F 3E 15
Brook Ct. SO15: South 6H 29
BROOKE'S HILL 5B 18
Brookes Hill Ind. Est.
SO40: Calm 5B 18
Brookfield Gdns.
SO31: Sar G 3D 48
Brookfield Pl. SO17: South 1D 30
Brookfield Rd. SO50: Fair O 5H 17
Brook Ho. SO19: South 2A 42
Brook La. SO30: Botl 4D 34
SO31: Sar G 3E 49
SO31: Sar G, Wars 6A 48
Brooklyn Cl. SO21: Ott 2C 10
Brooklyn Ct. *SO21: Ott 2C 10*
(off Main Rd.)
Brook Rd. SO18: South 4A 32
SO50: Fair O 1F 17
Brookside SO40: Tott 6F 27
Brookside Av. SO15: South 4D 28
Brookside Cen. SO15: South 4C 28
Brookside Dr. SO31: Sar G 4B 48
Brookside Ho. SO18: S'ing 5G 23
Brookside Way SO18: S'ing 5G 23
SO30: W End 1E 33
Brooks Way SO21: Hurs 1D 8
Brookvale Ct. SO17: South 2C 30
Brookvale Rd. SO17: South 2C 30
Brook Valley SO16: South 1E 29
Brook Wlk. SO40: Calm 2C 26
Brook Way SO51: Rom 3D 6
Brookwood Av. SO50: E'leigh . . .4H 15
Brookwood Ind. Est.
SO50: E'leigh 4A 16
Brookwood Rd. SO16: South . . .3B 28
Broomhill Way
SO50: E'leigh 6A 10
Brooms Gro. SO19: South 2D 42
Broomy Cl. SO45: Dib 2A 52
Broughton Cl. SO16: South 2E 29
Broughton Ho. SO18: South 3G 31
Brownhill Cl. SO53: Cha F 6E 9
Brownhill Ct. SO16: South 6C 20
Brownhill Gdns. SO53: Cha F 6E 9
Brownhill Ho. SO16: South 6C 20
Brownhill Rd. SO52: N Bad 3E 13
(not continuous)
SO53: Cha F 6E 9
Brownhill Way SO16: Nur 6A 20
Browning Av. SO19: South 5D 32
Browning Cl. PO15: White 4G 45
SO40: Tott 4D 26
SO50: E'leigh 4H 15
Brownlow Av. SO19: South 5H 31
Brownlow Gdns.
SO19: South 5A 32
Brownwich La. PO14: Titch 5G 51
Browsholme Cl.
SO50: E'leigh 1A 16
Broxburn Cl. SO53: Cha F 4G 9
Brue Cl. SO53: Cha F 6D 8
Brunei Ho. SO16: Bass 4C 22
Brunel Cl. SO30: Hed E 2B 34
Brunel Rd. SO15: South 3A 28
SO40: Tott 6D 18
Brunel Way PO15: Seg 2H 49
Brunswick Cl. SO50: Fair O 4H 17
Brunswick Pl.
SO15: South 1D 4 (5B 30)
SO40: Tott 4E 27
Brunswick Rd. SO50: Fair O 4H 17
Brunswick Sq.
SO14: South 6E 5 (2C 40)
Bryanston Rd. SO19: South 6F 31
Bryony Cl. SO31: Loc H 5D 48
Bubb La. SO30: W End 6H 25
Buchanan Rd. SO16: South 4D 20

A-Z Southampton 59

Buchan Av.—Chapel Rd.

Buchan Av. PO15: White 5G **45**
Buchan Ct. SO45: Dib P 4A **52**
Buckingham Ct. *SO17: South . . .3C 30*
(off Westwood Rd.)
Buckland Cl. SO50: E'leigh 1A **16**
Buckland Gdns. SO40: Calm 1C **26**
Buckley Ct. SO16: South 2F **29**
Buckthorn Cl. SO40: Tott 3B **26**
Budds Cl. SO30: Hed E 1A **34**
Budds La. SO51: Rom 3B **6**
Budds La. Ind. Est.
SO51: Rom 3B **6**
Bugle St.
SO14: South 6D **4** (2B **40**)
Bullar Rd. SO18: South 4G **31**
Bullar St. SO14: South 5D **30**
Bullfinch Cl. SO40: Tott 4C **26**
Bullrush Cl. SO45: Dib P 5D **52**
Bulls Copse Rd. SO40: Tott 1F **37**
Burbush Cl. SO45: Holb 5C **54**
Burgess Ct. SO16: Bass 5D **22**
Burgess Gdns. SO16: South 6A **22**
Burgess Rd.
SO16: Bass, South 6H **21**
(not continuous)
SO17: Bass, S'ing 5C **22**
Burghclere Rd. SO19: South . . .5H **41**
Burgoyne Rd. SO19: South 1E **43**
Burgundy Cl. SO31: Loc H 5D **48**
Burke Dr. SO19: South 5C **32**
Burley Cl. SO40: Tott 4B **26**
SO53: Cha F 3D **14**
Burley Ct. SO17: South 1C **30**
Burley Down SO53: Cha F 3D **14**
Burlington Ct. SO19: South 6B **32**
Burlington Ho. SO30: Hed E 3B **34**
Burlington Mans.
SO15: South 4G **29**
Burlington Rd. SO15: South 5A **30**
Burma Ho. SO18: S'ing 5G **23**
Burma Rd. SO51: Rom 6C **6**
Burma Way SO40: March 4D **38**
Burmese Cl. PO15: White 6G **45**
Burnbank Gdns. SO40: Tott 4E **27**
Burnett Cl. SO18: South 2G **31**
SO45: Hythe 4F **53**
Burnetts La. SO30: W End 6G **25**
Burney Pl. SO31: Sar G 3D **48**
Burnham Beeches
SO53: Cha F 1D **14**
Burnham Chase SO18: South . . .4B **32**
Burns Cl. SO50: E'leigh 6G **15**
Burns Pl. SO16: South 1E **29**
Burns Rd. SO19: South 5D **32**
SO50: E'leigh 6H **15**
Burr Cl. SO21: Col C 5F **11**
BURRIDGE **4F 45**
Burridge Rd.
SO30: Botl, Curd 5G **35**
SO31: Burr 3E **45**
Burrow Hill Pl. SO50: B'stke . . .2D **16**
BURSLEDON **5H 43**
Bursledon Brickworks Industrial Mus.
. . . .**5C 44**
Bursledon Hgts. SO31: Burs . . .4H **43**
Bursledon Rd. SO19: South 5A **32**
SO30: Hed E 1H **43**
SO31: Burs 3G **43**
Bursledon Station (Rail) **5A 44**
Bursledon Windmill **3G 43**
Burton Rd. SO15: South 5A **30**
Bury Brickfield Pk. Cvn. Site . . .1A **38**
Bury La. SO40: Elin 6H **27**
Bury Rd. SO40: March 2B **38**
Busketts Way SO40: A'hst 3A **36**
BUTLOCKS HEATH **1D 46**
Buttercup Cl. SO30: Hed E 5G **33**
SO45: Hythe 5E **53**
Buttercup Wlk. SO40: Tott 6D **26**
Buttercup Way SO31: Loc H 4C **48**
Butterfield Rd. SO16: Bass 6A **22**
Buttermere Cl. SO16: South 1C **28**
BUTTSASH **6E 53**
Butts Ash Av. SO45: Hythe 6E **53**
Butts Ash Gdns. SO45: Hythe . . .5E **53**
Butts Ash La. SO45: Hythe 6D **52**
Butts Bri. Hill SO45: Hythe 4E **53**
Buttsbridge Rd. SO45: Hythe . . .5E **53**
Butt's Cl. SO19: South 1D **42**
Butt's Cres. SO19: South 1C **42**
Butt's Rd. SO19: South 3B **42**
Butt's Sq. SO19: South 1C **42**
Byam's La. SO40: March 3E **39**
Bye Rd. SO31: Lwr Swan 5B **44**
Byeways SO45: Hythe 4D **52**
Byron Ct.
SO15: South 1A **4** (5A **30**)
Byron Rd. SO19: South 5C **32**
SO50: E'leigh 3B **16**
By The Wood SO40: Calm 1D **26**

C

Cable St.
SO14: South 1H **5** (6E **31**)
SO50: E'leigh 5A **16**
Cabot Cl. SO31: Loc H 4C **48**
Cabot Dr. SO45: Dib 3A **52**
Cabot Ho. SO14: South 4G **5**
Cadland Ct. SO14: South 2E **41**
Cadland Pk. Est. SO45: Hard . . .3C **54**
Cadland Rd. SO45: F'ley 1H **55**
SO45: Hard 2B **54**
Caerleon Av. SO19: South 5C **32**
Caerleon Dr. SO19: South 5B **32**
Caernarvon Gdns.
SO53: Cha F 3C **14**
Caigers Grn. SO31: Burr 4F **45**
Caistor Cl. SO16: South 5E **21**
Calabrese SO31: Swanw 6F **45**
Calbourne SO31: Net A 6C **42**
Calder Cl. SO16: South 3C **28**
Calderwood Dr. SO19: South . . .1A **42**
Caledonia Dr. SO45: Dib 3B **52**
California Cl. SO40: Tott 2B **26**
CALMORE **1B 26**
Calmore Cres.
SO40: Calm, Tott 1B **26**
Calmore Dr. SO40: Calm 2B **26**
Calmore Gdns. SO40: Tott 4C **26**
Calmore Ind. Est. SO40: Tott . . .1E **27**
(not continuous)
Calmore Rd. SO40: Calm 1B **26**
Calshot Ct. SO14: South 3E **41**
Calshot Dr. SO53: Cha F 4C **14**
Calshot Rd. SO45: F'ley 2H **55**
Camargue Cl. PO15: White 5F **45**
Camborne Cl. SO50: B'stke 5E **17**
Cambria Dr. SO45: Dib 3B **52**
Cambrian Cl. SO31: Burs 3G **43**
Cambridge Dr. SO53: Cha F 4E **15**
(not continuous)
Cambridge Grn.
PO14: Titch C 5G **49**
SO53: Cha F 4E **15**
Cambridge Rd. SO14: South . . .3C **30**
Camelia Gdns. SO18: South 1A **32**
Camelia Gro. SO50: Fair O 1H **17**
Camellia Cl. SO52: N Bad 2E **13**
Camellia Ho. SO14: South 6G **5**
Camellia Way PO15: White 5H **45**
Cameron Ct. SO16: South 4D **20**
Camilla Cl. SO40: Calm 2B **26**
Camino Ct. PO14: Titch C 6H **49**
Camley Cl. SO19: South 4G **41**
Campbell Rd. SO50: E'leigh 6B **16**
Campbell Way SO50: Fair O 1F **17**
Campion Cl. SO31: Wars 6C **48**
Campion Dr. SO51: Rom 3F **7**
Campion Rd. SO19: South 6D **32**
Canada Pl. SO16: Bass 5A **22**
Canada Rd. SO19: South 3G **41**
Canal Cl. SO51: Rom 3D **6**
Canal Wlk.
SO14: South 5E **5** (2C **40**)
SO51: Rom 4C **6**
Canberra Rd. SO16: Nur 5H **19**
Canberra Towers
SO19: South 5H **41**
Candlemas Pl. SO17: South 3C **30**
Candover Ct. SO19: South 5A **42**
Candy La. SO18: South 4E **33**
Canford Cl. SO16: South 1B **28**
Cannon St. SO15: South 3G **29**
Canoe Cl. SO31: Wars 6D **48**
Canon Ct. SO50: Fair O 1G **17**
Canon Pl. SO19: South 6D **32**
Cantell Community Sports Cen.
. . . .**5C 22**
Canterbury Av. SO19: South 2C **42**
Canterbury Dr. SO45: Dib 3B **52**
Canton St. SO15: South 5B **30**
Canute Ho. SO14: South 5F **5**
Canute Rd.
SO14: South 6G **5** (2D **40**)
Canvey Ct. SO16: South 1C **28**
Capella Gdns. SO45: Dib 3B **52**
Capon Cl. SO18: S'ing 5G **23**
Capstan Gdns. SO31: Loc H 4G **49**
Capstan Rd. SO19: South 3F **41**
Captain's Pl.
SO14: South 6G **5** (2D **40**)
Caraway PO15: White 6H **45**
Cardinal Pl. SO16: South 1D **28**
Cardinal Way SO31: Loc H 4F **49**
Cardington Ct. SO16: South 5D **20**
Carey Rd. SO19: South 6C **32**
Carisbrooke SO31: Net A 6C **42**
Carisbrooke Ct. SO51: Rom 3D **6**
Carisbrooke Cres.
SO53: Cha F 2G **15**
Carisbrooke Dr. SO19: South . . .5H **31**
Carlisle Rd. SO16: South 3F **29**
The Carlton Commerce Cen.
SO14: South 4D **30**
Carlton Ct. SO15: South 3B **30**
Carlton Cres. SO15: South 5B **30**
Carlton Pl. SO15: South 5B **30**
Carlton Rd. SO15: South 4B **30**
Carlyn Dr. SO53: Cha F 6F **9**
Carnation Rd. SO16: S'ing 4E **23**
Carne Cl. SO53: Cha F 5E **9**
Caroline Ct. SO15: South 3F **29**
Carolyn Cl. SO19: South 3G **41**
Carpathia Cl. SO18: W End 1A **32**
Carpathia Ct. SO14: South 6E **5**
Carpathia Dr.
SO14: South 5G **5** (2D **40**)
Carpenter Cl. SO45: Hythe 2E **53**
Carpenters Cl. SO30: Hed E 1H **43**
Carpenter Wlk. SO45: F'ley 3F **55**
Carpiquet Pk. SO52: N Bad 3E **13**
Carrington Ho. SO17: South 2C **30**
Carrol Cl. SO50: Fair O 2G **17**
Carroll Cl. PO15: White 4G **45**
The Carronades SO14: South 2F **5**
Carthage Cl. SO53: Cha F 6H **9**
Caspian Cl. PO15: White 6F **45**
Castilian Way PO15: White 6F **45**
Castle Ct. SO15: South 5E **29**
Castle Ho. SO14: South 5D **4**
Castle La.
SO14: South 5D **4** (2B **40**)
(not continuous)
SO52: Cha F, N Bad 3F **13**
SO53: Cha F 3C **14**
Castle Pl. SO14: South 6D **4**
Castle Rd. SO18: South 1G **31**
SO31: Net A 1B **46**
Castleshaw Cl. SO16: South . . .4D **28**
Castle Sq.
SO14: South 5D **4** (2B **40**)
Castle St. SO14: South 4C **30**
Castle Way
SO14: South 4D **4** (1B **40**)
Castlewood SO53: Cha F 3D **14**
Catamaran Cl. SO31: Wars 6D **48**
Cateran Cl. SO16: South 3D **28**
Cathay Gdns. SO45: Dib 3A **52**
Catherine Cl. SO30: W End 1E **33**
Catherine Gdns.
SO30: W End 1E **33**
Catmint Cl. SO53: Cha F 6B **8**
Causeway SO51: Rom 6A **6**
Causeway Cres. SO40: Tott 3G **27**
Causton Gdns. SO50: E'leigh 4A **16**
Cavalier Cl. SO45: Dib 3B **52**
Cavell Pl. SO19: South 4H **41**
Cavendish Cl. SO51: Rom 2E **7**
Cavendish Dr. SO31: Loc H 4C **48**
Cavendish Gro. SO17: South . . .3B **30**
Cavendish M. SO15: South 3B **30**
C Avenue
SO45: F'ley 2C **54**, 1E **55**
Caversham Cl. SO19: South 1A **42**
SO30: W End 3D **32**
Cawte Rd. SO15: South 5G **29**
Cawtes Reach SO31: Wars 4B **48**
Caxton Av. SO19: South 5B **32**
Cecil Av. SO16: South 2F **29**
SO40: A'hst 3C **36**
Cecil Gdns. SO31: Sar G 3E **49**
Cecil Rd. SO19: South 2H **41**
Cedar Av. SO15: South 3G **29**
Cedar Cl. SO30: Hed E 4A **34**
SO31: Burs 5F **43**
Cedar Cres. SO52: N Bad 2D **12**
Cedar Gdns. SO14: South 3C **30**
Cedar Lawn SO51: Rom 3F **7**
Cedar Lodge SO15: South 3E **29**
Cedar Rd. SO14: South 3C **30**
SO45: Hythe 6E **53**
SO50: E'leigh 6G **15**
Cedar Wood Cl. SO50: Fair O . . .1H **17**
Cedarwood Cl. SO40: Calm 3C **26**
Cedric Cl. SO45: Blac 5F **55**
Celandine Av. SO31: Loc H 5D **48**
Celandine Cl. SO53: Cha F 2B **14**
Cement Ter.
SO14: South 5D **4** (2B **40**)
Cemetery Rd. SO15: South 3A **30**
Centenary Plaza
SO19: South 3E **41**
Centenary Quay SO19: South . . .3E **41**
Central Bri.
SO14: South 5G **5** (2D **40**)
Central Cres. SO40: March 2E **39**
The Central Precinct
SO53: Cha F 2E **15**
Central Rd. SO14: South 3C **40**
Central Sta. Bri.
SO15: South 2A **4** (6A **30**)
Central Trad. Est.
SO14: South 3H **5** (1D **40**)
Centre 27 Retail Pk. 2G **33**
Centre Ct. SO15: South 3F **29**
Centre Way SO31: Loc H 4D **48**
Centurion Ind. Pk.
SO18: South 4E **31**
Century Ct. SO14: South 6E **5**
Cerdic Mews SO31: Hamb 3G **47**
Cerne Cl. SO18: W End 2B **32**
SO52: N Bad 3D **12**
Chadwell Av. SO19: South 1B **42**
Chadwick Rd. SO50: E'leigh 5H **15**
Chadwick Way SO31: Hamb 5F **47**
Chafen Rd. SO18: South 3F **31**
Chaffinch Cl. SO40: Tott 3C **26**
Chalcroft Distribution Pk.
SO30: W End 4H **25**
Chalewood Rd. SO45: Blac 6E **55**
Chalfont Ct. SO16: South 2E **29**
Chalice Ct. SO30: Hed E 5H **33**
Chalk Hill SO18: W End 3C **32**
Challenger Pl. SO45: Dib P 3B **52**
Challenger Way
SO45: Dib, Dib P 2B **52**
Challis Ct.
SO14: South 5F **5** (2C **40**)
Chalmers Way SO31: Hamb 4E **47**
Chaloner Cres. SO45: Dib P 5E **53**
Chalvington Rd. SO53: Cha F . . .2E **15**
Chalybeate Cl. SO16: South 1F **29**
Chamberlain Hall 5B **22**
Chamberlain Rd.
SO17: South 6C **22**
Chamberlayne Ct.
SO52: N Bad 2F **13**
Chamberlayne Ho.
SO31: Net A 1B **46**
Chamberlayne Leisure Cen. . . .**4A 42**
Chamberlayne Rd.
SO31: Burs 5F **43**
(not continuous)
SO31: Net A 1B **46**
SO50: E'leigh 6A **16**
Chambers Av. SO51: Rom 5E **7**
Chambers Cl. SO16: Nur 4A **20**
Chancel Rd. SO31: Loc H 4F **49**
Chancery Ga. Bus. Cen.
SO15: South 5C **28**
Chandlers Ct. SO14: South 6E **5**
CHANDLER'S FORD **6G 9**
Chandler's Ford Ind. Est.
SO53: Cha F 2D **14**
Chandler's Ford Station
(Rail) **1E 15**
Chandlers Gate SO53: Cha F . . .1E **15**
Chandlers Pl. SO31: Net A 1B **46**
Chandlers Way SO31: P Ga 1F **49**
Chandos Ho.
SO14: South 5F **5** (2C **40**)
Chandos St.
SO14: South 5F **5** (2C **40**)
Channels Farm Rd.
SO16: S'ing 4F **23**
Channel Way
SO14: South 6H **5** (2D **40**)
The Chantry PO14: Titch C 4G **49**
Chantry Hall SO14: South 4G **5**
Chantry Rd.
SO14: South 5H **5** (2D **40**)
Chantry Wlk. SO31: Net A 2C **46**
CHAPEL . . . .**4G 5 (1D 40)**
Chapel Cl. SO30: W End 1D **32**
Chapel Cres. SO19: South 1A **42**
Chapel Drove SO30: Hed E 5H **33**
Chapel Gro. SO21: Col C 4F **11**
Chapel La. SO21: Ott 4B **10**
SO32: Curd 2H **35**
SO40: Tott 6E **27**
SO45: Blac 5E **55**
SO45: F'ley 2G **55**
Chapel Rd.
SO14: South 4G **5** (1D **40**)
SO30: W End 1D **32**
SO31: Sar G 1C **48**

Chapel St.
SO14: South 4F 5 (1C 40)
Charden Ct. SO18: South 4B 32
Charden Rd. SO50: B'stke 5C 17
Charlecote Dr. SO53: Cha F 5C 8
Charlecote Ho. SO15: South 1A 4
Charles Arden Cl.
SO16: South 1D 28
Charles Knott Gdns.
SO15: South 4B 30
Charles Ley Ct. SO45: F'ley 2H 55
Charles Miller Ct.
SO15: South 3B 30
Charles St.
SO14: South 5F 5 (2C 40)
Charleston Rd. SO45: Hard ...6H 53
Charles Watts Way
SO30: W End 4E 33
Charles Wyatt Ho.
SO14: South 4C 30
Charlie Adams Ct.
SO45: Hythe 3F 53
(off Seward Grn.)
Charliejoy Gdns.
SO14: South 5D 30
Charlie Soar Ct.
SO50: E'leigh 5A 16
Charlotte Cl. SO19: South ...3H 41
SO53: Cha F 6G 9
Charlotte Mede SO21: Ott ...2B 10
Charlotte Pl.
SO14: South 1E 5 (5C 30)
Charlton Rd. SO15: South ...3H 29
Charmus Rd. SO40: Calm ...1B 26
Charmwen Cres.
SO30: W End 1C 32
Charnwood Cl. SO40: Tott ...2D 26
SO53: Cha F 3E 9
Charnwood Cres. SO53: Cha F ..3E 9
Charnwood Gdns.
SO53: Cha F 3E 9
Charnwood Way SO45: Blac ...6E 55
Charter Cl. SO51: Rom 5D 6
Charter Ho.
SO14: South 6G 5 (3D 40)
Charterhouse Way
SO30: Hed E 2A 34
Chartwell Cl. PO14: Titch C ...6G 49
SO50: E'leigh 1B 16
The Chase PO14: Titch C ...5H 49
Chatsworth Rd. SO19: South ..5A 32
SO50: E'leigh 1B 16
Chaucer Rd. SO19: South ...5D 32
Chaveney Cl. SO45: Dib P ...5D 52
Chavy water SO51: Rom 6B 6
Chawton Cl. SO18: South 3D 32
Cheam Way SO40: Tott 2D 26
Cheddar Cl. SO19: South ...2G 41
Cheltenham Ct. SO17: South ..2C 30
Cheltenham Gdns.
SO30: Hed E 1A 34
Chelveston Cres.
SO16: South 5C 28
Chelwood Ga. SO16: Bass ...4B 22
Cheping Gdns. SO30: Botl ...5E 35
Chepstow Cl. SO40: Tott ...3C 26
SO53: Cha F 1D 14
Cherbourg Rd. SO50: E'leigh ..6H 15
Cheriton Av. SO18: South ...4C 32
Cheriton Rd. SO50: E'leigh ..1H 23
Cherryton Gdns.
SO45: Holb 5B 54
Cherry Tree Ct. SO31: Wars ..6A 48
SO50: E'leigh 4G 15
Cherry Tree Farm Ind. Est.
SO31: Burr 3G 45
Cherry Wlk. SO15: South ...3G 29
SO31: Wars 1A 50
Cherrywood SO30: Hed E 5H 33
Cherrywood Gdns.
SO40: Tott 4C 26
SO50: B'stke 5H 17
Chervil Cl. SO53: Cha F 1B 14
Cherville M. SO51: Rom 5B 6
Cherville M. SO51: Rom 4B 6
Cherville St. SO51: Rom 5B 6
Cherwell Cres. SO16: South ..3C 28
Cherwell Gdns. SO53: Cha F ...2F 15
Cherwell Ho. SO16: South ...2C 28
Chessel Av. SO19: South 4G 31
Chessel Cres. SO19: South ...4G 31
Chester Cl. SO16: South 1G 29
Chester Rd. SO18: South 2A 32
Chesterton Pl. PO15: White ...5G 45
Chestnut Av. SO21: Col C 4F 11
SO50: E'leigh 6F 15
SO53: Cha F 4E 15

Chestnut Cl. SO30: W End 6D 24
SO51: Rom 6G 7
SO53: Cha F 4E 15
Chestnut Ct. SO17: South 1D 30
Chestnut Dr. SO40: A'hst 2C 36
Chestnut Lodge SO16: Bass ...6A 22
Chestnut M. SO19: South 1C 42
Chestnut Ri. SO16: South 6F 15
Chestnut Rd. SO16: South 1E 29
The Chestnuts SO31: Loc H ...5E 49
Chestnut Wlk. SO30: Botl 4D 34
Chestnut Way
PO14: Titch C 6G 49
Chettle Rd. SO19: South 6E 33
Chetwynd Dr. SO16: Bass 5B 22
Chetwynd Rd. SO16: Bass 5B 22
Cheviot Cres. SO16: South ...3C 28
Cheviot Dr. SO45: Dib 3B 52
Cheviot Grn. SO31: Wars 1B 50
Cheviot Rd. SO16: South 3C 28
Chevron Bus. Pk.
SO45: Holb 2B 54
Chichester Cl. SO30: Hed E ...2A 34
SO31: Sar G 4C 48
Chichester Rd. SO18: South ...4A 32
Chickenhall La.
SO50: E'leigh 4C 16
Chidden Holt SO53: Cha F ...2C 14
Chilbolt Cl. SO18: South 3C 32
Chilcott Cl. SO52: N Bad 3E 13
Chilham Cl. SO50: E'leigh 6A 10
Chillenden Ct. SO40: Tott 5C 26
Chillerton SO31: Net A 6C 42
Chilling La. SO31: Wars 4C 50
Chillington Gdns.
SO53: Cha F 4D 8
Chiltern Cl. SO40: Tott 6D 26
Chiltern Grn. SO16: South ...3C 28
CHILWORTH 6A 14
Chilworth Cl. SO16: Chil 6H 13
Chilworth Drove
SO16: Chil, South 3F 21
SO16: South 4F 21
Chilworth Golf Course 4F 13
Chilworth Grange SO16: Chil ..1C 22
CHILWORTH OLD VILLAGE 5G 13
Chilworth Rd.
SO16: Bass, Chil 6A 14
The Chimes SO31: Loc H 4F 49
Chine Av. SO19: South 6G 31
(not continuous)
Chine Cl. SO31: Loc H 3E 49
Chirk Pl. SO51: Rom 5D 6
Chisholm Cl. SO16: South ...4D 20
Chivers Rd. SO51: Rom 1E 7
Christie Av. PO15: White 5G 45
Church Cl. SO31: Loc H 4F 49
SO50: B'stke 3D 16
SO52: N Bad 3E 13
Church End SO15: South 3G 29
Church Farm Cvn. Site 6F 39
Church Farm Cl. SO45: Dib ...6F 39
Churchfields SO45: F'ley 2H 55
Church Hill SO30: W End 1C 32
Churchill Cl. PO14: Titch C ...6G 49
Churchill Ho. SO16: South ...3C 32
Church La.
SO14: South 5D 4 (2B 40)
SO16: Nur 3F 19
SO17: South 1D 30
SO21: Col C 5F 11
SO30: Botl 6E 35
SO30: Hed E 6H 33
SO31: Burs 5H 43
SO32: Curd 3H 35
SO45: F'ley 2G 55
SO51: Rom 5B 6
Church Path SO17: South 1D 30
SO19: South 2A 42
Church Pl. SO51: Rom 5B 6
Church Rd. PO14: Titch C ...4H 49
SO31: Loc H 4F 49
SO31: Wars 6B 48
SO50: B'stke 4D 16
SO51: Rom 5B 6
Church Vw. SO50: E'leigh 6A 16
Churchview SO19: South 2A 42
Church Vw. Cl. SO19: South ..2A 42
Churchward Gdns.
SO30: Hed E 1A 34
Cineworld Cinema
Southampton 6G 5 (3D 40)
Cineworld Cinema
PO15: White 5H 45

Cinnamon Ct. SO15: South 5A 30
SO18: South 3G 31
Cirrus Gdns. SO31: Hamb 5F 47
City Commerce Cen.
SO14: South 5G 5 (2D 40)
City Ct. SO14: South 6E 5
City Cruise Terminal ...5B 4 (2A 40)
City Gym 3F 29
City Ind. Pk.
SO15: South 3A 4 (1A 40)
Civic Cen. Rd.
SO14: South 6B 30
SO15: South 2C 4 (6B 30)
Clamp Grn. SO21: Col C 5F 11
Clandon Dr. SO50: E'leigh 1H 15
Clanfield Cl. SO53: Cha F 1F 15
Clanfield Dr. SO53: Cha F 1F 15
Clanfield Rd. SO18: South 4C 32
Clanfield Way SO53: Cha F ...1F 15
Clare Cl. PO14: Titch C 5G 49
Clare Gdns. SO45: Blac 6F 55
Claremont Cl. SO50: E'leigh ..1A 16
Claremont Cres.
SO15: South 4E 29
Claremont Rd. SO15: South ...4E 29
Clarence Ho. SO14: South 5E 31
Clarendon Cl. SO51: Rom 3E 7
Clarendon Cres.
PO14: Titch C 6F 49
Clarendon Rd. SO16: South ...3E 29
Claude Ashby Cl.
SO18: S'ing 5G 23
Claudeen Cl. SO18: S'ing 4G 23
Claudeen Ct. SO18: South ...5E 33
Claudius Cl. SO53: Cha F 6H 9
Claudius Gdns. SO53: Cha F ..6H 9
Clausentum Cl. SO53: Cha F ..6G 9
Clausentum Rd.
SO14: South 4C 30
Clayfields Sports Cen. 2B 52
CLAYPITS 4H 43
Claypits La. SO45: Dib 3A 52
Cleasby Cl. SO16: South 4B 28
Cleek Dr. SO16: Bass 4B 22
Cleethorpes Rd.
SO19: South 1B 42
The Cleeves SO40: Tott 5C 26
Cleland Rd. PO14: Titch C ...4H 49
Cleric Ct. PO14: Titch C 4H 49
Cleveland Ct. SO18: South ...2A 32
Cleveland Dr. SO45: Dib P ...4B 52
Cleveland Rd. SO18: South ...1H 31
Clevelands SO53: Cha F 4D 8
Cleverley Ri. SO31: Burs 5A 44
The Cliff SO19: South 3F 31
(off Portsmouth Rd.)
Cliffe Av. SO31: Hamb 4E 47
Clifford Dibben M.
SO14: South 3C 30
Clifford Pl. SO50: Fair O 1F 17
Clifford St.
SO14: South 2G 5 (6H 29)
Cliff Rd. SO15: South 6H 29
Clifton Gdns. SO15: South ...3E 29
SO18: W End 2C 32
Clifton Rd. SO15: South 3E 29
Clipper Cl. SO31: Wars 6C 48
Clipper Ho. SO14: South 4H 5
The Clock Ho. SO40: Calm ...1A 26
The Cloisters SO16: Bass 6C 22
SO51: Rom 3B 6
The Close SO18: South 4D 32
SO30: Hed E 5H 33
SO31: Hamb 3G 47
SO45: Holb 6D 54
SO50: B'dge 4D 10
Clovelly Rd.
SO14: South 1F 5 (5C 30)
Clover Cl. SO31: Loc H 5C 48
Clover Nooke SO15: South ...3A 28
Clover Way SO30: Hed E 5G 33
SO51: Rom 4F 7
Clyde Ho. SO14: South 6E 31
Clydesdale Rd.
PO15: White 6F 45
Clydesdale Way SO40: Tott ...3B 26
Coach Hill Cl. SO53: Cha F ...6D 8
Coachmakers M. SO51: Rom ..5B 6
Coachmans Copse
SO18: South 1A 32
Coach Rd. SO31: Hamb 5E 47
Coal Pk. La.
SO31: Lwr Swan 5B 44
Coalporters Amateur Rowing Club
..........5E 31
Coalville Rd. SO19: South ...1B 42

Coates Rd. SO19: South 1D 42
Coat Gdns. SO45: Hythe 3E 53
Cobalt Quarter SO14: South ...3D 40
(off Maritime Wlk.)
Cobbett Ct. SO18: South 4G 31
Cobbett Rd. SO18: South 4G 31
Cobbett Way SO30: Botl 4D 34
Cobden Av. SO18: South 2F 31
Cobden Bri. SO17: South 2F 31
SO18: South 2F 31
Cobden Cl. SO18: South 3G 31
Cobden Cres. SO18: South ...3H 31
Cobden Gdns. SO18: South ...2G 31
Cobden Hgts. SO18: South ...2G 31
Cobden Ri. SO18: South 2G 31
Coblands Av. SO40: Tott 4D 26
Coburg Ho. SO14: South 5E 31
Coburg St. SO14: South 5E 31
Cockerell Cl. PO15: Seg 2G 49
Cockleshell Cl.
SO31: Wars 6C 48
Cocklydown La. SO40: Tott ...1D 36
Colburn Cl. SO16: South 1B 28
COLBURY 3D 36
Colby St. SO16: South 1D 28
Colchester Av. SO50: B'stke ..3E 17
Coldeast Cl. SO31: Sar G 2D 48
Coldeast Way SO31: Sar G ...2D 48
COLDEN COMMON 5G 11
Coldharbour La. SO16: Nur ...1G 19
Colebrook Av. SO15: South ...2G 29
Coleman St.
SO14: South 3G 5 (1D 40)
Coleridge Cl. SO31: Wars 6B 48
Coleridge Ct. SO19: South ...6D 32
Coleridge Dr. PO15: White ...4G 45
Coles Cl. SO50: E'leigh 4B 16
Coles Mede SO21: Ott 2B 10
(not continuous)
Coleson Rd. SO18: South 3G 31
Coleville Av. SO45: F'ley 2H 55
College Cl. SO31: Hamb 5F 47
College Pl. SO15: South 5C 30
College Rd. SO19: South 3F 41
College St.
SO14: South 5F 5 (2C 40)
Collett Cl. SO30: Hed E 1H 33
Collier Cl. SO17: South 3E 31
Collingbourne Dr.
SO53: Cha F 1C 14
Collingworth Ri. SO31: P Ga ..1F 49
Collins Cl. SO53: Cha F 1B 14
Collins Ho. SO50: E'leigh 4C 16
SO53: Cha F 1F 15
Colne Av. SO16: South 6B 20
Colne Cl. SO16: South 1C 28
Colombus Ho. SO14: South ...4G 5
Colonel Crabbe M.
SO16: Bass 4B 22
The Colonnade SO19: South ..2F 41
Colt Cl. SO16: Rown 4G 28
Colton Copse SO53: Cha F ...1B 14
Coltsfoot Cl. SO30: Hed E ...4H 33
Coltsfoot Dr. SO31: Loc H ...5C 48
Coltsfoot Wlk. SO51: Rom ...3F 7
Colts Rd. SO16: Rown 2C 20
Columbine Wlk. SO40: Tott ...6D 26
Columbus Dr. SO31: Sar G ...2D 48
Colvedene Cl. SO21: Col C ...4F 11
Colvin Gdns. SO53: Cha F ...5D 8
Colwell Cl. SO16: South 3B 28
Combined Court
Southampton 5C 30
Comfrey Cl. SO51: Rom 3F 7
Comines Way SO30: Hed E ...5E 33
Commercial Rd.
SO14: South 1C 4 (6B 30)
SO15: South 1B 4 (6A 30)
SO40: Tott 4G 27
Commercial St. SO18: South ..4A 32
Commodore Ct.
SO14: South 6G 5 (2D 40)
The Common SO15: South ...2A 30
SO31: Burs 4G 43
Common Cl. SO53: Cha F 5E 9
Common Flds. SO30: Hed E ...5F 33
Common Gdns. SO53: Cha F ..5E 9
Common La. PO14: Titch 1H 51
Common Rd. SO53: Cha F ...5E 9
The Compass
SO14: South 4G 5 (1D 40)
Compass Cl. SO19: South 1A 42
Compass Ct. SO17: South ...2C 30
Compass Point SO31: Hamb ...5E 47
Compass Way
SO31: Lwr Swan 5A 44
Compton Cl. SO50: E'leigh ...1H 15

Compton Ho. SO16: South 3F **29**
   SO40: Tott 2D **26**
Compton Rd. SO40: Tott 3G **27**
Compton Wlk.
   SO14: South 1F **5** (6C **30**)
Concorde Cl. PO15: Seg 2H **49**
Concorde Way PO15: Seg 2H **49**
Condor Cl. SO19: South 2F **41**
Conduct Gdns.
   SO50: E'leigh 5G **15**
Conference Dr. SO31: Loc H ...4F **49**
Conifer Cl. SO45: Hythe 3C **52**
Conifer Rd. SO16: South 5E **21**
Coniston Gdns. SO30: Hed E ..6H **33**
Coniston Rd. SO16: South 3A **28**
   SO50: E'leigh 5H **15**
Connemara Cres.
   PO15: White 6F **45**
Conrad Gdns. PO15: White ...5G **45**
Consort Cl. SO50: E'leigh 2B **16**
Consort Rd. SO50: E'leigh 2B **16**
Constable Cl. SO19: South 3C **42**
Constantine Av. SO53: Cha F ..1G **15**
Constantine Cl. SO53: Cha F ..1H **15**
Consulate Ho.
   SO14: South 6H **5** (2D **40**)
Conway Cl. SO53: Cha F 4D **14**
Cook Ho. SO14: South 6G **5**
Cooks La. SO40: Calm 1B **26**
Cook St. SO14: South 4F **5** (1C **40**)
Coombedale SO31: Loc H 5F **49**
Cooper Rd. SO40: A'hst 2C **36**
Cooper's Cl. SO18: W End 2C **32**
Coopers Ct. SO14: South 6E **5**
Cooper's La. SO19: South 2F **41**
Copeland Rd. SO16: South 2B **28**
Copenhagen Towers
   SO19: South 5G **41**
Copinger Cl. SO40: Tott 5C **26**
Copper Cl. SO50: E'leigh 4H **15**
Copperfield Rd. SO16: Bass ...4C **22**
Copperfields SO40: Tott 4B **26**
Coppice Gdns. SO18: South ...4D **32**
Coppice Rd. SO40: Calm 1C **26**
The Copse SO51: Rom 3F **7**
   SO53: Cha F 2G **15**
Copse Bus. Cen. SO40: Tott ..1G **37**
Copse Cl. SO21: Ott 1C **10**
   SO40: Tott 5F **27**
   SO52: N Bad 3D **12**
Copse La. SO16: Chil 6B **14**
   SO31: Hamb 5F **47**
Copse Vw. SO19: South 6E **33**
Copsewood Rd. SO18: South ..1G **31**
   SO40: A'hst 2C **36**
   SO45: Hythe 3D **52**
Copthorne La. SO45: F'ley ...2H **55**
Coracle Cl. SO31: Wars 6D **48**
Corbiere Cl. SO16: South 6C **20**
Corbould Rd. SO45: Dib P 5D **52**
Cordelia Cl. SO45: Dib P 3B **52**
Coriander Dr. SO40: Tott 4C **26**
Coriander Way PO15: White ...5H **45**
Corinna Gdns. SO45: Dib 3B **52**
Corinthian Rd. SO53: Cha F ...6G **9**
Cork La. SO40: March 3D **38**
Cormorant Dr. SO45: Hythe ..4G **53**
Cornel Rd. SO19: South 6H **31**
Cornfield Cl. SO53: Cha F 1B **14**
Cornflower Cl. SO31: Loc H ...5C **48**
Cornforth Rd. SO40: Calm 2C **26**
Cornmarket SO51: Rom 5B **6**
Cornwall Cl. SO18: South 1A **32**
Cornwall Cres. SO18: South ...1H **31**
Cornwall Rd. SO18: South 1H **31**
   SO53: Cha F 4E **15**
Coronation Av. SO15: South ..6A **22**
Coronation Homes
   SO18: South 3D **32**
Coronation Pde.
   SO31: Hamb 4E **47**
   (off Kings Av.)
Corsair Dr. SO45: Dib 3B **52**
Cortina Way SO30: Hed E 6B **34**
Corvette Av. SO31: Wars 6D **48**
Corylus Cl. SO40: Tott 2B **26**
Cosford Cl. SO50: B'stke 5G **17**
Cossack Grn.
   SO14: South 3F **5** (1C **40**)
Cosworth Dr. SO45: Dib 3B **52**
Cotsalls SO50: Fair O 2F **17**
Cotswold Cl. SO45: Dib P 3B **52**
Cotswold Rd. SO16: South 3D **28**
Cotton Cl. SO50: B'stke 4E **17**
Coulsdon Rd. SO30: Hed E ...5A **34**
Coultas Cl. SO53: Cha F 3G **9**

COUNTESS MOUNTBATTEN HOUSE
   ....1E **33**
COURSE PARK 5G **49**
Course Pk. Cres.
   PO14: Titch C 5G **49**
Court Cl. SO18: South 5A **32**
   SO40: Calm 1D **26**
Courtenay Cl. PO15: Seg 4H **49**
Courtier Cl. SO45: Dib 3A **52**
Courtland Gdns. SO16: Bass ..4D **22**
Court Rd. SO15: South 4B **30**
Court Royal M. SO15: South ..3B **30**
Coventry Rd. SO15: South 5B **30**
The Covert SO51: Rom 6E **7**
Cowdray Cl. SO16: South 5F **21**
Cowes La. SO31: Wars 4B **50**
Cowley Cl. SO16: South 1C **28**
Cowper Rd. SO19: South 5D **32**
Cowslip Cl. SO31: Loc H 5C **48**
Cowslip Wlk. SO40: Tott 6D **26**
   (Denbigh Cl.)
Cowslip Way SO51: Rom 3F **7**
   (Trevone Cl.)
Cox Dale PO14: Titch C 6G **49**
COXFORD 1E **29**
Coxford Cl. SO16: South 1E **29**
Coxford Drove SO16: South ...6E **21**
Coxford Rd. SO16: South 1D **28**
Cox Row SO53: Cha F 4E **15**
Cox's Dr. SO19: South 3B **42**
Cox's La. SO19: South 3F **41**
Cozens Cl. SO19: South 4G **41**
Crabapple Cl. SO40: Tott 4C **26**
Crabbe La. SO16: Bass 4C **22**
   (not continuous)
Crabbs Way SO40: Tott 4B **26**
Crableck La. SO31: Sar G 2A **48**
Crabtree SO16: South 2D **28**
Crabwood Cl. SO16: South ...1D **28**
Crabwood Dr. SO30: W End ..2E **33**
Crabwood Rd. SO16: South ...1C **28**
Cracknore Hard SO40: March ..4E **39**
Cracknore Hard La.
   SO40: March 3E **39**
Cracknore Ind. Pk.
   SO40: March 3G **39**
Cracknore Rd. SO15: South ...6H **29**
CRAMPMOOR 3H **7**
Crampmoor La. SO51: Cram ...3G **7**
Cranberry Cl. SO40: March 4D **38**
Cranborne Gdns. SO53: Cha F ..4D **8**
Cranbourne Cl. SO15: South ..1H **29**
Cranbourne Dr. SO21: Ott 2B **10**
Cranbourne Pk. SO30: Hed E ..1A **44**
The Cranbury SO14: South 5C **30**
   (off Cranbury Ter.)
Cranbury Av. SO14: South 5C **30**
Cranbury Cl. SO21: Ott 3B **10**
Cranbury Ct. SO19: South 2H **41**
   (off Cranbury Rd.)
Cranbury Gdns. SO31: Old N ..4F **43**
Cranbury Pl. SO14: South 5C **30**
Cranbury Rd. SO19: South 2H **41**
   SO50: E'leigh 6A **16**
   (not continuous)
Cranbury Ter. SO14: South ...5C **30**
Cranbury Towers
   SO14: South 5C **30**
   (off Cranbury Pl.)
Cranford Gdns. SO53: Cha F ..5D **8**
Cranford Ho. SO17: South 1C **30**
Cranford Way SO17: South 1C **30**
Cranleigh Ct. SO17: South 3C **30**
Cranleigh Rd. SO30: Hed E ...5A **34**
Cranmer Dr. SO16: Nur 4A **20**
Cranmore SO31: Net A 6C **42**
Cranwell Cl. SO16: South 4D **20**
Cranwell Rd. SO53: Cha F 1F **15**
Craven St.
   SO14: South 2F **5** (6C **30**)
Craven Wlk.
   SO14: South 2E **5** (6C **30**)
Crawford Cl. SO16: Nur 4B **20**
Crawte Av. SO45: Holb 6D **54**
Creedy Gdns. SO18: W End ...6A **24**
Creighton Rd. SO15: South ...5D **28**
The Crescent SO19: South 3A **42**
   SO31: Net A 1C **46**
   SO40: March 4C **38**
   SO50: E'leigh 3A **16**
   SO51: Rom 4E **7**
   SO52: N Bad 2D **12**
Cressey Rd. SO51: Rom 5C **6**

Crest Way SO19: South 1C **42**
Crestwood College Leisure Cen.
   ....2H **15**
Crestwood Vw. SO19: South ..2H **15**
Crete Cotts. SO45: Dib P 6C **52**
Crete La. SO45: Dib P 5D **52**
Crete Rd. SO45: Dib P 6D **52**
Crichton Ho. SO31: Net A 1B **46**
Crigdon Cl. SO16: South 3C **28**
Crispin Cl. SO31: Loc H 3F **49**
The Croft SO40: Calm 1C **26**
   SO50: E'leigh 5A **16**
   SO53: Cha F 4E **15**
Croft Cl. SO45: Hythe 4E **53**
Crofton Cl. SO17: South 2C **30**
Crofton Way SO31: Wars 6A **48**
Cromalt Cl. SO45: Dib P 4B **52**
Cromarty Rd. SO16: South 4C **20**
Cromer Rd. SO16: South 2B **28**
Crompton Way PO15: Seg 2G **49**
Cromwell Rd. SO15: South 4B **30**
Crooked Hays Cl.
   SO40: March 4D **38**
Crookham Rd. SO19: South ...5H **41**
Crossbow Ho. SO19: South ...3F **41**
   (off John Thornycroft Rd.)
CROSSHOUSE 5H **5** (2D **40**)
Cross Ho. Cen.
   SO14: South 5H **5** (2E **41**)
Crosshouse Rd.
   SO14: South 6H **5** (2E **41**)
Crossley Ct. SO15: South 5G **29**
Crossley Pl. SO15: South 5A **30**
Cross Rd. SO19: South 4G **31**
Crosstrees SO31: Sar G 1D **48**
The Crossways SO53: Cha F ...3E **15**
Crosswell Cl. SO19: South 6C **32**
Crowders Grn. SO21: Col C ...5F **11**
CROWDHILL 3H **17**
Crowlin Ho. SO40: Tott 3C **26**
Crown St. SO15: South 3F **29**
Crows Nest La. SO32: Botl 2D **34**
CROWSPORT 4G **47**
Crowsport SO31: Hamb 4G **47**
Crowther Cl. SO19: South 1C **42**
Croydon Cl. SO16: South 5E **21**
Crummock Rd. SO53: Cha F ..5C **8**
Crusader Rd. SO30: Hed E 6B **34**
Crusaders Way SO53: Cha F ..1B **14**
Cuckmere La. SO16: South ...3A **28**
CUCKOO BUSHES 5E **9**
Cuckoo Bushes La.
   SO53: Cha F 5D **8**
Cuckoo La.
   SO14: South 6D **4** (2B **40**)
Cudworth Mead SO30: Hed E ..2B **34**
Culford Av. SO40: Tott 5F **27**
Culford Way SO40: Tott 5F **27**
Culver SO31: Net A 6C **42**
Culver Cl. SO16: South 1B **28**
Culvery Gdns. SO18: W End ..2A **32**
Cumberland Av. SO53: Cha F ..1G **15**
Cumberland Cl. SO53: Cha F ..1G **15**
Cumberland Pl.
   SO15: South 1C **4** (6B **30**)
Cumberland St.
   SO14: South 3G **5** (1D **40**)
Cumberland Way SO45: Dib ...3A **52**
Cumber Rd. SO31: Loc H 4C **48**
Cumbrian Way SO16: South ...3C **28**
Cummins Grn. SO31: Burs 4G **43**
Cunard Av. SO15: South 3G **29**
Cunard Rd. SO14: South 3C **40**
Cunningham Cres.
   SO19: South 1B **42**
Cunningham Dr. SO31: Loc H ..3F **49**
Cunningham Gdns.
   SO31: Old N 5F **43**
CUPERNHAM 3E **7**
Cupernham Cl. SO51: Rom ...3D **6**
Cupernham La. SO51: Rom ...1D **6**
Cupid Ho. SO17: South 6E **23**
CURBRIDGE 1H **45**
Curbridge Nature Reserve 1G **45**
CURDRIDGE 3H **35**
Curlew Cl. SO16: South 4F **21**
   SO45: Hythe 4F **53**
Curlew Dr. SO45: Hythe 4F **53**
Curlew Sq. SO50: E'leigh 5G **15**
Curlew Wlk. SO45: Hythe 4F **53**
Curzon Cl. SO16: South 5H **21**
Cutbush La. SO18: South 1A **32**
   (not continuous)
Cutforth Way SO51: Rom 2E **7**
Cutter Av. SO31: Wars 6C **48**
Cygnus Gdns. SO45: Dib 3A **52**
Cypress Av. SO19: South 6H **31**

Cypress Gdns. SO30: Botl 4E **35**
   SO40: Tott 4C **26**
Cypress Gro. SO53: Cha F 5E **9**
Cyprus Rd. PO14: Titch C 6G **49**

D

Daffodil Rd. SO16: S'ing 5E **23**
Dahlia Rd. SO16: Bass 5C **22**
Daintree Cl. SO19: South 2D **42**
Dairy La. SO16: Nur 5G **19**
Daisy La. SO31: Loc H 4F **49**
Daisy Rd. SO16: Bass 5D **22**
Dakota Way SO50: E'leigh 1H **23**
Dale Grn. SO53: Cha F 4D **8**
Dale Rd. SO16: South 1G **29**
   SO45: Hythe 3D **52**
Dales Way SO40: Tott 3B **26**
Dale Valley Cl. SO16: South ..1G **29**
Dale Valley Gdns.
   SO16: South 1G **29**
Dale Valley Rd. SO16: South ..1G **29**
Dalmally Gdns. SO18: South ..3H **31**
Damen Cl. SO30: Hed E 6H **33**
Damson Cres. SO50: Fair O ...6G **17**
Danbury Gdns. SO53: Cha F ..3C **14**
Danbury Way SO16: Nur 6B **20**
Dane Cl. SO45: Blac 4F **55**
Danehurst Pl. SO31: Loc H ...5E **49**
Daniels Wlk. SO40: Calm 2B **26**
Danube Dr. SO31: Swanw 6F **45**
Dapple Pl. SO40: March 4E **39**
Dark La. SO45: Blac 4E **55**
Darlee Ga. SO31: Old N 4F **43**
Darlington Gdns.
   SO15: South 2H **29**
Dart Ho. SO18: South 3H **31**
Dartington Rd. SO50: B'stke ..2D **16**
Dart Rd. SO18: W End 6B **24**
Darwin Rd. SO15: South 4H **29**
   SO50: E'leigh 3B **16**
D Avenue SO45: F'ley ..2D **54**, 1F **55**
David Ct. SO51: Rom 6D **6**
David Lloyd Leisure
   Southampton 6B **20**
   West End 2F **33**
David Lockhart Ct.
   SO14: South 2D **30**
David Moxon Annexe
   SO14: South 4G **5**
Davidson Cl. SO45: Hythe 2F **53**
Dawlish Av. SO15: South 3H **29**
Dawnay Cl. SO16: S'ing 4F **23**
Dawson Lodge SO30: W End ..2F **33**
Dawson Rd. SO19: South 3C **42**
Dawtrey Ct. SO17: South 1E **31**
Dayrell Cl. SO40: Calm 2B **26**
Deacon Cl. SO19: South 6A **32**
Deacon Cres. SO19: South 6A **32**
Deacon Rd. SO19: South 6A **32**
   SO31: Loc H 5F **49**
Deacon Trad. Est.
   SO50: E'leigh 5C **16**
Deakin Ct. SO53: Cha F 2E **15**
Dean Ct. SO18: South 3G **31**
   SO30: Hed E 4H **33**
The Deanery SO53: Cha F 4D **8**
Deanery Halls SO14: South ...5G **5**
Deanfield Cl. SO31: Hamb 5F **47**
Deanfields Ct. SO18: South ...3B **32**
Dean M. SO18: South 4A **32**
Dean Pl. SO53: Cha F 1E **15**
Dean Rd. SO18: South 3A **32**
   SO50: Fair O 6H **17**
Deansfield Cl. SO51: Rom 4E **7**
Dee Cl. SO53: Cha F 2D **14**
The Deepdene SO18: South ...3G **31**
Deeping Cl. SO19: South 4H **41**
Deerbrook Cl. SO31: Sar G ...2D **48**
Deerhurst Cl. SO40: Tott 5D **26**
Deerleap Cl. SO45: Hythe 3E **53**
Deerleap La.
   SO40: March, Tott 2D **36**
Deerleap Way SO45: Hythe ...3E **53**
Deer Pk. Farm Ind. Est.
   SO50: Fair O 2H **17**
Deer Wlk. SO30: Hed E 3B **34**
Defender Rd. SO19: South 2F **41**
Defender Wlk. SO19: South ...2F **41**
Defoe Cl. PO15: White 5G **45**
De Grouchy La. SO17: South ..2C **30**
Delamere Gdns.
   SO14: South 3H **17**
Delft Cl. SO31: Loc H 4D **48**
Delius Av. SO19: South 2D **42**
The Dell SO15: South 5A **30**

Dell Cl.—Exmouth St.

Dell Cl. SO50: Fair O 2F **17**
Dell Rd. SO18: South 1H **31**
Delta Ho. SO16: Chil 6G **13**
Dempsey Cl. SO19: South 1B **42**
Denbigh Cl. SO40: Tott 6D **26**
SO50: E'leigh 2H **15**
Denbigh Gdns. SO16: Bass 5B **22**
Dene Cl. SO16: Chil 2B **22**
SO31: Sar G 3C **48**
Dene Rd. SO40: A'hst 3C **36**
Dene Way SO40: A'hst 2C **36**
Denham Flds. SO50: Fair O 4H **17**
Denham Gdns. SO31: Net A 2B **46**
Denmead Rd. SO18: South 3C **32**
Dennison Ct. SO15: South 3F **29**
Denny Cl. SO45: F'ley 2H **55**
Denyer Wlk. SO19: South 3E **41**
Denzil Av. SO14: South 5C **30**
SO31: Net A 1C **46**
Depden Gdns. SO45: Dib P 5B **52**
Depedene Cl. SO45: Holb 4B **54**
Derby Rd.
SO14: South 1G **5** (6D **30**)
SO50: E'leigh 5G **15**
Deridene Ct. SO40: Tott 5D **26**
Derwent Cl. SO18: W End 2B **32**
Derwent Dr. SO40: Tott 3B **26**
Derwent Rd. SO16: South 2C **28**
Desborough Rd.
SO50: E'leigh 6A **16**
Devine Gdns. SO50: B'stke 5E **17**
Devon Cl. SO53: Cha F 4E **15**
Devon Dr. SO53: Cha F 4E **15**
Devon M. SO15: South 1A **4**
Devonshire Gdns.
SO31: Burs 3G **43**
SO45: Hythe 6E **53**
Devonshire Mans.
SO15: South 1C **4**
Devonshire Rd.
SO15: South 1C **4** (5B **30**)
Dewar Cl. PO15: Seg 2G **49**
Dew La. SO50: E'leigh 4H **15**
Dewsbury Ct. SO18: South 1A **32**
Dibben Wlk. SO51: Rom 3F **7**
Dibble Dr. SO52: N Bad 4D **12**
DIBDEN 1A **52**
Dibden Golf Course 1A **52**
Dibden Lodge Cl.
SO45: Hythe 1D **52**
DIBDEN PURLIEU 5C **52**
Dibles Pk. SO31: Wars 6C **48**
Dibles Rd. SO31: Wars 6B **48**
(not continuous)
Dibles Wharf SO14: South 6E **31**
Dickens Dell SO40: Tott 4B **26**
Dickens Dr. PO15: White 4G **45**
Didcot Rd. SO15: South 2G **29**
Diligence Cl. SO31: Burs 4G **43**
Diment Cres. SO51: Rom 2E **7**
Dimond Cl. SO18: South 2G **31**
Dimond Hill SO18: South 2G **31**
Dimond Rd. SO18: South 1G **31**
Dingle Way SO31: Loc H 3E **49**
Dirty Dr. SO52: N Bad 2H **13**
Disa Ho. SO15: South 5A **30**
Dodwell La. SO31: Burs 4H **43**
Dodwell Ter. SO31: Burs 4H **43**
Doe Wlk. SO30: Hed E 3B **34**
Dolphin Cl. SO50: B'stke 5F **17**
Dolton Rd. SO16: South 6D **20**
Dominy Cl. SO45: Hythe 2F **53**
Doncaster Drove
SO50: E'leigh 2G **23**
Doncaster Rd. SO50: E'leigh . . .1A **24**
Donkey La. SO30: Botl 4E **35**
Donnington Dr. SO53: Cha F 4C **14**
Donnington Gro.
SO17: South 1D **30**
Dorchester Ct. SO15: South 3B **30**
Doric Cl. SO53: Cha F 6H **9**
Dorland Gdns. SO40: Tott 5D **26**
Dormy Cl. SO31: Sar G 4B **48**
Dornan Ho. SO14: South 4C **30**
Dorrick Ct. SO15: South 4B **30**
The Dorrits SO40: Tott 4B **26**
Dorset Rd. SO53: Cha F 4E **15**
Dorset St. SO15: South 5C **30**
Dorval Ho. SO15: South 4A **30**
Dorval Mnr. SO15: South 4A **30**
Douglas Cres. SO19: South 5C **32**
Douglas Way SO45: Hythe 2D **52**
Dove Dale SO50: E'leigh 5F **15**
Dove Gdns. SO31: P Ga 2F **49**
Dover St. SO14: South 4C **30**
Dowds Cl. SO30: Hed E 3H **33**
Downing Ct. PO14: Titch C 6G **49**
Downland Cl. SO30: Botl 4D **34**
SO31: Loc H 3E **49**
Downland Pl. SO30: Hed E 6H **33**
Down La. SO51: Rom 4E **7**
Downscroft Gdns.
SO30: Hed E 4H **33**
Downside Av. SO19: South 5A **32**
Downs Pk. Av. SO40: Elin 5G **27**
Downs Pk. Cres. SO40: Elin 5G **27**
Downs Pk. Rd. SO40: Elin 5G **27**
Downton Rd. SO18: South 1H **31**
Downwood Cl. SO45: Dib P 4A **52**
Doyle Ct. SO19: South 4H **41**
Dragonfly Way SO50: E'leigh . . .6C **10**
Dragoon Cl. SO19: South 1C **42**
Drake Cl. SO31: Loc H 2F **49**
SO40: March 3E **39**
Drake Ho. SO14: South 6G **5**
Drake Rd. SO50: B'stke 3E **17**
Drakes Cl. SO45: Hythe 4D **52**
Drakes Ct. SO40: March 2D **38**
Drapers Copse Res. Pk.
SO45: Dib 2B **52**
Drayton Cl. SO19: South 5H **41**
Drayton Pl. SO40: Tott 4D **26**
Driftstone Gdns.
SO31: Loc H 3F **49**
Driftwood Gdns. SO40: Tott 5C **26**
Drinkwater Cl. SO50: E'leigh . . .4H **15**
The Drive SO30: W End 6B **24**
SO40: Tott 6F **27**
The Driveway SO45: Blac 4E **55**
Droffatts Ho. SO15: South 4H **29**
The Drove SO18: South 4A **32**
SO30: W End 6F **25**
SO40: Calm 2B **26**
SO45: Blac 4E **55**
Drove Rd. SO19: South 6B **32**
Drummond Ct. SO19: South 2G **41**
SO50: E'leigh 2B **16**
Drummond Dr. SO14: South 3E **31**
Drummond Rd. PO15: Seg 3H **49**
SO30: Hed E 2A **34**
SO45: Hythe 2E **53**
Drummond Way SO53: Cha F 5D **8**
Drum Rd. SO50: E'leigh 5H **15**
Dryden Rd. SO19: South 6E **33**
Duchess Ho. *SO19: South 3F 41*
(off John Thornycroft Rd.)
Duddon Cl. SO18: W End 2B **32**
Duke Rd. SO30: Hed E 6B **34**
Dukes Keep SO14: South 5G **5**
Dukes Mill Cen. SO51: Rom 5B **6**
Dukes Rd. SO14: South 3D **30**
Duke St. SO14: South . . .5G **5** (2D **40**)
Dukeswood Dr. SO45: Dib P 5D **52**
Dumas Dr. PO15: White 4G **45**
Dumbleton Cl. SO19: South 6F **33**
Dumbleton's Towers
SO19: South 1E **43**
Dunbar Cl. SO16: South 4D **20**
Duncan Cl. SO19: South 4G **41**
Duncan Ct. SO19: South 6C **32**
Duncan Hood Ct.
SO17: South 6E **23**
Duncan Rd. SO31: P Ga 1F **49**
Dundee Rd. SO17: South 2E **31**
Dundonald Cl. SO19: South 4F **41**
Dundry Way SO30: Hed E 4A **34**
Dunkirk Cl. SO16: South 5H **21**
Dunkirk Rd. SO16: South 5G **21**
Dunnings La. SO52: N Bad 2C **12**
Dunster Cl. SO16: South 4G **21**
Dunvegan Dr. SO16: South 4G **21**
Durban Cl. SO51: Rom 3D **6**
Durley Cres. SO40: Tott 6D **26**
Durlston Rd. SO16: South 2B **28**
Durnford Rd. SO14: South 5D **30**
Dutton La. SO50: E'leigh 3B **16**
Duttons Rd. SO51: Rom 2B **6**
Dyer Rd. SO15: South 4G **29**
Dymott Cl. SO15: South 6H **29**
Dyneley Grn. SO18: South 2A **32**
Dyram Cl. SO50: E'leigh 2H **15**
Dyserth Cl. SO19: South 4B **42**

E

Eagle Cl. SO53: Cha F 3D **14**
Earls Cl. SO50: B'stke 5G **17**
Earl's Rd. SO14: South 3C **30**
East Bargate
SO14: South 4E **5** (1C **40**)
Eastbourne Av. SO15: South 3H **29**
Eastbrook Cl. SO31: P Ga 2E **49**
Eastchurch Cl. SO16: South 5D **20**
Eastcot Cl. SO45: Holb 5C **54**
East Dr. SO50: B'stke 3D **16**
Eastern Rd. SO30: W End 2D **32**
Eastfield Rd. SO17: South 3E **31**
Eastgate St.
SO14: South 5E **5** (2C **40**)
East Horton Golf Cen. 2H **17**
East Horton Golf Course 2H **17**
Eastlands Boatyard
SO31: Lwr Swan 4B **44**
EASTLEIGH 5B **16**
Eastleigh Bus Station 4B **16**
Eastleigh FC 2G **23**
Eastleigh Lakeside Steam Railway 1H **23**
Eastleigh Mus. 5A **16**
Eastleigh Rd. SO50: Fair O 2F **17**
Eastleigh Station (Rail) 4B **16**
Eastmeare Ct. SO40: Tott 5C **26**
East Pk. Ter.
SO14: South 1E **5** (6C **30**)
East Rd. SO40: March 2E **39**
SO45: Hard 6H **53**
East St. SO14: South 4E **5** (1C **40**)
Eastville Rd. SO50: Fair O 2F **17**
Eastwood Ct. SO51: Rom 5B **6**
Eaton Ho. *off Radcliffe Rd. 5D 30*
(off Radcliffe Rd.)
Eddystone Rd. SO40: Tott 1D **26**
Edelvale Rd. SO18: South 2B **32**
Edenbridge Way
SO31: Sar G 1D **48**
Eden Rd. SO18: W End 6B **24**
Eden Wlk. SO53: Cha F 2D **14**
Edgehill Rd. SO18: South 2H **31**
Edgehurst SO31: Loc H 5D **48**
Edinburgh Ct. *SO15: South 5E 29*
(off Regent's Pk. Rd.)
Edith Haisman Cl.
SO15: South 1A **4** (6H **29**)
Edmunds Cl. SO30: Botl 6B **34**
Edney Path SO31: Sar G 1B **48**
Edward Av. SO50: B'stke 3D **16**
Edward Cl. SO45: Blac 4E **55**
Edward Rd. SO15: South 4G **29**
SO45: Hythe 2E **53**
Edwina Cl. SO19: South 5H **31**
SO52: N Bad 3F **13**
Edwina Ho. SO18: S'ing 5G **23**
Edwina Mountbatten Ho.
SO51: Rom 5B 6
(off Broadwater Rd.)
Edwin Jones Grn.
SO15: South 3A **30**
Effingham Gdns.
SO19: South 1C **42**
Eight Acres SO51: Rom 5D **6**
Ekless Ct. SO31: Sar G 1D **48**
Elan Cl. SO18: W End 2B **32**
Elderberry Cl. SO50: Fair O 5G **17**
Elder Cl. SO31: Loc H 5D **48**
SO40: March 4E **39**
Elder Grn. SO21: Col C 5G **11**
Eldon Ho.
SO14: South 5F **5** (2C **40**)
Eldridge Gdns. SO51: Rom 4C **6**
Electron Way SO53: Cha F 1E **15**
Elfin Ct. *SO17: South 3C 30*
(off Westwood Rd.)
Elgar Cl. SO19: South 2C **42**
Elgar Rd. SO19: South 2C **42**
Elgin Cl. SO45: Hythe 3E **53**
Elgin Rd. SO15: South 6H **29**
ELING 6H **27**
Elingfield Ct. SO40: Tott 4G **27**
Eling Hill SO40: Elin 6H **27**
Eling La. SO40: Tott, Elin 4G **27**
Eling Sailing Club 5H **27**
Eling Tide Mill 5H **27**
Eling Vw. SO15: South 4B **28**
Eling Wharf SO40: Elin 5H **27**
Eliot Cl. PO15: White 4G **45**
Eliot Ho. SO17: South 1E **31**
Elizabeth Cl. SO30: W End 2D **32**
Elizabeth Ct. SO17: South 2E **31**
SO30: W End 2D **32**
SO50: E'leigh 3A **16**
Elizabeth Gdns. SO45: Dib P . . .5E **53**
Elizabeth Ho. SO40: Calm 1B **26**
Elizabeth Way SO50: E'leigh 2B **16**
Elkins Sq. SO50: B'stke 5G **17**
Elland Cl. SO50: Fair O 2F **17**
Elldene Ct. SO40: Tott 6E **27**
Ellen Gdns. SO53: Cha F 2C **14**
Elliot Cl. SO40: Tott 4D **26**
Elliot Ri. SO30: Hed E 1A **34**
Ellis Rd. SO19: South 6E **33**
Ellwood Av. SO19: South 6E **33**
Ellwood Cl. SO19: South 5E **33**
Elm Cl. SO16: Bass 5B **22**
Elm Ct. SO19: South 2H **41**
Elm Cres. SO45: Hythe 1A **54**
Elmdale Cl. SO31: Wars 6B **48**
Elmes Dr. SO15: South 4D **28**
Elmfield Nth. Block
SO15: South 1A **4** (6H **29**)
Elmfield West Block
SO15: South 2A **4** (6H **29**)
Elm Gdns. SO30: W End 6D **24**
Elm Gro. SO50: E'leigh 5H **15**
Elmsleigh Ct. SO16: Bass 5C **22**
Elmsleigh Gdns. SO16: Bass 5C **22**
Elmslie Gdns. SO31: Old N 4F **43**
Elm St. SO14: South 4H **5** (1D **40**)
Elm Ter. SO14: South . . .5H **5** (2D **40**)
Elmtree Cl. SO40: A'hst 3B **36**
Elmtree Gdns. SO51: Rom 6F **7**
Elmwood Ct. SO16: South 1F **29**
Elsanta Cres. PO14: Titch C 6H **49**
Elstree Rd. SO19: South 6G **31**
Elver Ct. SO40: Elin 5G **27**
The Embankment
SO15: South 6G **29**
Embley Cl. SO40: Calm 1D **26**
Embsay Rd. SO31: Lwr Swan 5B **44**
Emerald Cl. SO19: South 5B **32**
Emerald Cres. SO45: Hythe 2F **53**
Emer Cl. SO52: N Bad 2E **13**
Emily Davies Halls
SO15: South 2C **4**
Emmanuel Cl. PO14: Titch C . . .5G **49**
Emmett Rd. SO16: Rown 4D **20**
Emmons Cl. SO31: Hamb 6F **47**
Emperor Ho. SO18: South 4E **31**
Empire La.
SO15: South 1C **4** (6B **30**)
Empire Vw.
SO15: South 2C **4** (6B **30**)
Empress Pk. SO14: South 4D **30**
Empress Rd. SO14: South 4D **30**
Emsworth Rd. SO15: South 3F **29**
Endeavour Cl. SO15: South 4F **29**
SO31: Wars 6B **48**
Endeavour Ct.
SO14: South 6H **5** (2D **40**)
Endeavour Way SO45: Hythe . . .1D **52**
Enderwood Cl. SO40: Tott 3B **26**
Endle St. SO14: South . . .5H **5** (2E **41**)
Enfield Gro. SO19: South 2G **41**
Englefield Rd. SO18: South 4F **31**
English Rd. SO15: South 4F **29**
Ennel Copse SO52: N Bad 3E **13**
Ennerdale Gdns.
SO18: W End 2B **32**
Ennerdale Rd. SO16: South 1C **28**
Ensign Pk. SO31: Hamb 5E **47**
Ensign Way SO31: Hamb 5E **47**
Enterprise Cl. SO31: Wars 6C **48**
Enterprise Rd. SO16: Chil 6G **13**
Epping Cl. SO18: South 2B **32**
Epsilon Ho. SO16: Chil 6H **13**
Epsom Ct. *PO15: White 5G 45*
(off Timor Cl.)
Erica Cl. SO31: Loc H 4D **48**
Eric Meadus Cl. SO18: S'ing 5F **23**
Erskine Ct. SO16: South 4D **20**
Escombe Rd. SO50: B'stke 4D **16**
Essex Grn. SO53: Cha F 5E **15**
Estridge Cl. SO31: Burs 4G **43**
Ethelburt Av. SO16: S'ing 4E **23**
Ethelred Gdns. SO40: Tott 5C **26**
European Way SO14: South 3D **40**
Evans St. SO14: South . . .4F **5** (1C **40**)
Evelyn Cres. SO15: South 3H **29**
Evenlode Rd. SO16: South 2C **28**
Evergreen Cl. SO40: March 4D **38**
Evergreens SO40: Elin 5G **27**
Evesham Cl. SO16: Bass 4D **22**
Ewart Ct. SO45: Hythe 1E **53**
Ewell Way SO40: Tott 2D **26**
Exbury Cl. SO50: B'stke 5F **17**
Exbury Rd. SO45: Blac 4E **55**
Exeter Cl. SO18: South 2A **32**
SO31: Loc H 4D **48**
SO50: E'leigh 2H **15**
Exeter Rd. SO18: South 3A **32**
Exford Av. SO18: South 4C **32**
Exford Dr. SO18: South 4C **32**
Exleigh Cl. SO18: South 5B **32**
Exmoor Cl. PO15: White 6F **45**
SO40: Tott 4B **26**
Exmoor Rd. SO14: South 5D **30**
Exmouth St.
SO14: South 2E **5** (6C **30**)

Eyeworth Wlk.—Gento Cl.

Eyeworth Wlk. SO45: Dib 2A **52**
Eynham Av. SO19: South 5C **32**
Eynham Cl. SO19: South 5C **32**
Eynham Gdns. SO19: South 5B **32**
Eyre Cl. SO40: Tott 5D **26**

F

Faber M. SO51: Rom 4E **7**
Factory Rd. SO50: E'leigh 5A **16**
Fairbairn Wlk. SO53: Cha F 1B **14**
Fairbourne Ct. SO19: South 3E **41**
Faircross Cl. SO45: Holb 5C **54**
Fairfax Ct. SO19: South 5E **33**
Fairfax M. SO19: South 5E **33**
Fair Fld. SO51: Rom 3D **6**
Fairfield Cl. SO45: Hythe 2D **52**
Fairfield Lodge SO16: South 5G **21**
Fairfield Rd. SO21: Shaw 1D **10**
Fair Grn. SO19: South 6B **32**
Fairholme Ct. SO50: E'leigh 4A **16**
Fairisle Rd. SO16: South 5C **20**
Fairlawn Cl. SO16: Rown 3D **20**
Fairlawns SO31: Burr 4F **45**
Fairlea Grange SO16: Bass 5B **22**
Fairlie Cl. SO30: Hed E 6H **25**
Fairmead Ct. SO31: Wars 6C **48**
Fairmead Way SO40: Tott 6E **27**
FAIR OAK 5H **17**
Fair Oak Ct. SO50: Fair O 1F **17**
Fair Oak Rd.
SO50: B'stke, Fair O 4D **16**
Fair Oak Squash Club 1F **17**
Fairthorne Manor Golf Course
....5G **35**
Fairview Cl. SO45: Hythe 3E **53**
SO51: Rom 3E **7**
Fairview Dr. SO45: Hythe 4D **52**
SO51: Rom 3E **7**
Fairview Pde. SO45: Hythe 4E **53**
The Fairway SO31: Wars 6D **48**
Fairway Gdns. SO16: Rown 4C **20**
Fairway Rd. SO45: Hythe 2D **52**
Falaise Cl. SO16: South 5G **21**
Falconer Ct. SO45: Hard 2C **54**
Falcon Flds. SO45: F'ley 2H **55**
Falcon Sq. SO50: E'leigh 6G **15**
Falcon Way SO32: Botl 2D **34**
Falkland Ct. SO53: Cha F 4E **15**
Falkland Rd. SO15: South 3E **29**
SO53: Cha F 5E **15**
Fallow Cres. SO30: Hed E 3B **34**
Falstaff Way SO40: Tott 6D **26**
Fanshawe St. SO14: South 5C **30**
FAREHAM COMMUNITY
HOSPITAL 2E **49**
Faringdon Rd. SO18: South 4D **32**
Farley Cl. SO50: Fair O 2G **17**
Farley Ct. SO16: South 1H **29**
Farm Cl. SO31: Hamb 5G **47**
SO40: Calm 1B **26**
Farmery Cl. SO18: S'ing 5F **23**
Farm La. SO40: A'hst 3B **36**
Farm Rd. PO14: Titch 5H **49**
Farrell Flds. SO40: March 3D **38**
Farringford Rd. SO19: South 5D **32**
The Farthings PO14: Titch C 1G **51**
Fastnet Cl. SO16: South 4C **20**
FAWLEY 2H **55**
Fawley Bus. Cen.
SO45: F'ley 2G **55**
Fawley By-Pass SO45: F'ley 2H **55**
Fawley Rd. SO15: South 5E **29**
SO45: F'ley 2E **55**
SO45: Hard, Hythe 4E **53**
SO45: Hythe 6F **53**
Fawn Cres. SO30: Hed E 3B **34**
Fell Cl. SO31: Loc H 3E **49**
Feltham Cl. SO51: Rom 4F **7**
Felton Cl. SO31: Net A 1C **46**
Fenwick Ho. *off Meridian Way* *5E 31*
(off Meridian Way)
Fernacre Bus. Pk. SO51: Rom 3A **6**
Fern Cl. SO19: South 5F **33**
Ferndale SO30: Hed E 6B **34**
Ferndale Rd. SO40: March 4D **38**
Ferndene Way SO18: South 3H **31**
Fernhill SO53: Cha F 1G **15**
Fernhills Rd. SO45: Hythe 5F **53**
Fernhurst Cl. SO21: Col C 4F **11**
Fernlea Gdns. SO16: Bass 6A **22**
Fernlea Way SO45: Dib P 3B **52**
Fern Rd. SO19: South 3H **41**
SO45: Hythe 3D **52**
Fernside Cl. SO16: South 3D **28**
SO45: Holb 5C **54**
Fernside Ct. SO16: Bass 5A **22**
Fernside Wlk. SO50: Fair O 1G **17**
Fernside Way SO50: Fair O 1G **17**
Fern Way PO15: Seg 4H **49**
Fernwood Cres.
SO18: South 3H **31**
Fernyhurst Av. SO16: Rown 4D **20**
Ferrybridge Grn.
SO30: Hed E 5A **34**
Ferrymans Quay SO31: Net A 2B **46**
Ferry Rd. SO45: Hythe 3D **52**
Field Cl. SO16: S'ing 4E **23**
SO31: Loc H 5E **49**
SO51: Rom 5D **6**
Fielden Cl. SO52: N Bad 3D **12**
Fielders Ct. SO30: W End 2E **33**
Fieldfare Ct. SO40: Tott 3C **26**
Fielding Rd. PO15: White 4G **45**
Fields Cl. SO45: Blac 4E **55**
Field Vw. SO53: Cha F 1B **14**
Filton Cl. SO40: Calm 2C **26**
The Finches SO16: South 3F **29**
SO17: South 1D **30**
Finches Cl. SO21: Col C 5G **11**
Finlay Cl. SO19: South 1C **42**
Finley Cl. SO40: Calm 2B **26**
Finzi Cl. SO19: South 2C **42**
Fircroft Dr. SO53: Cha F 2F **15**
Firecracker Dr. SO31: Sar G 4C **48**
Firecrest Cl. SO16: South 4F **21**
Firgrove Cl. SO52: N Bad 3D **12**
Firgrove Ct. SO15: South 4G **29**
Firgrove Rd. SO15: South 4G **29**
SO52: N Bad 3D **12**
Fir Rd. SO40: A'hst 3B **36**
The Firs SO16: Bass 5B **22**
Firs Dr. SO30: Hed E 6G **33**
First Av. SO15: South 4B **28**
First St. SO45: Hard 6H **53**
Fir Tree Ct. SO18: South 3B **32**
Firtree Gro. SO45: Hythe 6E **53**
Fir Tree La. SO50: Hor H 1G **25**
Firtree Way SO19: South 6B **32**
Firwood Cl. SO53: Cha F 5E **9**
FISHER'S POND 6H **11**
Fisher's Rd. SO40: Elin 5G **27**
Fishlake Mdws. SO51: Rom 3B **6**
Fitzgerald Cl. PO15: White 5G **45**
FITZHUGH 4B **30**
Fitzhugh Pl. SO15: South 4B **30**
Fitzhugh St.
SO15: South 2C **4** (6B **30**)
Fitzroy Cl. SO16: Bass 2B **22**
Five Elms Dr. SO51: Rom 6E **7**
Flamborough Cl.
SO16: South 6B **20**
Flanders Fld. La.
SO16: South 3A **28**
Flanders Ind. Pk.
SO30: Hed E 3H **33**
Flanders Rd. SO30: Hed E 3H **33**
FLEETEND 6D **48**
Fleet End Bottom
SO31: Wars 1D **50**
Fleet End Rd. SO31: Wars 6D **48**
Fleet Ter. SO21: Ott 4A **10**
Fleming Av. SO52: N Bad 3E **13**
Fleming Cl. PO15: Seg 3H **49**
Fleming Ct. SO52: N Bad 3F **13**
Fleming Ho. SO50: E'leigh 5G **15**
Fleming Pl. SO21: Col C 4F **11**
SO51: Rom 4C **6**
Fleming Rd. SO16: S'ing 5F **23**
Fletcher Cl. SO45: Dib 3B **52**
Fletchwood La.
SO40: A'hst, Tott 3A **36**
(not continuous)
Fletchwood Meadows
Nature Reserve 2B **36**
Fletchwood Rd. SO40: Tott 5B **26**
Fleuret Cl. SO45: Hythe 5E **53**
FLEXFORD 5C **8**
Flexford Cl. SO53: Cha F 4C **8**
Flexford Nature Reserve 4C **8**
Flexford Rd. SO52: N Bad 1G **13**
Flint Cl. SO19: South 1E **43**
Floating Bri. Rd.
SO14: South 6H **5** (2E **41**)
Florence Rd. SO19: South 3F **41**
The Florins PO14: Titch C 6E **49**
Flowerdown Cl. SO40: Calm 3C **26**
Flowers Cl. SO31: Hamb 4E **47**
Folland Cl. SO52: N Bad 3E **13**
Font Cl. PO14: Titch C 4G **49**
Fontwell Cl. SO40: Calm 2C **26**
Foord Rd. SO30: Hed E 6G **33**
Footner Cl. SO51: Rom 2F **7**
Forbes Cl. SO16: South 3D **20**
Ford Av. SO53: Cha F 3F **15**
Fordington Vs. SO53: Cha F 1E **15**
Forest Cl. SO52: N Bad 2C **12**
SO53: Cha F 5E **9**
Forest Edge SO45: F'ley 2G **55**
Foresters Rd. SO45: F'ley 3F **55**
Forest Front SO45: Hythe 6D **52**
Forest Ga. SO45: Blac 6F **55**
Forest Hills Dr. SO18: South 6G **23**
Forest Hill Way SO45: Dib P 4D **52**
Forest La. SO45: Hard 2B **54**
Forest Mdw. SO45: Hythe 6E **53**
Forest M. SO40: Tott 1D **26**
Forest Rd. SO53: Cha F 5F **9**
Forest Side SO45: Hythe 6D **52**
Forest Vw.
SO14: South 5D **4** (1B **40**)
Forest Way SO40: Calm 1A **26**
Forge Cl. SO31: Burs 4G **43**
Forge La. SO45: F'ley 2H **55**
Forge Rd. SO45: Blac 6F **55**
Forster Rd. SO14: South 4C **30**
Forsythia Cl. SO30: Hed E 3H **33**
SO45: Hythe 1A **54**
Forsythia Pl. SO19: South 6H **31**
Forth Cl. SO53: Cha F 2D **14**
Forth Ho. SO14: South 5E **31**
Fort Rd. SO19: South 2G **41**
Fortune Ct. SO53: Cha F 1E **15**
Foster Way SO51: Rom 1E **7**
Foundry Ct. SO19: South 3F **41**
Foundry Cres. SO31: Burs 5F **43**
Foundry La. SO15: South 3F **29**
Fountain Ct. SO21: Col C 4F **11**
SO30: Hed E 5H **33**
Fountains Pk. SO31: Net A 6A **42**
Four Acres SO30: Botl 5E **35**
FOURPOSTS 1A **4** (6A **30**)
Fourposts Hill
SO15: South 1A **4** (6A **30**)
Fourshells Cl. SO45: F'ley 3F **55**
The Fowey SO45: Blac 3E **55**
Fowey Cl. SO53: Cha F 6D **8**
Fowlers Rd. SO30: Hed E 3H **33**
Fowlers Wlk. SO16: Chil 5H **13**
Foxbury Cl. SO45: Hythe 4E **53**
Fox Cl. SO50: B'stke 5F **17**
Foxcott Cl. SO19: South 5H **41**
Foxcroft Dr. SO45: Holb 5B **54**
Foxfield SO31: P Ga 1F **49**
Foxglade SO45: Blac 6F **55**
The Foxgloves SO30: Hed E 6B **34**
Foxhayes La. SO45: Blac 6F **55**
FOXHILLS 1C **36**
Foxhills SO40: A'hst 1C **36**
Foxhills Cl. SO40: A'hst 2C **36**
Foxlands SO45: Blac 6F **55**
Fox's Wlk. SO45: Blac 6F **55**
Foxtail Dr. SO45: Dib P 5D **52**
Foxy Paddock SO45: Blac 6F **55**
Foyes Ct. SO15: South 4H **29**
Foy Gdns. SO31: Wars 6A **48**
Foyle Rd. SO53: Cha F 1D **14**
Fragorum Flds.
PO14: Titch C 5G **49**
Frampton Cl. SO21: Col C 4F **11**
Frampton Way SO40: Tott 5F **27**
Francis Copse SO21: Col C 4G **11**
Franconia Dr. SO16: Nur 6H **19**
Frankie's Fun Factory 3B **6**
Franklyn Av. SO19: South 1A **42**
Fraser Cl. SO16: South 3D **20**
Fratton Way SO50: Fair O 2F **17**
Frayslea SO45: Dib P 4E **53**
Freda Routh Gdns.
SO50: Fair O 1G **17**
Frederick St. SO14: South 5D **30**
Freegrounds Av.
SO30: Hed E 5A **34**
Freegrounds Cl.
SO30: Hed E 5A **34**
Freegrounds Rd.
SO30: Hed E 5A **34**
FREEMANTLE 5G **29**
Freemantle Bus. Cen.
SO15: South 6G **29**
Freemantle Cl. SO19: South 6H **31**
Freemantle Comn. Rd.
SO19: South 6H **31**
Freemantle Rd. SO51: Rom 1E **7**
French Ct. SO14: South 6D **4**
French St.
SO14: South 6D **4** (2B **40**)
Frensham Cl. SO30: Hed E 5A **34**
Frensham Ct. SO30: Hed E 5A **34**
Freshfield Rd. SO15: South 4F **29**
Freshfield Sq. SO15: South 4F **29**
Freshwater Ct. SO53: Cha F 4G **9**
Friars Cft. SO31: Net A 6B **42**
SO40: Calm 1C **26**
Friars Rd. SO50: E'leigh 6H **15**
Friars Way SO18: S'ing 5F **23**
Fritham Cl. SO40: Tott 4C **26**
Fritham Rd. SO18: South 3D **32**
Frobisher Ct. SO40: March 2E **39**
Frobisher Gdns.
SO19: South 1C **42**
Frobisher Ind. Cen.
SO51: Rom 3B **6**
Froghall SO45: Dib P 5E **53**
Frogmore La. SO16: Nur 6B **20**
Frome Cl. SO40: March 4E **39**
Frome Rd. SO18: W End 6A **24**
FROSTLANE 5G **53**
Frost La. SO45: Hythe 5E **53**
Fry Cl. SO31: Hamb 3G **47**
SO45: F'ley 3F **55**
Fryern Arc. SO53: Cha F 6F **9**
Fryern Cl. SO53: Cha F 1G **15**
FRYERN HILL 1F **15**
Fryers Cl. SO51: Rom 5D **6**
Fuchsia Gdns. SO16: South 1H **29**
Fulcrum PO15: White 6H **45**
Fulford Rd. SO52: N Bad 3E **13**
Fullerton Cl. SO19: South 5H **41**
Fullerton Pl. SO17: South 3D **30**
Fulmar Cl. SO16: South 4F **21**
Fulmar Dr. SO45: Hythe 4F **53**
Furze Cl. SO19: South 6A **32**
Furzedale Gdns.
SO45: Hythe 5F **53**
Furzedale Pk. SO45: Hythe 5F **53**
Furzedown M. SO45: Hythe 5F **53**
Furzedown Rd. SO17: South 1C **30**
Furze Dr. SO51: Rom 2E **7**
Furze Rd. SO19: South 6A **32**
Furzey Av. SO45: Hythe 4F **53**
Furzey Cl. SO45: F'ley 4F **55**
Fyeford Cl. SO16: Rown 3D **20**
Fyfield Cl. PO15: White 5G **45**

G

Gables Ct. SO16: Bass 4B **22**
Gage Cl. SO40: March 3E **39**
Gainsborough Cl.
SO19: South 3C **42**
Gainsborough Ct.
SO52: N Bad 3F **13**
Gainsford Rd. SO19: South 6F **31**
Gala Bingo
Southampton 5D **20**
Galleon Cl. SO31: Wars 6D **48**
The Gallops PO14: Titch C 5H **49**
Galsworthy Rd. SO40: Tott 4D **26**
Gamble Cl. SO19: South 1H **41**
Gamma Ho. SO16: Chil 6G **13**
Gammon Cl. SO30: Hed E 1H **33**
Ganger Farm La. SO51: Rom 2F **7**
Ganger Rd. SO51: Rom 2F **7**
Gang Warily Recreation &
Community Cen. 3E **55**
Gannet Cl. SO16: South 4F **21**
SO45: Hythe 4F **53**
Gantry Ct. SO15: South 2C **4**
Garden M. SO31: Wars 6A **48**
Gardiner Cl. SO40: March 3E **39**
Gardner Way SO53: Cha F 5D **8**
Garfield Rd. SO19: South 4G **31**
SO31: Net A 1A **46**
Garland Way SO40: Tott 3B **26**
Garnier Dr. SO50: B'stke 2C **16**
(not continuous)
Garnock Rd. SO19: South 3F **41**
Garratt Cl. SO30: Hed E 1A **34**
Garretts Cl. SO19: South 4A **42**
Garrick Gdns. SO19: South 3A **42**
The Garth SO45: Dib P 4D **52**
Garton Rd. SO19: South 2G **41**
Gashouse Hill SO31: Net A 2C **46**
Gaston Gdns. SO51: Rom 4C **6**
Gatcombe SO31: Net A 6C **42**
Gatcombe Gdns.
SO18: W End 1A **32**
The Gatehouse SO18: South 3G **31**
SO30: W End 1C **32**
Gateley Hall SO15: South 4B **30**
Gaters Hill SO18: W End 6A **24**
Gatwick Cl. SO16: South 5E **21**
Gavan St. SO19: South 6D **32**
Gemini Cl. SO16: South 5D **20**
Gento Cl. SO30: Botl 5C **34**

64 A-Z Southampton

George Curl Way—Hardy Cl.

George Curl Way
SO18: S'ton A 3H 23
George Perrett Way
SO53: Cha F 3B 14
George Raymond Rd.
SO50: E'leigh 5H 15
George St. SO50: E'leigh 4B 16
Georges Way SO50: E'leigh 4G 15
George Wright Cl.
SO50: E'leigh 5H 15
Georgina Cl. SO40: Tott 2B 26
Gerard Cres. SO19: South 5D 32
Gibbs Cl. SO45: Hythe 6E 53
Gibbs Rd.
SO14: South 2D 4 (6B 30)
Gilbury Cl. SO18: S'ing 5G 23
Gilchrist Gdns. SO31: Wars 2A 50
Giles Cl. SO30: Hed E 2B 34
Gillcrest PO14: Titch C 3G 49
Gilman Ct. SO50: B'stke 3D 16
Gilpin Cl. SO19: South 6E 33
Gipsy Gro. SO15: South 4G 29
Girton Cl. PO14: Titch C 6G 49
The Glade SO45: Blac 6E 55
SO53: Cha F 4H 9
The Glades SO31: Loc H 3E 49
Gladstone Ho. SO14: South 2G 5
Gladstone Rd. SO19: South 6B 32
Glasslaw Rd. SO18: South 3A 32
Glebe Ct. SO17: South 1C 30
SO30: Botl 3E 35
SO50: Fair O 1G 17
Glebe Rd.
SO14: South 5H 5 (2D 40)
The Glen *SO50: E'leigh 5A 16*
(off Grantham Rd.)
Glencarron Way SO16: Bass 6A 22
Glencoyne Gdns.
SO16: South 1D 28
Glenda Cl. SO31: Wars 1B 50
Glendale SO31: Loc H 5E 49
Glendowan Rd. SO53: Cha F 6C 8
Gleneagles Equestrian Cen. . . .4D 24
Glen Eyre Cl. SO16: Bass 5C 22
Glen Eyre Dr. SO16: Bass 4C 22
Glen Eyre Halls SO16: Bass 4C 22
Glen Eyre Rd. SO16: Bass 4B 22
Glen Eyre Way SO16: Bass 5C 22
Glenfield Av. SO18: South 4H 31
Glenfield Cres. SO18: South . . .4H 31
Glenfield Way SO18: South 4H 31
Glenlea Cl. SO30: W End 2D 32
Glenlea Dr. SO30: W End 2D 32
Glen Lee SO18: South 3A 32
Glenmore Ct. SO17: South 3C 30
Glenn Rd. SO30: W End 1D 32
Glen Pk. Mobile Home Pk.
SO21: Col C 4G 11
Glen Rd. SO19: South 4F 41
SO31: Sar G, Swanw 6C 44
(not continuous)
Glenside SO30: W End 2D 32
SO45: Hythe 3D 52
Glenside Av. SO19: South 1D 42
Glenwood Av. SO16: Bass 4C 22
Glenwood Ct. SO50: Fair O 1H 17
Gloster Ct. PO15: Seg 2G 49
Gloucester Dr. SO31: Sar G 2E 49
Gloucester Sq. SO14: South 6E 5
Glyn Jones Cl. SO45: F'ley 3F 55
Goals Soccer Cen.
Southampton 5E 29
Godfrey Olson Ho.
SO50: E'leigh 4B 16
God's House Tower 6E 5 (3C 40)
Goldcrest Gdns.
SO16: South 4E 21
Goldcrest La. SO40: Tott 3C 26
Golden Ct. SO30: W End 6F 25
Golden Gro.
SO14: South 2G 5 (6D 30)
Golden Hind Pk.
SO45: Hythe 4D 52
Goldsmith Cl. SO40: Tott 4D 26
Goldsmith Rd. SO50: E'leigh 6H 15
Goldsmiths Ct. SO14: South 6E 5
Goldwire Dr. SO53: Cha F 2B 14
Golf Course Rd. SO16: Bass 4A 22
Goodacre Dr. SO53: Cha F 2B 14
Goodalls La. SO30: Hed E 4H 33
Goodison Cl. SO50: Fair O 6H 17
Goodlands Va. SO30: Hed E 4G 33
Goodwin Cl. SO16: South 1B 28
Goodwood Cl. PO14: Titch C 5H 49
Goodwood Gdns. SO40: Tott 3C 26
Goodwood Rd. SO50: E'leigh . . .2G 15
Gordon Av. SO14: South 3C 30
Gordon Rd. SO53: Cha F 4F 9
Gordon Ter. SO19: South 3A 42
Gorse Cl. SO31: Loc H 5D 48
Gorselands Rd. SO18: South . . .2B 32
Gort Cres. SO19: South 1B 42
Gover Rd. SO16: South 2A 28
Grace Dieu Gdns.
SO31: Burs 4F 43
Graddidge Way SO40: Tott 4D 26
Grafton Gdns. SO16: South 4G 21
Graham Ct. SO19: South 5A 32
Graham Ho. SO14: South 5E 31
Graham Rd. SO14: South 5C 30
Graham St. SO14: South 5E 31
Grainger Gdns. SO19: South . . .2C 42
Granada Rd. SO30: Hed E 6G 33
Granary La. SO50: E'leigh 4A 16
Granby Gro. SO17: South 6D 22
Grange Cl. SO18: S'ing 5G 23
Grange Ct. SO18: S'ing 4G 23
SO31: Net A 1B 46
Grange Dr. SO21: Ott 5B 10
SO30: Hed E 3B 34
SO50: E'leigh 5B 10
Grange Farm SO31: Net A 6B 42
Grange M. SO51: Rom 3F 7
Grange Pk. SO30: Hed E 2A 34
Grange Rd. SO16: South 2F 29
SO30: Botl, Hed E 3A 34
SO31: Net A 1A 46
Grangewood Ct.
SO50: Fair O 5H 17
Grangewood Gdns.
SO50: Fair O 5H 17
Grantham Av. SO31: Hamb 4E 47
Grantham Rd. SO19: South 5H 31
SO50: E'leigh 5H 15
Granville St.
SO14: South 4H 5 (1D 40)
Grasdean Cl. SO18: South 2A 32
Grasmere SO50: E'leigh 5H 15
Grasmere Cl. SO18: W End 2B 32
Grasmere Ct. SO16: South 1C 28
Grassymead PO14: Titch C 3G 49
Grateley Cl. SO19: South 5H 41
Gravel Wlk. SO45: F'ley 3F 55
Gray Cl. SO31: Wars 5D 48
Grayling Mead SO51: Rom 3C 6
Graylings SO15: South 3E 29
Grays Av. SO45: Hythe 3F 53
Grays Cl. SO21: Col C 5F 11
SO51: Rom 5D 6
Greatbridge Rd. SO51: Rom 1B 6
Gt. Elms Cl. SO45: Holb 5B 54
Gt. Farm Rd. SO50: E'leigh 4H 15
Gt. Well Dr. SO51: Rom 4D 6
Greatwood Cl. SO45: Hythe 4E 53
The Green SO31: Sar G 1C 48
SO51: Rom 3F 7
Greenacres Dr. SO21: Ott 2C 10
Greenacres Rd.
SO31: Loc H, Sar G 4C 48
Greenaway La. SO31: Wars 5B 48
Greenbank Cres. SO16: Bass . . .4B 22
Green Cl. SO45: Hythe 2E 53
Greendale Cl. SO53: Cha F 1G 15
Greenfield Cl. SO30: Hed E 1H 43
Greenfields Av. SO40: Tott 2E 27
Greenfields Cl. SO40: Tott 2E 27
Greenfinch Cl. SO50: E'leigh 6F 15
Greenhill La. SO16: Rown 1C 20
Greenhill Ter. SO51: Rom 6A 6
Greenhill Vw. SO51: Rom 5A 6
Greenlands Vw. SO30: Botl 4C 34
Green La. SO16: Chil 6B 14
SO16: South 1C 28
SO31: Burr 4E 45
SO31: Burs, Old N 3F 43
SO31: Hamb 5G 47
SO31: Lwr Swan 5B 44
SO31: Wars 6D 48
SO40: Calm 5B 18
SO45: Blac 6B 54
(Roughdown La.)
SO45: Blac 5F 55
(Walker's La. Nth.)
SO51: Ampf, Rom 4H 7
Greenlea Cres. SO16: S'ing 4F 23
Green Pk. Rd. SO16: South 4C 28
Greenridge Ct. *SO15: South 3B 30*
(off Marshall Sq.)
Greens Cl. SO50: B'stke 6G 17
Greenway Ct. SO16: South 1G 29
Greenways SO16: S'ing 4F 23
SO53: Cha F 1G 15
The Greenwich SO14: South 6E 5
SO45: Blac 3E 55
Greenwood Av. SO16: Rown 3B 20
Greenwood Cl. SO50: E'leigh . . .6H 15
SO51: Rom 4D 6
Gregory Gdns. SO40: Calm 2C 26
Grenadier Cl. SO31: Loc H 5F 49
Grendon Cl. SO16: Bass 4D 22
Grenville Ct. SO15: South 4A 30
SO18: South 6H 23
Grenville Gdns. SO45: Dib P . . .5E 53
Gresley Gdns. SO30: Hed E 1A 34
Greville Rd. SO15: South 4H 29
Greyhound Cl. SO30: Hed E 6H 25
Greywell Av. SO16: South 5G 21
Greywell Ct. SO16: South 5G 21
Griffen Cl. SO50: B'stke 5E 17
Griffin Ct. SO17: South 3E 31
Griffin Ind. Pk. SO40: Tott 6E 19
Griffon Cl. SO31: Burs 4G 43
Grosvenor Cl. SO17: South 1E 31
Grosvenor Ct. *SO17: South 2E 31*
(off Grosvenor Rd.)
SO51: Rom 5F 7
Grosvenor Gdns.
SO17: South 1E 31
SO30: W End 3D 32
Grosvenor Mans.
SO15: South 1C 4
Grosvenor M. SO17: South 1E 31
Grosvenor Rd. SO17: South 1E 31
SO53: Cha F 4G 9
Grosvenor Sq.
SO15: South 1D 4 (5B 30)
The Grove SO19: South 4B 42
SO31: Burs 4G 43
SO31: Net A 6D 42
Grovebury SO31: Loc H 5E 49
Grove Bus. Pk. SO51: Rom 3A 6
Grove Copse SO19: South 4C 42
Grove Gdns. SO19: South 4B 42
Grovely Way SO51: Cram 3H 7
Grove M. SO19: South 3B 42
Grove Pl. SO19: South 3B 42
Grove Rd. SO15: South 4G 29
SO21: Shaw 1C 10
Grove St.
SO14: South 4G 5 (1D 40)
Guardian Ct. SO17: South 2C 30
Guernsey Cl. SO16: South 6C 20
Guest Rd. SO50: B'stke 4D 16
Guildford Dr. SO53: Cha F 4D 14
Guildford St.
SO14: South 1H 5 (6D 30)
Guildhall Pl. SO14: South 2D 4
Guildhall Sq.
SO14: South 2D 4 (6B 30)
Guild Ho. SO14: South 6E 5
Guillemot Cl. SO45: Hythe 3F 53
Gull Coppice PO15: White 6G 45
The Gulls SO40: March 3D 38
Gullycroft Mead
SO30: Hed E 4H 33
Gurney Rd. SO15: South 3G 29
Gwelo Dr. SO30: Hed E 1H 43

H

Hack Dr. SO21: Col C 5F 11
Hackworth Gdns.
SO30: Hed E 6H 25
Haddon Dr. SO50: E'leigh 2A 16
Hadleigh Gdns.
SO50: E'leigh 2A 16
Hadley Fld. SO45: Hard 3B 54
Hadrians Cl. SO53: Cha F 6G 9
Hadrian Way SO16: Chil 2A 22
Haflinger Dr. PO15: White 5F 45
Haig Rd. SO50: B'stke 5G 17
Haileybury Gdns.
SO30: Hed E 2A 34
Halden Cl. SO51: Rom 3E 7
Hales Dr. SO30: Hed E 6G 33
Halifax Ct. SO30: W End 1C 32
Hallett Cl. SO18: South 1A 32
Hall Lands La. SO50: Fair O 1G 17
Halstead Rd. SO18: South 1H 31
HALTERWORTH 5F 7
Halterworth Cl. SO51: Rom 5E 7
Halterworth La.
SO51: Cram, Rom 5F 7
Haltons Cl. SO40: Tott 2D 26
Halyard Cl. SO31: Lwr Swan . . .5B 44
Halyards SO31: Hamb 3G 47
Hambert Way SO40: Tott 6E 27
HAMBLE CLIFF 4D 46
Hamblecliff Ho.
SO31: Hamb 4D 46
Hamble Cliff Stables
SO31: Hamb 4D 46
Hamble Cl. SO31: Wars 6A 48
Hamble Ct. SO53: Cha F 2F 15
Hamble Ct. Bus. Pk.
SO31: Hamb 4E 47
Hamble Ho. Gdns.
SO31: Hamb 5G 47
Hamble La. SO31: Burs, Hamb,
Hou, Old N 1E 47
HAMBLE-LE-RICE 5G 47
Hamble Mnr. Ct.
SO31: Hamb 5G 47
Hamble Pk. SO31: Wars 6D 48
Hambleside Ct.
SO31: Hamb 5F 47
Hamble Sports Complex 2F 47
Hamble Station (Rail) 2E 47
Hamble Wood SO30: Botl 5E 35
Hamblewood Ct. SO30: Botl 5F 35
Hameldon Cl. SO16: South 4D 28
Hamilton Bus. Pk.
SO30: Hed E 2H 33
Hamilton Ct. *SO17: South 2C 30*
(off Winn Rd.)
SO45: Holb 4D 54
Hamilton Ho. 5E 31
Hamilton M. SO45: Hythe 5F 53
Hamilton Rd. SO31: Sar G 2D 48
SO45: Hythe 6F 53
SO50: B'stke 4D 16
Hamlet Ct. SO45: F'ley 2H 55
Hammonds Cl. SO40: Tott 3E 27
HAMMOND'S GREEN 3D 26
Hammond's Grn. SO40: Tott 2D 26
Hammonds La. SO40: Tott 3E 27
Hammonds Way SO40: Tott 3E 27
Hampshire Corporate Pk.
SO53: Cha F 4D 14
Hampshire County Cricket Club
. . . . .2F 33
Hampshire Ct. SO53: Cha F 4E 15
The Hampshire Rose Bowl 2F 33
Hampton Cl. SO45: Blac 5E 55
Hampton Gdns. SO45: Blac 5E 55
Hampton La. SO45: Blac 3E 55
HAMPTON PARK 6D 22
Hampton Towers
SO19: South 5G 41
Hamtun Cres. SO40: Tott 2E 27
Hamtun Gdns. SO40: Tott 2E 27
Hamtun Rd. SO19: South 2C 42
Hamtun St.
SO14: South 5D 4 (2B 40)
Hamwic Hall 4F 5
Handel Rd.
SO15: South 1C 4 (5B 30)
Handel Ter.
SO15: South 1B 4 (6A 30)
Handford Pl. SO15: South 5B 30
Hanger Farm Arts Cen. 3B 26
Hanley Rd. SO15: South 3H 29
Hannay Ri. SO19: South 6D 32
Hann Rd. SO16: Rown 3C 20
Hanns Way SO50: E'leigh 4A 16
Hanover Bldgs.
SO14: South 4E 5 (1C 40)
Hanover Cl. SO51: Rom 5B 6
Hanover Ct. SO45: Hythe 2E 53
Hanover Gables
SO17: South 3C 30
(off Westwood Rd.)
Hanover Ho. SO40: Tott 3G 27
Hanoverian Way
PO15: White 6G 45
Hansen Gdns. SO30: Hed E 2H 33
Harborough Rd.
SO15: South 5B 30
Harbour Cl. SO40: March 3G 39
Harbour Lights Picturehouse . . .3D 40
Harbourne Gdns.
SO18: W End 1B 32
Harbour Pde.
SO15: South 3B 4 (1A 40)
Harcourt Rd. SO18: South 3F 31
Hardings La. SO50: Fair O 4H 17
HARDLEY 2C 54
Hardley Ind. Est.
SO45: Hard 2A 54
Hardley La.
SO45: Hard, Hythe 1A 54
(not continuous)
Hardwicke Cl. SO16: South 1D 28
Hardwicke Way SO31: Hamb . . .5D 46
Hardwick Rd. SO53: Cha F 1F 15
Hardy Cl. SO15: South 5F 29
SO31: Loc H 3F 49

A-Z Southampton 65

Hardy Dr.—Hollyoak Ct.

Hardy Dr. SO45: Hythe 4F 53
Hardy Rd. SO50: E'leigh 6A 16
HAREFIELD
SO18 4C 32
SO51 4E 7
Harefield Ct. SO51: Rom 4E 7
Harefield Rd. SO17: South 5E 23
Hare La. SO21: Twy 1G 11
Harewood Cl. SO50: E'leigh 1A 16
Hargreaves Wlk.
SO50: B'stke 3D 16
Harland Cres. SO15: South 2H 29
Harlaxton Cl. SO50: E'leigh 2H 15
Harlech Dr. SO53: Cha F 3C 14
Harley Ct. SO31: Wars 6B 48
Harlyn Rd. SO16: South 2D 28
Harold Cl. SO40: Tott 5D 26
Harold Rd. SO15: South 4G 29
The Harrage SO51: Rom 5C 6
Harrier Cl. SO16: South 3F 21
Harrier Grn. SO45: Hard 2B 54
Harrier M. SO31: Hamb 4E 47
Harrier Way SO45: Hard 2B 54
Harris Av. SO30: Hed E 3A 34
Harrison Rd. SO17: South 6E 23
Harrison's Cut SO15: South 2F 29
Harrisons Cut
SO14: South 4F 5 (1D 40)
Harris Way SO52: N Bad 3E 13
Hart Ct. SO19: South 2H 41
Hart Hill SO45: Hythe 5G 53
Hartington Rd.
SO14: South 1H 5 (6D 30)
Hartley Av. SO17: South 1D 30
Hartley Cl. SO45: Dib P 5E 53
SO50: B'stke 6G 17
Hartley Ct. *SO17: South 3C 30*
(off Winn Rd.)
Hartley Gro. SO16: Bass 5C 22
Hartley Rd. SO50: B'stke 6G 17
Hartley Wlk. SO45: Dib P 5E 53
Hartsgrove Av. SO45: Blac 5E 55
Hartsgrove Cl. SO45: Blac 4E 55
Hartswood SO51: Rom 4D 6
Harvest Rd. SO53: Cha F 1B 14
Harvey Ct. SO45: Blac 3E 55
Harvey Cres. SO31: Wars 6D 48
Harvey Gdns. SO45: Hythe 3F 53
Harvey Rd. SO50: B'stke 4E 17
Harwood Cl. SO40: Tott 3E 27
Haselbury Rd. SO40: Tott 4F 27
Haselfoot Gdns.
SO30: W End 4E 33
HATCH BOTTOM 1E 33
Hatch Mead SO30: W End 1C 32
Hathaway Cl. SO50: E'leigh 3B 16
Hatherell Cl. SO30: W End 2D 32
Hatherley Mans.
SO15: South 4G 29
Hatley Rd. SO18: South 3A 32
Havelock Ct. SO31: Wars 6A 48
Havelock Rd.
SO14: South 1C 4 (6B 30)
SO31: Wars 6A 48
The Haven SO16: Bass 3C 22
SO30: Hed E 1H 43
SO31: Loc H 3G 49
SO50: E'leigh 1B 16
Havendale SO30: Hed E 6B 34
(not continuous)
Havenstone Way
SO18: S'ing 5G 23
Havre Towers SO19: South 5G 41
Haweswater Cl.
SO16: South 2D 28
Hawfinch Cl. SO16: South 3F 21
Hawke Ho. *SO19: South 3F 41*
(off John Thornycroft Rd.)
Hawkers Cl. SO40: Tott 2E 27
Hawkes Ho. SO14: South 5G 5
Hawkeswood Rd.
SO18: South 4E 31
Hawkhill SO45: Dib 3A 52
Hawkhurst Cl. SO19: South 4A 42
Hawkins Ct. SO40: March 2D 38
Hawkins Way SO50: E'leigh 4A 16
Hawkley Grn. SO19: South 4H 41
Hawksworth Pl.
PO14: Titch C 1G 51
Hawthorn Cl. SO21: Col C 5G 11
SO30: Hed E 5B 34
SO50: Fair O 1F 17
Hawthorne Ct. SO31: Sar G 2E 49
Hawthorne Rd. SO40: Tott 3D 26
Hawthorn La. SO31: Sar G 2C 48
Hawthorn Rd. SO17: South 1C 30
SO45: Hythe 3D 52
The Hawthorns SO40: March 4D 38
(Baytree Gdns.)
SO40: March 4E 39
(The Limes)
SO50: E'leigh 6G 15
The Hawthorns
Urban Wildlife Cen. 3B 30
Hayburn Rd. SO16: South 1B 28
Haydock Cl. SO40: Tott 3C 26
Hayes Mead SO45: Hard 3B 54
Hayle Rd. SO18: W End 1B 32
Hayley Cl. SO45: Hythe 6D 52
Haynes Rd. SO18: South 4A 32
Haynes Way SO45: Dib P 5C 52
Hayter Gdns. SO51: Rom 4D 6
Hayton Ct. SO40: Tott 4F 27
Hayward Cl. SO40: Tott 4D 26
Hayward Ct. SO45: Holb 4C 54
Hazel Cl. SO21: Col C 4G 11
SO53: Cha F 3E 9
Hazeldown Rd. SO16: Rown 4C 20
Hazeleigh Av. SO19: South 3G 41
Hazel Farm Rd. SO40: Tott 4C 26
Hazel Gro. SO31: Loc H 5F 49
SO40: A'hst 2A 36
Hazel Rd. SO19: South 1F 41
Hazelwood Gro.
SO50: E'leigh 6A 10
Hazelwood Rd. SO18: South 2A 32
Headland Dr. SO31: Loc H 3E 49
Heath Cl. SO50: Fair O 2G 17
Heathcote Rd. SO53: Cha F 1F 15
Heatherbrae Gdns.
SO52: N Bad 3D 12
Heather Chase SO50: B'stke 5G 17
Heather Cl. SO40: Tott 4E 27
Heather Ct. SO18: South 4C 32
SO19: South 2G 41
Heatherdeane Rd.
SO17: South 1C 30
Heatherdene Rd. SO53: Cha F 4G 9
Heatherdown SO45: Dib P 6D 52
Heatherlands Rd. SO16: Chil 1B 22
Heather Rd. SO45: F'ley 3F 55
The Heathers SO50: E'leigh 5G 15
Heatherstone Av.
SO45: Dib P 6D 52
Heatherview Cl.
SO52: N Bad 2D 12
Heathfield SO45: Hythe 4D 52
Heathfield Cl. SO19: South 2C 42
SO53: Cha F 3E 9
Heathfield Rd. SO19: South 2B 42
SO53: Cha F 3E 9
Heath Gdns. SO31: Net A 6D 42
Heath Ho. Cl. SO30: Hed E 1H 43
Heath Ho. Gdns.
SO30: Hed E 1H 43
Heath Ho. La. SO30: Hed E 1H 43
Heathlands Cl. SO53: Cha F 5E 9
Heathlands Ct. SO45: Dib P 6C 52
Heathlands Rd. SO53: Cha F 5E 9
Heath Rd. SO19: South 6A 32
SO31: Loc H 4D 48
SO52: N Bad 4E 13
Heath Rd. Nth. SO31: Loc H 4D 48
Heath Rd. Sth. SO31: Loc H 4D 48
Hebron Ct. SO15: South 5A 30
Hedera Rd. SO31: Loc H 4D 48
(not continuous)
HEDGE END 5A 34
Hedge End Bus. Cen.
SO30: Hed E 2H 33
Hedge End Golf Cen. 5G 33
Hedge End Retail Pk. 4G 33
Hedge End Station (Rail) 1B 34
Hedge End Trade Pk.
SO30: Hed E 2G 33
Hedge End Way SO30: Hed E 1G 43
Hedgerow Cl. SO16: Rown 2C 20
Hedgerow Dr. SO18: South 2B 32
The Hedges *SO50: E'leigh 5A 16*
(off Grantham Rd.)
Hedley Cl. SO45: F'ley 4F 55
Hedley Gdns. SO30: Hed E 1H 33
Hedley Wlk. SO45: F'ley 4F 55
The Heights SO30: Hed E 5G 33
Heinz Burt Cl. SO50: E'leigh 4H 15
Helford Gdns. SO18: W End 1B 32
Helica Trade Cen.
SO15: South 4C 28
Hellyar Ri. SO30: Hed E 1G 43
Helvellyn Rd. SO16: South 3D 28
Hemdean Gdns.
SO30: W End 2D 32
Hemingway Gdns.
PO15: White 5G 45
Hemlock Way SO53: Cha F 2B 14
Hemming Cl. SO40: Tott 5E 27
Hendy Ct. *SO15: South 4G 29*
(off Selby Pl.)
Henry Cl. SO45: Hard 2B 54
Henry Rd. SO15: South 4F 29
SO31: Sar G 2D 48
SO50: B'stke 3D 16
Henry St. SO15: South 5B 30
Henstead Ct. SO15: South 5B 30
Henstead Rd. SO15: South 5B 30
Hensting La.
SO50: Fis P, Hens 6H 11
Henty Rd. SO16: South 3F 29
Hepworth Cl. SO19: South 3C 42
Herald Ind. Est. SO30: Hed E 2H 33
Herald Rd. SO30: Hed E 2H 33
Herbert Walker Av.
SO15: South 4A 4 (6E 29)
(not continuous)
Hereward Cl. SO51: Rom 5E 7
Heron Sq. SO50: E'leigh 5G 15
Herons Wood SO40: Calm 1D 26
Herrick Cl. SO19: South 1D 42
Hertsfield PO14: Titch C 4G 49
Hesketh Ho. SO15: South 5G 29
Hestia Cl. SO51: Rom 4F 7
Hewetts Ri. SO31: Wars 1A 50
Hewitt's Rd. SO15: South 6H 29
The Hexagon Cen.
SO53: Cha F 5E 15
Heye's Dr. SO19: South 2C 42
Heysham Rd. SO15: South 3F 29
Heywood Grn. SO19: South 6E 33
Hibberd Ri. SO30: Hed E 1H 33
Hickory Gdns. SO30: W End 6C 24
Highbay Cl. SO50: E'leigh 5H 15
HIGHBRIDGE 6D 10
Highbridge Rd. SO21: Twy 5E 11
SO50: B'dge, Highb 6C 10
Highbury Cl. SO50: Fair O 2F 17
Highclere Rd. SO16: South 6H 21
Highclere Way SO53: Cha F 4C 14
Highcliff Av. SO14: South 3C 30
Highcliffe Dr. SO50: E'leigh 6A 10
Highcrown M. SO17: South 1C 30
Highcrown St. SO17: South 1C 30
HIGHFIELD 1C 30
Highfield Av. SO17: South 6B 22
Highfield Cl. SO17: South 1C 30
SO53: Cha F 1G 15
Highfield Cres. SO17: South 1D 30
Highfield Hall SO17: South 1C 30
Highfield La. SO17: South 1C 30
Highfield Rd. SO17: South 2B 30
SO53: Cha F 1G 15
Highfields SO17: South 2D 30
SO31: Wars 6D 48
High Firs Gdns. SO51: Rom 5F 7
High Firs Rd. SO19: South 6B 32
SO51: Rom 4F 7
Highgrove Cl. SO40: Tott 6D 26
Highlands Cl. SO45: Dib P 4E 53
SO52: N Bad 2C 12
Highlands Ho. SO19: South 2F 41
Highlands Way SO45: Dib P 4D 52
High Mdw. SO19: South 5C 32
Highnam Gdns. SO31: Sar G 3D 48
High Oaks Cl. SO31: Loc H 4E 49
Highpoint Cen. SO19: South 1E 43
High Rd. SO16: S'ing 6F 23
High St.
SO14: South 4D 4 (1C 40)
SO21: Twy 1F 11
SO30: Botl 4D 34
SO30: W End 1C 32
SO31: Burs 6G 43
SO31: Hamb 5G 47
SO40: Tott 4G 27
SO45: Hythe 1E 53
SO50: E'leigh 6A 16
(Desborough Rd., not continuous)
SO50: E'leigh 5A 16
(Wells Pl.)
HIGHTOWN 2D 42
Hightown Towers
SO19: South 1E 43
High Trees SO50: Fair O 1H 17
High Vw. Way SO18: South 3H 31
Highwood La. SO51: Rom 4F 7
Hilda Pl. SO14: South 1H 5
HILL 5A 30
Hill Coppice Rd.
PO15: White 1H 49
Hill Cottage Gdns.
SO18: W End 6A 24
Hillcrest Av. SO53: Cha F 1F 15
Hillcrest Cl. SO52: N Bad 2D 12
Hillcrest Dr. SO53: Cha F 1F 15
Hill Cft. PO15: Seg 4H 49
Hilldene Way SO30: W End 2D 32
Hilldown Rd. SO17: South 1D 30
Hill Farm Rd. SO15: South 5A 30
Hillgrove Rd. SO18: South 6H 23
Hill La. SO15: South 1A 4 (6H 21)
SO16: South 6H 21
SO21: Col C 4F 11
Hill Pl. SO31: Burs 5H 43
Hillside Av. SO18: South 2G 31
SO51: Rom 5D 6
Hillside Cl. SO53: Cha F 1F 15
Hillside M. SO31: Sar G 1B 48
Hillsons Rd. SO30: Curd 4F 35
HILLSTREET 4C 18
Hill St. SO19: South 2F 41
SO40: Calm 3C 18
Hilltop Dr. SO19: South 1D 42
Hillview Rd. SO45: Hythe 3D 52
The Hillway SO53: Cha F 6F 9
HILLYFIELDS 6B 20
Hillyfields SO16: Nur 5B 20
HILTINGBURY 4F 9
Hiltingbury Cl. SO53: Cha F 4F 9
Hiltingbury Ct. SO53: Cha F 4D 8
Hiltingbury Rd. SO53: Cha F 4D 8
Hilton Rd. SO30: Hed E 4A 34
Hindmarch Cres.
SO30: Hed E 6A 34
Hinkler Ct. SO19: South 1D 42
Hinkler Rd. SO19: South 5E 33
Hinton Cres. SO19: South 6E 33
Hirst Rd. SO45: Hythe 3F 53
Hispano Av. PO15: White 6G 45
Hobart Dr. SO45: Hythe 3E 53
Hobb La. SO30: Hed E 6B 34
Hobbs Ct. SO50: Fair O 4H 17
Hobson Way SO45: Holb 5D 54
HOCOMBE 3D 8
Hocombe Dr. SO53: Cha F 3D 8
Hocombe Mead
Nature Reserve 3D 8
Hocombe Pk. Cl. SO53: Cha F 3D 8
Hocombe Rd. SO53: Cha F 3D 8
Hocombe Wood Rd.
SO53: Cha F 3C 8
Hodder Cl. SO53: Cha F 2D 14
Hoddinott Rd. SO50: E'leigh 5H 15
Hodinott Cl. SO51: Rom 2E 7
Hoe La. SO51: Toot 5A 12
SO52: N Bad 4D 12
Hogarth Cl. SO19: South 3C 42
SO51: Rom 3E 7
Hogwood La. SO30: W End 3D 24
HOLBURY 4D 54
Holbury Drove SO45: Holb 5B 54
Holcroft Ho. SO19: South 5E 33
Holcroft Rd. SO19: South 6E 33
Holkham Cl. SO16: South 6C 20
Holland Cl. SO53: Cha F 4E 15
Holland Pk. SO31: Loc H 4D 48
Holland Pl. SO16: South 2F 29
Holland Rd. SO19: South 3F 41
SO40: Tott 4C 26
Hollingbourne Cl.
SO18: South 3F 31
Hollman Dr. SO51: Rom 4A 6
Hollowbread Gdns.
SO31: Old N 4F 43
Hollybank Cl. SO45: Hythe 3E 53
Hollybank Cres.
SO45: Hythe 2D 52
Hollybank Rd. SO45: Hythe 2D 52
Hollybrook Av. SO16: South 6G 21
Hollybrook Cl. SO16: South 1F 29
Hollybrook Gdns.
SO31: Loc H 2E 49
Hollybrook Rd. SO16: South 1G 29
Holly Cl. SO31: Sar G 4C 48
SO45: Hythe 1A 54
Holly Ct. PO15: White 5H 45
Holly Dell SO16: Bass 4A 22
Hollydene Vs. SO45: Hythe 2E 53
Holly Gdns. SO30: W End 6D 24
Holly Hatch Rd. SO40: Tott 5E 27
Holly Hill SO16: Bass 4A 22
Holly Hill Cl. SO16: Bass 4A 22
Holly Hill La. SO31: Sar G 3A 48
Holly Hill Mans.
SO31: Sar G 3C 48
Holly Hill Woodland Pk. 3B 48
Holly Lodge SO17: South 2D 30
SO53: Cha F 4E 15
Holly M. SO16: Bass 5B 22
Hollyoak Ct. SO16: South 5E 21

Holly Oak Rd.—Kensington Cl.

Holly Oak Rd. SO16: South 6E **21**
(not continuous)
Holly Pl. SO16: South 6H **21**
Holly Rd. SO40: A'hst 3B **36**
SO45: Blac 5E **55**
Hollywood Bowl 4D 4 (1B 40)
Hollywood Bowling
Eastleigh 5B 16
Hollywood Cl. SO52: N Bad 3D **12**
Holmes Cl. SO31: Net A 1B **46**
Holmesland Dr. SO30: Botl 4D **34**
Holmesland La. SO30: Botl 4D **34**
Holmesland Wlk. SO30: Botl . . .4D **34**
Holmgrove PO14: Titch C 4G **49**
Holmsley Cl. SO18: South 4C **32**
Holmsley Ct. SO40: Tott 3B **26**
Holt Ct. SO19: South 5G **41**
Holt Rd. SO15: South 4B **30**
Holt Vw. SO50: B'stke 5F **17**
Holyborne Rd. SO51: Rom 5E **7**
Holyrood Av. SO17: South 1D **30**
Holy Rood Est. SO14: South 5F **5**
Holyrood Ho.
SO14: South 5E **5** (2C **40**)
Holyrood Pl.
SO14: South 5E **5** (2C **40**)
Homeborough Ho.
SO45: Hythe 1E **53**
Home Farm Cl. SO45: Hythe 3F **53**
Homefield SO51: Rom 3D **6**
Home Fld. Dr. SO16: Nur 4A **20**
Homemead Ho. SO51: Rom 6B **6**
Homepoint Ho. SO18: South . . .4A **32**
Homer Farm La. SO45: Blac 6E **55**
Home Rule Rd. SO31: Loc H . . .3F **49**
Homespinney Ho.
SO18: South 1F **31**
Honeysuckle Cl.
SO31: Loc H 2E **49**
Honeysuckle Cotts.
SO16: S'ing 5E **23**
Honeysuckle Rd.
SO16: Bass, S'ing 5C **22**
Honeysuckle Way
SO53: Cha F 1C **14**
Honeywood Cl. SO40: Tott 2D **26**
Honister Cl. SO16: South 3C **28**
Hood Cl. SO31: Loc H 3F **49**
Hood Rd. SO18: South 3A **32**
HOOK 2E 51
Hook Cl. SO51: Ampf 3C **8**
Hook Cres. SO51: Ampf 3C **8**
Hook La. PO14: Abs 2E **51**
SO31: Wars 2E **51**
HOOK PARK 3B 50
Hook Pk. Est. SO31: Wars 3B **50**
Hook Pk. Rd. SO31: Wars 2A **50**
Hook Rd. SO51: Ampf 2A **8**
Hookwater Cl. SO53: Cha F 3D **8**
Hookwater Rd. SO53: Cha F 3C **8**
Hook with Warsash
Local Nature Reserve 3B 50
Hookwood La. SO51: Ampf 3B **8**
Hooper Dr. SO51: Rom 1E **7**
Hope Rd. SO30: W End 1E **33**
Horder Cl. SO16: Bass 6B **22**
Hornbeam Cl. SO30: Hed E 5B **34**
Hornbeam Gdns.
SO30: W End 6D **24**
Hornbeam Rd. SO53: Cha F 1A **14**
Hornby Cl. SO31: Wars 1B **50**
Hornchurch Rd.
SO16: South 4D **20**
Horne Cl. SO18: W End 1B **32**
Horns Drove SO16: Rown 4B **20**
Horns Hill SO16: Nur 3B **20**
Horns Hill Cl. SO16: Nur 3B **20**
Horsebridge Way
SO16: Rown 4C **20**
Horsecroft SO51: Rom 4C **6**
The Horsefair SO51: Rom 5B **6**
Horsefair Ct. SO51: Rom 5B **6**
Horsefair M. SO51: Rom 5B **6**
Horseshoe Bri. SO17: South 3D **30**
Horseshoe Cl. PO14: Titch C . . .5H **49**
Horseshoe Dr. SO40: Calm 1A **26**
SO51: Rom 2E **7**
Horseshoe Lodge
SO31: Wars 6C **48**
Horton Way SO50: B'stke 5F **17**
Hotspur Cl. SO45: Hythe 1D **52**
HOUND 1E 47
Hound Cl. SO31: Net A 2D **46**
Hound Rd. SO31: Hou, Net A . . .2C **46**
Hound Rd. Gdns.
SO31: Net A 1D **46**
Hound Way SO31: Net A 1C **46**
Houndwell Pl.
SO14: South 4F **5** (1C **40**)
HOUNSDOWN 6F 27
Hounsdown Av. SO40: Tott 6F **27**
Hounsdown Bus. Pk.
SO40: Tott 1F **37**
Hounsdown Cl. SO40: Tott 6F **27**
Hoveton Gro. SO53: Cha F 5D **8**
Howard Cl. SO18: S'ing 5G **23**
SO50: Fair O 1F **17**
SO53: Cha F 3F **15**
Howard Oliver Ho.
SO45: Hythe 3F **53**
Howard Rd. SO15: South 5H **29**
Howard's Gro. SO15: South 3G **29**
Howell Cl. SO14: South 6E **31**
Howerts Cl. SO31: Wars 2B **50**
The Hub
Eastleigh 4C 16
Hudson Ct. SO40: Tott 5D **26**
Hudson Ho. SO14: South 6G **5**
Hughes Cl. SO45: Blac 4E **55**
Hulles Way SO52: N Bad 3D **12**
Hulse Lodge SO15: South 3B **30**
Hulse Rd. SO15: South 3B **30**
Hulton Cl. SO19: South 4F **41**
Humber Gdns. SO31: Burs 4G **43**
The Hundred SO51: Rom 5B **6**
Hungerford SO31: Burs 6F **43**
Hunt Av. SO31: Net A 1C **46**
Hunter Cl. SO45: Hard 2B **54**
Hunter Ct. SO15: South 2F **29**
Hunters Ct. SO31: Burs 1H **43**
Hunters Cres. SO40: Tott 5B **26**
SO51: Rom 2F **7**
Hunters Hill SO40: Tott 2D **36**
Hunter's Ride SO21: Hurs 1A **8**
Hunters Way SO50: B'stke 5G **17**
Huntingdon Cl.
PO14: Titch C 6G **49**
SO40: Tott 2E **27**
Huntly Way SO18: South 4H **31**
Hunton Cl. SO16: South 6H **21**
Hunts Cl. SO21: Col C 4G **11**
Hunts Pond Rd.
PO14: Titch C 5G **49**
SO31: P Ga 2F **49**
The Hurdles PO14: Titch C 5H **49**
Hurlingham Gdns.
SO16: Bass 4C **22**
Hurricane Dr. SO16: Rown 3C **20**
Hursley Ct. SO53: Cha F 4D **8**
Hursley Dr. SO45: Blac 6E **55**
Hursley Rd. SO21: Hurs 2D **8**
SO53: Cha F 2D **8**
Hurstbourne Pl.
SO19: South 5H **41**
Hurst Cl. SO40: Tott 3F **27**
SO53: Cha F 3C **14**
Hurst Grn. Cl. SO19: South 4A **42**
Hurworth Ho. *SO19: South 3F 41*
(off John Thornycroft Rd.)
Hut Farm Pl. SO53: Cha F 2E **15**
Hutwood Rd. SO16: Chil 1C **22**
Huxley Cl. SO31: Loc H 5F **49**
Huxley Ct. SO45: Dib P 4A **52**
Hyde Cl. SO15: South 2G **29**
SO40: Tott 4B **26**
Hymans Way SO40: Tott 4F **27**
Hyssop Cl. PO15: White 6H **45**
HYTHE 1E 53
Hythe By-Pass SO45: Dib 3A **52**
HYTHE HOSPITAL 4E 53
Hythe Marine Pk.
SO45: Hythe 2F **53**
Hythe Rd. SO40: March 5C **38**
Hythe Sailing Club 3G 53
Hythe Spartina Marsh
Nature Reserve 3G 53

I

Ibbotson Way SO40: Tott 6D **26**
Ibsen Cl. PO15: White 5G **45**
Ida Ct. SO19: South 3H **41**
Ideal Pk. Homes Cvn. Site 1E **17**
Ilex Cres. SO31: Loc H 4D **48**
Imber Way SO19: South 1C **42**
Imperial Av. SO15: South 3F **29**
Imperial Pk. Ind. Est.
SO14: South 4D **30**
Imperial Rd. SO14: South 4D **30**
Imperial Way SO15: South 6G **29**
Ingersley Ri. SO30: W End 2E **33**
Ingle Glen SO45: Dib P 5E **53**
Ingle Grn. SO40: Calm 2B **26**
Ingleside SO31: Net A 6C **42**
Ingleton Rd. SO16: South 2B **28**
Inglewood Gdns.
SO50: Fair O 1F **17**
Ingram Ct. SO17: South 3E **31**
Inkerman Rd. SO19: South 2F **41**
International Way
SO19: South 5G **41**
Ionic Cl. SO53: Cha F 6H **9**
Ipley Way SO45: Hythe 4E **53**
Irene Ct. SO16: South 1F **29**
Iris Rd. SO16: Bass 5D **22**
Ironbridge Cres. SO31: P Ga . . .1E **49**
Ironside Ct. SO14: South 5D **4**
Irving Rd. SO16: South 2D **28**
Irwell Cl. SO53: Cha F 2C **14**
Isis Cl. SO16: South 3C **28**
Islander Wlk. SO50: E'leigh 1H **23**
Isle of Wight Car Ferry Terminal
. . . . .6D 4 (3B 40)
ITCHEN 2F 41
Itchen Av. SO50: B'stke 5F **17**
The Itchen Bri.
SO14: South 6H **5** (2E **41**)
SO19: South 2E **41**
Itchen Bus. Pk. SO17: South . . .1E **31**
Itchen College Sports Cen. 6A 32
Itchen Grange SO50: E'leigh 4D **16**
Itchenside Cl. SO18: S'ing 5H **23**
Itchen Valley Country Pk. 4C 24
Itchen Valley Country Pk.
Visitor Cen. 4B 24
Itchen Valley Nature Reserve
. . . . .5A 24
Itchen Vw. SO18: S'ing 5H **23**
Itchin Cl. SO40: Tott 5D **26**
Ivanhoe Rd. SO15: South 2H **29**
Ivor Cl. SO45: Holb 4C **54**
Ivy Cl. SO40: Tott 1E **27**
Ivy Dene SO19: South 1D **42**
Ivy La. SO18: W End 1B **32**
SO30: W End 1C **32**
Ivy Rd. SO17: South 3E **31**
Ivy Ter. SO30: Hed E 5H **33**

J

Jacaranda Cl. PO15: Seg 3H **49**
Jack Cl. SO53: Cha F 1A **14**
Jackdaw Ri. SO50: E'leigh 6F **15**
Jackie Wigg Gdns.
SO40: Tott 4G **27**
Jackman's Cl. SO19: South 2F **41**
Jacksons Rd. SO30: Hed E 1A **34**
Jacobs Cl. SO51: Rom 5D **6**
Jacob's Gutter La.
SO40: Elin, Tott 6F **27**
(not continuous)
Jacob's Wlk. SO40: Tott 1E **37**
James Ct. SO51: Rom 6D **6**
James Grieve Av.
SO31: Loc H 5E **49**
Jameson Rd. SO19: South 2H **41**
James St.
SO14: South 3G **5** (1D **40**)
James Weld Cl. SO15: South . . .4B **30**
Janaway Gdns. SO17: South . . .3F **31**
Janes Cl. SO45: Blac 5E **55**
Janson Rd. SO15: South 4G **29**
Jarvis Flds. SO31: Burs 5H **43**
Jasmine Ct. PO15: White 4H **45**
SO17: South 3B 30
(off Westwood Rd.)
Jasmine Rd. SO30: Hed E 3H **33**
Java Dr. PO15: White 6G **45**
Jazmine Ct. SO31: Net A 1C **46**
Jeffries Cl. SO16: Rown 4C **20**
Jelico Ct. SO16: Bass 4C **22**
Jellicoe Dr. SO31: Sar G 3D **48**
Jellicoe Ho. SO30: Hed E 3B **34**
Jenkyns Cl. SO30: Botl 4E **35**
Jenner Way SO51: Rom 4F **7**
Jennings Rd. SO40: Tott 3G **27**
Jensen Ct. SO15: South 3B **30**
Jermyns La. SO51: Ampf 1F **7**
Jerome Ct. SO19: South 5D **32**
Jerome St. PO15: White 4G **45**
Jerram Pl. SO31: Sar G 3E **49**
Jerrett's La. SO16: Nur 6B **20**
Jersey Cl. SO16: South 6C **20**
Jesmond Gro. SO31: Loc H 6E **49**
Jessamine Rd. SO16: South 1F **29**
Jessica Cres. SO40: Tott 2B **26**
Jessie Ter.
SO14: South 6F **5** (2C **40**)
Jessop Cl. SO45: Hythe 1D **52**
Jessop Wlk. *SO45: Hythe 1D 52*
(off Waterside Sq.)
Jex Blake Cl. SO16: South 5F **21**
Jockey La. SO50: B'stke 2E **17**
Joe Bigwood Cl. SO16: Nur 4B **20**
John Bunyan Cl.
PO15: White 5G **45**
John Darling Mall
SO50: E'leigh 3A **16**
John Hansard Gallery . . .1D 4 (6B 30)
Johnson St.
SO14: South 3F **5** (1C **40**)
(not continuous)
John's Rd. SO19: South 3F **41**
John St. SO14: South 6F **5** (2C **40**)
John Thornycroft Rd.
SO19: South 3E **41**
Joiners M. SO19: South 3F **41**
Jo Jo's Health & Fitness 3C 30
Jonas Nichols Sq.
SO14: South 3G **5** (1D **40**)
Jones La. SO45: Hythe 2D **52**
Jordan Ho. SO15: South 6G **29**
Josian Wlk.
SO14: South 2G **5** (6D **30**)
Jubilee Cl. SO50: E'leigh 6H **15**
Jubilee Ct. SO30: Hed E 6H **33**
Jubilee Gdns. SO18: South 4B **32**
Jubilee M. SO31: Net A 1A **46**
Jubilee Rd. SO51: Rom 4B **6**
Jubilee Sports Cen.
Southampton 6C 22
Judd Cl. SO50: E'leigh 3G **15**
Judges Gully Cl.
SO50: B'stke 2D **16**
Jukes Wlk. SO30: W End 1F **33**
Julian Cl. SO16: Chil 3A **22**
Julian Ct. SO18: South 1G **31**
Julian Rd. SO19: South 2B **42**
Julius Cl. SO53: Cha F 1G **15**
Jumar Cl. SO31: Wars 2B **50**
Junction Rd. SO40: Tott 4G **27**
Juniper Cl. SO52: N Bad 2D **12**
Juniper Ct. SO18: South 4G **31**
Juniper Rd. SO18: South 4H **31**
Juno Ho. *SO19: South 3F 41*
(off John Thornycroft Rd.)
Jupiter Cl. SO16: South 6D **20**
Jurds Lake Way SO19: South . . .4F **41**
Jurd Way SO31: Burs 4F **43**
Justinian Cl. SO53: Cha F 6H **9**
Jutland Cl. PO15: White 6F **45**

K

Kanes Hill SO19: South 5E **33**
Kanes Hill Cvn. Site 1F **43**
Kathleen Rd. SO19: South 2A **42**
Kathryn Cl. SO40: Calm 2B **26**
Katrine Cres. SO53: Cha F 5C **8**
Kayak Cl. SO31: Wars 6C **48**
Kayleigh Cl. SO40: Tott 5D **26**
Keats Cl. PO15: White 4F **45**
Keats Rd. SO19: South 5C **32**
Keble Cl. SO53: Cha F 2E **15**
Keble Rd. SO53: Cha F 3E **15**
Keepers Cl. SO53: Cha F 1D **14**
Kelburn Cl. SO53: Cha F 6D **8**
Kellett Rd. SO15: South 3A **30**
Kelly Ho. SO18: S'ing 5G **23**
Kelmscott Gdns. SO53: Cha F . . .4D **8**
Kelsey Cl. PO14: Titch C 6F **49**
Kelston Cl. SO15: South 4E **29**
Kelvin Cl. SO45: Hythe 3E **53**
Kelvin Gro. SO31: Net A 1C **46**
Kelvin Rd. SO50: E'leigh 5H **15**
Kemps Quay Ind. Pk.
SO18: South 4F **31**
Kempton Ct. *PO15: White 5G 45*
(off Timor Cl.)
Kendal Av. SO16: South 2B **28**
Kendal Cl. SO53: Cha F 6G **9**
Kendal Ct. SO16: South 2B **28**
Kenilworth Dr. SO50: E'leigh . . .1A **16**
Kenilworth Gdns.
SO30: W End 2E **33**
Kenilworth Ho. *SO14: South 5E 31*
(off Kent St.)
SO30: W End 2E **33**
Kenilworth Rd. SO15: South . . .5B **30**
Kenmore Cl. SO40: Tott 1E **37**
Kennedy Rd. SO16: South 6D **20**
Kennet Cl. SO18: W End 6B **24**
Kennett Cl. SO51: Rom 4F **7**
Kennett Rd. SO51: Rom 4F **7**
Kensington Cl. SO50: B'stke 2D **16**

A-Z Southampton 67

Kensington Flds.
SO45: Dib P 4B 52
Kensington Gdns.
PO14: Titch C 5G 49
Kenson Gdns. SO19: South 1A 42
Kent Gdns. SO40: Tott 6D 26
Kent Ho. SO14: South . . .1H 5 (5E 31)
Kentish Rd. SO15: South 4G 29
Kent Rd. SO17: South 2E 31
SO53: Cha F 4E 15
Kent St. SO14: South 1H 5 (6E 31)
Kenwyn Cl. SO18: W End 1B 32
Keppel Ri. SO19: South 3F 41
(off Capstan Rd.)
Kern Cl. SO16: South 6D 20
Kerrigan Ct. SO17: South 3C 30
Kerry Cl. SO53: Cha F 1E 15
Kersley Gdns. SO19: South 1A 42
Kesteven Way SO18: South 3A 32
Kestrel Cl. SO16: South 4F 21
SO32: Botl 2D 34
SO40: March 4C 38
Kestrel Rd. SO50: E'leigh 5F 15
The Kestrels SO31: Burs 5F 43
Keswick Rd. SO19: South 2F 41
Kevlyn Cres. SO31: Old N 4E 43
Kew La. SO31: Burs 6G 43
Keynsham Rd. SO19: South 5B 32
Khartoum Rd. SO17: South 1C 30
Kielder Cl. SO53: Cha F 6C 8
Kilford Cl. SO30: Botl 5E 35
Killarney Cl. SO19: South 2E 43
Kilmeston Cl. SO50: E'leigh 6A 16
Kiln Cl. SO45: Dib P 3C 52
Kiln Grn. SO21: Col C 5G 11
Kiln La. SO21: Ott 3B 10
SO50: B'dge 4D 10
Kilnyard Cl. SO40: Tott 2D 26
Kimber Hall SO14: South 4F 5
Kimber Ho. SO14: South 6D 4
Kimberley Cl. SO30: Hed E 6H 33
SO50: Fair O 1G 17
Kimberley Ct. SO19: South 3G 41
Kimbridge Cl. SO16: Rown 4C 20
Kineton Rd. SO15: South 2A 30
Kingcup Av. SO31: Loc H 4D 48
Kingdom Cl. PO15: Seg 2H 49
King Edward Av.
SO16: South 3E 29
King Edward Pk. SO52: N Bad 4B 8
Kingfisher Cl. SO31: Hamb 3G 47
Kingfisher Copse
SO31: Loc H 4F 49
Kingfisher Rd. SO50: E'leigh 5F 15
Kingfisher Way SO40: March 4C 38
SO51: Rom 4C 6
King George's Av.
SO15: South 5D 28
King John's House & Heritage Cen.
. . . . .5B 6
Kings Av. SO31: Hamb 4E 47
Kingsbridge La.
SO15: South 2C 4 (6B 30)
Kingsbury Rd. SO14: South 4D 30
Kingsclere Av. SO19: South 4H 41
Kingsclere Cl. SO19: South 4H 41
Kings Cl. SO53: Cha F 6F 9
Kings Copse Av.
SO30: Botl, Hed E 1B 44
Kings Copse Rd.
SO30: Hed E 1B 44
Kingsdown Way
SO18: South 1H 31
Kings Fld. SO31: Burs 4G 43
Kingsfield Gdns. SO31: Burs 4G 43
Kingsfold Av. SO18: South 6H 23
Kings Ho.
SO14: South 5F 5 (2C 40)
Kingsland Ct.
SO14: South 3F 5 (1C 40)
Kingsland Ho. SO14: South 2E 5
KINGSLAND PLACE 2F 5
Kingsland Sq.
SO14: South 3F 5 (1C 40)
Kingsley Gdns. SO40: Tott 4B 26
Kingsley Rd. SO15: South 4F 29
Kingsley Way PO15: White 4F 45
Kingsmead Cl. SO15: South 2F 29
King's Pk. Rd. SO15: South 5C 30
Kings Ride SO45: Blac 6E 55
King's Rd. SO53: Cha F 1E 15
Kingston SO31: Net A 6C 42
Kingston Rd. SO15: South 5H 29
King St. SO14: South 5F 5 (2C 40)
Kingsway
SO14: South 2F 5 (6C 30)
SO53: Cha F 6F 9

Kingsway Ct. SO53: Cha F 5G 9
Kingsway Gdns. SO53: Cha F 5G 9
Kingswood SO40: March 4E 39
Kingswood Cl. PO15: White 5H 45
Kinloss Cl. SO16: South 4E 21
Kinross Rd. SO40: Tott 4F 27
Kinsbourne Cl. SO19: South 5E 33
Kinsbourne Ri. SO19: South 5F 33
Kinsbourne Way
SO19: South 5E 33
Kinterbury Ct. SO17: South 3C 30
Kinver Cl. SO51: Rom 3E 7
Kinver Cres. SO50: Fair O 3H 17
Kipling Cl. PO15: White 4F 45
Kipling Ct. SO19: South 4H 41
Kirk Gdns. SO40: Tott 6F 27
Kitchener Rd. SO17: South 6E 23
Kite's Croft Bus. Pk.
PO14: Titch 6H 49
Kites Croft Cl. PO14: Titch C 6G 49
KITNOCKS 4H 35
Kleves Ct. SO19: South 5B 32
Knellers La. SO40: Tott 1D 36
Knighton Rd. SO19: South 1H 41
Knights Cl. SO31: Wars 6C 48
Knightstone Grange
SO45: Hythe 4E 53
Knightwood Cl. SO40: A'hst 3B 36
SO19: South 3G 41
Knightwood Cres.
SO53: Cha F 1C 14
Knightwood Glade
SO53: Cha F 6B 8
Knightwood Leisure Cen. 2B 14
Knightwood M. SO53: Cha F 1C 14
Knightwood Rd. SO45: Hythe 4F 53
SO53: Cha F 5B 8
Knightwood Vw. SO53: Cha F 2E 15
Knotgrass Rd. SO31: Loc H 5C 48
Knowle Hill SO50: E'leigh 6B 10
Knowle La. SO50: Hor H 2H 17
Knowles Cl. SO16: Nur 4B 20
Knyght Cl. SO51: Rom 6D 6
Kootenay Av. SO18: South 4E 33
Kornwestheim Way
SO50: E'leigh 4G 15

L

Laburnum Cl. SO52: N Bad 2E 13
Laburnum Cl. SO19: South 2F 41
Laburnum Cres.
SO45: Hythe 1A 54
Laburnum Gro. SO50: E'leigh 4A 16
Laburnum Rd. SO16: S'ing 5E 23
SO30: Hed E 5B 34
Lackford Av. SO40: Tott 5E 27
Lackford Way SO40: Tott 5F 27
Lacon Cl. SO18: South 3G 31
LADWELL 1D 8
Lady Betty's Dr. PO15: White 1H 49
Ladycross Rd. SO45: Hythe 4E 53
Ladywood SO50: E'leigh 1H 15
Laidlaw Gdns. SO53: Cha F 4D 8
Lake Cl. SO21: Hurs 2B 8
Lake Farm Cl. SO30: Hed E 3A 34
Lake Ho. SO15: South 5G 29
Lakeland Gdns.
SO40: March 4C 38
Lakelands Dr. SO15: South 5G 29
Laker Ho. SO15: South 4B 30
Lake Rd. SO19: South 3F 41
SO53: Cha F 5G 9
Lakeside Av. SO16: Rown 4C 20
Lakeside Country Pk. 1H 23
Lakewood Cl. SO53: Cha F 5F 9
Lakewood Rd. SO40: A'hst 2C 36
SO53: Cha F 6F 9
Lamberhurst Cl.
SO19: South 5A 42
Lambourne Cl. SO45: Dib P 5D 52
Lambourne Dr. SO31: Loc H 4E 49
Lambourne Ho. SO30: Hed E 5H 33
Lambourne Rd.
SO18: W End 1B 32
Lamburn Sq. SO53: Cha F 1D 14
Lammas Rd. SO45: Hythe 4E 53
Lancaster Cl. SO31: Burs 4G 43
Lancaster Rd. SO30: W End 1C 32
Lancaster Rd. SO16: South 6D 20
Landguard Rd. SO15: South 5H 29
Landseer Rd. SO19: South 2C 42
Lands End Rd. SO31: Burs 6H 43

The Lane SO45: F'ley 2H 55
Lanehays Rd. SO45: Hythe 3D 52
Langbar Cl. SO19: South 5G 31
Langdale Cl. SO16: South 3D 28
LANGDOWN 3E 53
Langdown Ct. SO45: Hythe 3E 53
Langdown Firs SO45: Hythe 3E 53
Langdown Lawn
SO45: Hythe 4E 53
Langdown Lawn Cl.
SO45: Hythe 4E 53
Langdown Rd. SO45: Hythe 3E 53
Langham Cl. SO52: N Bad 3D 12
Langhorn Rd. SO16: S'ing 5E 23
LANGLEY 6E 55
Langley Lodge Gdns.
SO45: Blac 6F 55
Langley Rd. SO15: South 5E 29
Langrish Rd. SO16: South 5F 21
Langstaff Way SO18: South 3A 32
Langtry Ct. SO31: Burs 3G 43
Lansdowne Cl. SO51: Rom 4B 6
Lansdowne Ct. SO51: Rom 4B 6
Lansdowne Gdns. SO51: Rom 4B 6
LANSDOWNE HILL 5D 4 (2B 40)
Lansdowne Hill
SO14: South 5D 4 (2B 40)
Lansdowne Rd. SO15: South 4E 29
Lapwing Dr. SO40: Tott 3C 26
Larch Av. SO45: Hard 3C 54
Larch Cl. SO30: W End 6D 24
Larchdale Cl. SO31: Wars 1B 50
Larch Rd. SO16: South 6E 21
Larch Way SO31: Burs 5F 43
Larchwood Cl. SO15: South 6H 29
Larchwood Rd. SO40: Tott 5C 26
Lark Rd. SO50: E'leigh 6F 15
Larkspur Chase SO19: South 6E 33
Larkspur Cl. SO31: Loc H 5C 48
Larkspur Dr. SO40: March 5C 38
SO53: Cha F 1B 14
Larkspur Gdns. SO30: Hed E 5A 34
SO45: Holb 4B 54
Laser Cl. SO31: Wars 6C 48
Latchmore Dr. SO45: Dib 2A 52
Latelie Cl. SO31: Net A 2C 46
Latham Cl. SO50: Fair O 5H 17
Latham Ct. SO15: South 4F 29
Latham Rd. SO50: Fair O 5H 17
SO51: Rom 4C 6
Latimer Gate SO14: South 6F 5
Latimer St.
SO14: South 6F 5 (2C 40)
SO51: Rom 5B 6
Latimer Wlk. SO51: Rom 2E 7
Launcelyn Cl. SO52: N Bad 4D 12
Launceston Dr.
SO50: E'leigh 2H 15
Laundry Rd. SO16: South 6E 21
Laurel Cl. SO19: South 2F 41
SO31: Loc H 3F 49
SO45: Hythe 3D 52
Laurel Gdns. SO31: Loc H 3F 49
Laurel Rd. SO31: Loc H 3F 49
The Laurels SO32: Botl 2D 34
Laurence Cl. SO50: Fair O 1F 17
Laurence M. SO51: Rom 4C 6
Lauren Way SO40: Calm 2B 26
Laurie Wlk. SO45: F'ley 4F 55
Lauriston Dr. SO53: Cha F 4D 8
Lavender Cl. SO19: South 6H 31
Lavender Ct. PO15: White 4H 45
Lavender Gro. SO31: Loc H 4E 49
Laverstoke Cl. SO16: Rown 4C 20
Lavington Gdns.
SO52: N Bad 4D 12
Lawes Wlk. SO51: Rom 2E 7
Lawford Way SO40: Tott 4E 27
Lawn Cl. SO17: South 3D 30
Lawn Dr. SO31: Loc H 5E 49
Lawn Rd. SO17: South 3D 30
SO50: E'leigh 3B 16
Lawnside Rd. SO15: South 3E 29
Lawnswood SO50: Fair O 2G 17
Lawnswood Cl. SO45: Dib P 5C 52
Lawrence Cl. SO19: South 3H 41
Lawrence Gro. SO19: South 3H 41
Lawrence Ho. SO45: Hythe 2F 53
Lawson Cl. SO31: Lwr Swan 5A 44
Laxton Cl. SO19: South 3A 42
SO31: Loc H 4F 49
Leabrook SO31: Sar G 2E 49
Leafy La. PO15: White 1H 49
Leah Cl. SO16: South 1H 29
Leander Cl. SO50: E'leigh 2A 16
Lea Rd. SO45: Blac 6E 55

Leaside Way
SO16: Bass, S'ing 4E 23
Leatherhead Gdns.
SO30: Hed E 1B 34
Lebanon Rd. SO15: South 4B 28
Lebburn Mdws. SO30: Hed E 2H 33
Leckford Cl. SO18: South 3D 32
Lecole Wlk. SO30: Botl 4E 35
Ledbury Ho. SO19: South 3F 41
(off John Thornycroft Rd.)
LEE 1G 19
Lee Church La. SO51: Lee 1F 19
Lee Drove SO51: Lee 6A 12
Lee La. SO16: Nur 2G 19
SO51: A'field, Lee 1G 19
Legion Cl. SO16: Bass 5E 23
Leicester Rd. SO15: South 1H 29
Leigh Ct. SO50: E'leigh 4G 15
Leigh Rd. SO17: South 2C 30
SO50: E'leigh 4G 15
SO53: Cha F 3E 15
Leighton Av. SO15: South 3F 29
Leighton Rd. SO19: South 2G 41
Leisure World
Southampton 4B 4 (1A 40)
Le Marechal Av. SO31: Old N 3F 43
Lemon Rd. SO15: South 4B 28
Lennox Cl. SO16: South 4D 20
SO53: Cha F 5G 9
Leonards Ct. SO16: South 3A 28
Lepe Rd. SO45: Blac, F'ley 6E 55
Leroux Cl.
SO15: South 1C 4 (6B 30)
Leslie Loader Ct.
SO50: E'leigh 2A 16
Leslie Loader M.
SO19: South 6G 31
Le Tissier Ct. SO15: South 5A 30
Leven Cl. SO53: Cha F 5C 8
Lewes Cl. SO50: E'leigh 1A 16
Lewin Cl. SO21: Col C 5F 11
Lewins Wlk. SO31: Burs 4F 43
Lewis Cl. SO45: Dib P 4A 52
Lewis Ho.
SO14: South 2F 5 (6C 30)
Lewis Silkin Way
SO16: South 5E 21
Lewry Cl. SO30: Hed E 4A 34
Lexby Rd. SO40: Elin 5G 27
Leybourne Av. SO18: South 3H 31
Leyton Rd. SO14: South 5E 31
Liberty Row SO31: Hamb 5G 47
(off Meadow La.)
Library Rd. SO40: Tott 4G 27
Lichen Way SO40: March 3D 38
Lichfield Rd. PO14: Titch C 4G 49
Liddel Way SO53: Cha F 2D 14
Lightning Cl. SO45: F'ley 3F 55
Lilac Rd. SO16: Bass 5D 22
Lilley Cl. SO40: March 3D 38
Lime Av. SO19: South 6A 32
Lime Cl. SO19: South 6A 32
SO21: Col C 5G 11
SO45: Dib P 4C 52
Lime Gdns. SO30: W End 6D 24
Lime Kiln La. SO45: Holb 3B 54
Lime Kiln La. Est.
SO45: Holb 3B 54
The Limes SO40: March 4E 39
Lime St. SO14: South 5F 5 (2C 40)
Lime Wlk. SO30: Botl 4C 52
SO45: Dib P 4C 52
Linacre Rd. SO19: South 6D 32
Lincoln Cl. PO14: Titch C 4G 49
SO51: Rom 3E 7
Lincoln Ct. SO15: South 1A 30
SO30: W End 1C 32
Lincoln Pl. SO53: Cha F 3F 15
Lincolns Ri. SO50: E'leigh 4B 10
Linda Rd. SO45: F'ley 2H 55
Linden Cl. SO18: W End 6B 24
SO31: Loc H 3F 49
SO51: Rom 5B 6
Linden Gdns. SO30: Hed E 6B 34
SO51: Rom 5C 6
Linden Gro. SO53: Cha F 5E 9
Linden Rd. SO16: South 5E 21
SO51: Rom 5C 6
Linden Wlk. SO52: N Bad 2D 12
Lindoe Cl. SO15: South 4B 30
Lindsay Rd. SO19: South 5E 33
Lindway SO31: P Ga 1E 49
Liners Ind. Est. SO15: South 5G 29
Linford Cl. SO50: Fair O 1F 17
Linford Cres. SO16: South 6H 21
Ling Dale SO16: Chil 2B 22
Lingdale Pl. SO17: South 3C 30

Lingfield Gdns. SO18: South ...1H 31
Lingwood Cl. SO16: Bass 2B 22
Lingwood Wlk. SO16: Bass ...2B 22
Link Rd. SO16: South 6D 20
Links Vw. Way SO16: Bass ...3B 22
The Linnets SO40: Tott 3C 26
Linnet Sq. SO50: E'leigh 6F 15
Linwood Cl. SO45: Hythe 4E 53
Lionheart Way SO16: Burs ...4F 43
Lipizzaner Flds. PO15: White .5F 45
Lisbon Rd. SO15: South 5H 29
Litchfield Cres. SO18: South ..2H 31
Litchfield Rd. SO18: South ...2H 31
Lit. Abshot Rd. PO14: Abs 1F 51
Littlefield Cres. SO53: Cha F .1A 14
Lit. Fox Dr. SO31: P Ga 2F 49
LITTLE HOLBURY 3B 54
Lit. Holbury Pk. Homes
  SO45: Holb 3B 54
Lit. Kimble Wlk.
  SO30: Hed E 5A 34
Lit. Lance's Hill
  SO19: South 4H 31
Little Meads SO51: Rom 5A 6
Lit. Oak Rd. SO16: Bass 5B 22
Lit. Park Cl. SO30: Hed E 5H 33
Lit. Park Farm Rd.
  PO15: Seg 2G 49
Little Reynolds SO40: Tott ...6D 26
Littlewood Gdns.
  SO30: W End 2D 32
  SO31: Loc H 4C 48
Liverpool St. SO14: South 4C 30
Livingstone Rd. SO14: South ..3C 30
Lloyd Av. SO40: March 4C 38
Loane Rd. SO19: South 2H 41
Lobelia Rd. SO16: S'ing 5E 23
Lockerley Cres. SO16: South ..2D 28
Locke Rd. SO30: Hed E 3A 34
LOCKS HEATH 4E 49
Locks Heath Cen. 4E 49
Locks Heath Pk. Rd.
  SO31: Loc H 6F 49
Locksley Ct. SO16: South 4B 30
Locksley SO50: E'leigh 6G 15
Locks Rd. SO31: Loc H 5E 49
Lockswood Keep
  SO31: Loc H 3E 49
Lockswood Rd.
  SO31: Loc H, Sar G, Wars
  ....6C 48
The Lodge SO15: South 4B 30
Lodge Dr. SO45: Dib P 5D 52
Lodge Rd. SO14: South 4C 30
  SO31: Loc H 4F 49
Lofting Cl. SO50: B'stke 5E 17
Logan Cl. SO16: South 4D 20
Lomax Cl. SO30: Hed E 2A 34
London Rd.
  SO15: South 1D 4 (5B 30)
Lone Eagle Cl. SO19: South ..6D 32
Longacres PO14: Titch C 3G 49
Long Beech Dr. SO40: Tott ...5D 26
Longbridge Cl. SO40: Calm ...1D 26
Longbridge Ct. SO40: Calm ...1D 26
Longbridge Ind. Pk.
  SO14: South 6H 5 (2E 41)
LONG COMMON 1D 34
Long Copse SO45: Holb 5D 54
LONG DOWN 6G 37
Longdown Activity Farm 3D 36
Long Dr. SO30: W End 1E 33
Longfield Rd. SO50: Fair O 2G 17
Long La. SO31: Burs 5G 43
  SO40: March 4B 38
  SO45: Hard, Holb 2B 54
Long La. SO45: Holb 5D 54
Longleat Gdns. SO16: South ..5F 21
Longmead Av. SO50: B'stke ..3D 16
Longmeadow Gdns.
  SO45: Hythe 2E 53
Longmead Rd. SO18: South ..1A 32
Longmore Av. SO19: South ...3F 41
Longmore Cres. SO19: South ..3F 41
Longridge Rd. SO30: Hed E ..5A 34
Longstock Cl. SO19: South ...5A 42
Longstock Cres. SO40: Tott ...4D 26
Lonsdale Gdns. SO31: Burs ...3G 43
Loperwood
  SO40: Calm, Wins 1A 26
Loperwood La. SO40: Calm ..5A 18
  (not continuous)
Lord Mountbatten Cl.
  SO18: S'ing 5G 23
Lordsdale SO16: South 1G 29

LORD'S HILL 5D 20
Lords Hill Centre E.
  SO16: South 5D 20
Lords Hill Centre W.
  SO16: South 5D 20
Lord's Hill District Cen.
  SO16: South 5D 20
Lords Hill Way SO16: South ..5C 20
Lordswood Cl. SO16: South ...5H 21
Lordswood Ct. SO16: South ...5G 21
Lordswood Gdns.
  SO16: South 5H 21
Lordswood La. SO16: Chil 1H 21
Lordswood Rd. SO16: South ..5G 21
Loreille Gdns. SO16: Rown ...2C 20
Lorne Pl. SO14: South 4A 32
Loroux Wlk. SO40: Tott 3F 27
Lortemore Pl. SO51: Rom 5B 6
Loughwood Cl. SO50: E'leigh .1A 16
Louis Rd. PO14: Titch C 1H 51
Lovage Gdns. SO40: Tott 4C 26
Lovage Rd. PO15: White 6H 45
Love La. SO51: Rom 5B 6
Loveridge Way SO50: E'leigh ..4A 16
Lwr. Alfred St. SO14: South ...5D 30
Lwr. Banister St.
  SO15: South 5B 30
Lwr. Brownhill Rd.
  SO16: South 1A 28
Lwr. Canal Wlk.
  SO14: South 6E 5 (3C 40)
Lwr. Church Rd.
  PO14: Titch C 4G 49
Lwr. Duncan Rd. SO31: P Ga ..2F 49
Lwr. Moors Rd. SO21: Col C ...4F 11
Lwr. Mortimer Rd.
  SO19: South 2F 41
Lwr. Mullins La.
  SO45: Hythe 3C 52
Lwr. New Rd. SO30: W End ...1D 32
Lwr. Northam Rd.
  SO30: Hed E 5A 34
Lower St Helens Rd.
  SO30: Hed E 6A 34
Lower Spinney SO31: Wars ...2A 50
LOWER SWANWICK 5B 44
Lwr. Swanwick Rd.
  SO31: Lwr Swan 5B 44
Lower Test Nature Reserve ...2G 27
Lwr. Vicarage Rd.
  SO19: South 2F 41
Lwr. William St.
  SO14: South 5F 31
Lwr. William St. Ind. Est.
  SO14: South 5F 31
Lwr. York St. SO14: South 5F 31
LOWFORD 3F 43
Lowford Hill SO31: Burs 4F 43
Lowford Hill Cl. SO31: Burs ...4G 43
Lowry Gdns. SO19: South 3C 42
Lucas Cl. SO16: Rown 4D 20
Luccombe Pl. SO15: South ...1H 29
Luccombe Rd. SO15: South ...1H 29
Lucerne Gdns. SO30: Hed E ..4G 33
Lucia Foster Welch Halls
  SO14: South 6G 5
Ludlow Rd. SO19: South 1G 41
Lukes Cl. SO31: Hamb 5G 47
Lulin Dr. SO16: Nur 3A 20
Lulworth Bus. Cen.
  SO40: Tott 1E 27
Lulworth Cl. SO16: South 1C 28
  SO53: Cha F 4D 14
Lulworth Ct. SO16: South 1C 28
Lumpy La.
  SO14: South 1H 5 (6D 30)
Lumsden Mans.
  SO15: South 4G 29
Lundy Cl. SO16: South 4C 20
Lunedale Rd. SO45: Dib P 6C 52
Luton Rd. SO16: S'ing 4E 23
Lutyens Cl. SO19: South 2D 42
Luxton Cl. SO30: Botl 3D 34
Luzborough La.
  SO51: A'field, Rom 3A 12
Lyburn Cl. SO16: South 5G 21
Lyburn Cl. SO16: South 5G 21
Lydgate SO40: Tott 4D 26
Lydgate Cl. SO19: South 1D 42
Lydgate Grn. SO19: South 1D 42
Lydgate Rd. SO19: South 1D 42
Lydiard Cl. SO50: E'leigh 2A 16
Lydlynch Rd. SO40: Tott 4E 27
Lydney Rd. SO31: Loc H 4D 48

Lyme Cl. SO50: E'leigh 2H 15
Lymer La. SO16: Nur 3A 20
Lymer Vs. SO16: Nur 3A 20
Lyndale Rd. SO31: P Ga 3F 49
Lynden Ga. SO19: South 2A 42
Lyndhurst Rd. SO40: A'hst ...5A 36
Lyndock Cl. SO19: South 3G 41
Lyndock Ct. SO19: South 3G 41
Lynn Cl. SO18: W End 6B 24
Lynn Cres. PO14: Titch C 6H 49
Lynton Ct. SO40: Tott 5E 27
Lynton Rd. SO30: Hed E 4A 34
Lynx Cl. SO50: B'stke 5F 17
Lyons Pl. SO30: Hed E 6H 33
Lytham Rd. SO18: South 2A 32
Lytton Rd. SO45: Hythe 4F 53

M

M3 Trade Pk. SO50: E'leigh ..3G 15
Macarthur Cres.
  SO18: South 3A 32
McGovern M. SO31: Wars ...1B 50
Mackenzie Cl. SO31: Wars ...6B 48
Macnaghten Rd.
  SO19: South 4F 31
Maddison St.
  SO14: South 4D 4 (1B 40)
Maddoxford La. SO32: Botl ...1D 34
Maddoxford Way SO32: Botl ..2D 34
Maffey Ct. SO30: Botl 4E 35
Magazine La. SO40: March ...3D 38
Magdalene Way
  PO14: Titch C 5G 49
Magellan Ho. SO14: South ...6G 5
Magistrates' Court
  Southampton 5C 30
Magnolia Cl. SO45: Dib 2A 52
Magnolia Gro. SO50: Fair O ..1H 17
Magnolia Rd. SO19: South ...6H 31
Magnolia Wlk. SO51: Rom ...1D 6
Magpie Dr. SO40: Tott 4C 26
Magpie Gdns. SO19: South ...1C 42
Magpie La. SO50: E'leigh 5G 15
Maidman Pl. SO30: Hed E 1H 43
Main Rd. SO21: Col C 4G 11
  SO21: Ott 3B 10
  SO40: March 4D 38
  SO40: Tott 1E 37
  SO45: Dib 1A 52, 6E 39
  SO45: Hard 2C 54
  SO50: Fis P 5H 11
Mainstone SO51: Rom 6A 6
Mainstream Ct.
  SO50: B'stke 4D 16
Majestic Rd. SO16: Nur 6H 19
Malcolm Cl. SO31: Loc H 4F 49
Malcolm Rd. SO53: Cha F 4G 9
Malcroft M. SO40: March 4E 39
Maldon Cl. SO50: B'stke 4D 16
Maldon Rd. SO19: South 6G 31
Malibres Rd. SO53: Cha F 5H 9
Malin Cl. SO16: South 5C 20
The Mall SO53: Cha F 6G 9
Mallard Cl. SO51: Rom 4C 6
Mallard Gdns. SO30: Hed E ..1A 34
The Mallards SO40: Tott 3G 27
Mallards Rd. SO31: Burs 6F 43
Mallett Cl. SO30: Hed E 1C 34
Mallow Cl. SO31: Loc H 5D 48
Mallow Rd. SO30: Hed E 5G 33
Malmesbury Cl. SO50: Fair O ..1F 17
Malmesbury St. SO31: Net A ..2A 46
Malmesbury Pl.
  SO15: South 4H 29
Malmesbury Rd.
  SO15: South 4H 29
  SO51: Rom 4B 6
Malory Cl. SO19: South 5D 32
The Malthouse SO31: Rom 4B 6
Malthouse Cl. SO51: Rom 4B 6
Malthouse Gdns.
  SO40: March 4D 38
Malvern Cl. SO50: Fair O 3H 17
Malvern Dr. SO45: Dib P 3B 52
Malvern Gdns. SO30: Hed E ..1A 34
Malvern Rd. SO16: South 1G 29
Malwood Av. SO16: South 3C 20
Malwood Gdns. SO40: Tott ...3C 26
Malwood Rd. SO45: Hythe ...2D 52
Malwood Rd. W.
  SO45: Hythe 2D 52
Manaton Way SO30: Hed E ...2H 33
Manchester Rd. SO31: Net A ..2A 46

Mandela Way
  SO15: South 1A 4 (6A 30)
Manley Rd. SO31: Burs 4F 43
The Manners SO31: Net A 1B 46
Manns Cl. SO18: W End 1C 32
Manor Cl. SO31: Old N 4F 43
  SO40: Tott 5E 27
Manor Ct. PO15: Seg 3H 49
Manor Cres. SO31: South 4F 43
Manor Farm
  Botley 1D 44
Mnr. Farm Cl. SO31: B'stke ...5E 17
Manor Farm Country Pk. 2B 44
Mnr. Farm Grn. SO21: Twy ...1F 11
Mnr. Farm Gro. SO50: B'stke ..5E 17
Mnr. Farm Rd. SO18: South ...2F 31
Manor Ho. Av. SO15: South ...5C 28
Manor Pk. Ind. Est.
  SO18: South 4H 27
Manor Quay SO18: South 4F 31
Manor Rd. SO16: Chil 1H 21
  SO45: Holb 4C 54
  SO50: B'stke 5E 17
Manor Rd. Nth. SO19: South ..1G 41
Manor Rd. Sth. SO19: South ..2G 41
Manor Ter. SO31: Old N 4E 43
Manor Way SO50: E'leigh 3G 15
Manor Wharf SO18: South 4E 31
Mansbridge Cotts.
  SO18: S'ing 5H 23
Mansbridge Rd. SO18: S'ing ..5G 23
  SO50: E'leigh 6A 16
Mansel Cl. SO16: South 1C 28
Mansell Cl. SO45: Dib P 5C 52
Mansel Rd. E. SO16: South ...2C 28
Mansel Rd. W. SO16: South ...1B 28
Mansergh Wlk. SO40: Tott ...3B 26
Mansfield Pk. St.
  SO18: South 4C 32
Mansion Ho. Cl.
  SO31: Sar G 2D 48
Mansion Rd. SO15: South 5G 29
Manston Ct. SO16: South 5D 20
Maple Cl. SO31: Burs 5F 43
  SO51: Rom 6F 7
Maple Gdns. SO40: Tott 5C 26
Maple Ri. PO15: White 5H 45
Maple Rd. SO18: South 4G 31
  SO45: Hythe 6F 53
The Maples SO53: Cha F 5E 9
Mapleton Rd. SO30: Hed E ...5B 34
Maplewood Cl. SO40: Tott ...5C 26
Maplin Rd. SO16: South 1B 28
Marathon Pl. SO50: B'stke ...5H 17
MARCHWOOD 4D 38
  SO40: Tott 5F 27
Marchwood By-Pass
  SO40: March 2E 39
Marchwood Ind. Pk.
  SO40: March 2E 39
Marchwood Rd. SO15: South ..5F 29
  SO40: Elin 1H 37
Marchwood Ter.
  SO40: March 3D 38
  (off Main Rd.)
Marchwood Village Cen.
  SO40: March 4D 38
Marchwood Yacht Club 2E 39
Marcus Cl. SO50: B'stke 5H 17
Marcus Liebherr Pavilion 4B 38
Mardale Rd. SO16: South 3B 28
Mardale Wlk. SO16: South ...3B 28
Mardon Cl. SO18: S'ing 4G 23
Margam Av. SO19: South 6H 31
Marianne Cl. SO15: South ...5D 28
Marie Rd. SO19: South 2C 42
Marina Dr. SO31: Hamb 5G 47
Marine Cl. SO45: Hythe 2D 52
Marine Pde.
  SO14: South 4H 5 (1D 40)
Mariners Cl. SO31: Hamb 3G 47
Mariners M. SO45: Hythe 2E 53
Mariners Way SO31: Wars 6A 48
Marion Ho. SO31: P Ga 1F 49
Maritime Av. SO40: March ...2E 39
Maritime Chambers
  SO14: South 6G 5
Maritime Wlk. SO14: South ...3D 40
Maritime Way SO14: South ...3C 40
Marjoram Way PO15: White ..6H 45
Mark Cl. SO15: South 4F 29
Marken Cl. SO31: Loc H 4D 48
Market Bldgs. SO16: S'ing ...5F 23
Market Pl. SO51: Rom 5B 6
Market St. SO50: E'leigh 6B 16
  (not continuous)
Marlands Shop. Cen. 2D 4 (1B 40)

Marlborough Ct. SO45: Dib P 4C 52
  SO53: Cha F 3C 14
Marlborough Gdns.
  SO30: Hed E 6H 25
Marlborough Ho.
  SO15: South 3B 30
Marlborough Rd.
  SO15: South 3F 29
  SO53: Cha F 4G 9
Marlhill Cl. SO18: South 1H 31
Marlowe Ct. SO19: South 4H 41
Marls Rd. SO30: Botl 4C 34
Marne Rd. SO18: South 4A 32
The Marsh SO45: Hythe 1E 53
Marshall Ct. SO15: South . . .4B 30
Marshall Dr. SO30: W End . . .2F 33
Marshall Sq. SO15: South . . .4B 30
Marshfield Cl. SO40: March . .4B 38
Marsh Gdns. SO30: Hed E . . .1A 34
Marsh Ho.
  SO14: South 5F 5 (2C 40)
Marsh La.
  SO14: South 5G 5 (2D 40)
  SO45: F'ley 1H 55
Marsh Pde. SO45: Hythe 2E 53
          (off The Marsh)
Marston Rd. SO19: South . . .6D 32
Martindale Ter. SO16: South . .3C 28
          (off Severn Rd.)
The Martins SO50: Fair O . . .2G 17
Martley Gdns. SO30: Hed E . .1A 34
Marvin Cl. SO30: Botl 4C 34
Marvin Way SO18: South 5C 32
  SO30: Botl 4C 34
Maryat Way PO15: White 4G 45
Marybridge Cl. SO40: Tott . . .5E 27
Mary Drake Cl. SO45: Holb . .5C 54
Maryfield
  SO14: South 4G 5 (1D 40)
Mary Key Cl. SO19: South . . .5A 42
Maryland Cl. SO18: South . . .6H 23
Masefield Cl. SO50: E'leigh . .4H 15
Masefield Grn. SO19: South . .5D 32
Matheson Rd. SO16: South . .3D 20
Matley Gdns. SO40: Tott 4B 26
Matrix Pk. PO15: Titch 4H 49
Maud Av. PO14: Titch C 6H 49
Maunsell Way
  SO30: Hed E 6H 25, 1A 34
Mauretania Ho. SO14: South . .5E 31
Mauretania Rd. SO16: Nur . . .5H 19
Maxwell Rd. SO19: South 2A 42
Maybray King Way
  SO18: South 4H 31
MAYBUSH 1C 28
Maybush Ct. SO16: South 2E 29
Maybush Rd. SO16: South . . .1C 28
May Cl. SO45: Holb 5D 54
May Copse SO45: Holb 5D 54
May Cres. SO45: Holb 5D 54
Maycroft Ct. SO15: South 3B 30
Mayfair Cl. SO30: Botl 4E 35
Mayfair Gdns. SO15: South . .4B 30
Mayfield Av. SO40: Tott 3E 27
Mayfield Rd. SO17: South . . .6D 22
Mayflower Cl. SO53: Cha F . . .2D 14
Mayflower Ct. SO16: South . . .3F 29
Mayflower Cruise Terminal . . .1G 39
The Mayflower Gym . . .1C 4 (6B 30)
Mayflower Memorial 6D 4
Mayflower Rd. SO15: South . .3F 29
The Mayflowers SO16: Bass . .5C 22
Mayflower Theatre . . .1C 4 (6B 30)
Maynard Rd. SO40: Tott 4F 27
Maypole Vs. SO50: E'leigh . . .5B 10
Mayridge PO14: Titch C 4G 49
May Rd. SO15: South 4G 29
Maytree Cl. SO31: Loc H 4E 49
  SO50: Fair O 1G 17
Maytree Rd. SO18: South 5A 32
  SO53: Cha F 3E 9
Mayvale Cl. SO40: March 4D 38
Meacher Cl. SO40: Tott 3E 27
The Mead SO45: Hythe 3C 52
Meadbrook Gdns.
  SO53: Cha F 1E 15
Mead Cl. SO51: Rom 5E 7
Mead Ct. SO53: Cha F 1E 15
     (off Meadbrook Gdns.)
Mead Cres. SO18: S'ing 6F 23
Meadcroft Cl. SO31: Wars . . .1B 50
Meadow Av. SO31: Loc H 3E 49
Meadow Cl. SO30: W End 1E 33
  SO40: Tott 6F 27
  SO52: N Bad 4E 13
Meadowcroft Cl. SO21: Ott . . .2C 10
Meadow Gro. SO53: Cha F . . .3E 15

Meadowhead Rd.
  SO16: Bass 6B 22
Meadow La. SO31: Hamb 5G 47
  SO50: E'leigh 5A 16
Meadowmead Av.
  SO15: South 4E 29
The Meadows SO18: S'ing . . .5G 23
  SO51: Rom 3C 6
Meadowside Cl. SO18: S'ing . .5G 23
Meadow Way SO45: F'ley 2G 55
Mead Rd. SO53: Cha F 1E 15
The Meads SO51: Rom 5A 6
  SO53: Cha F 2C 14
Mears Rd. SO50: Fair O 2G 17
Medieval Merchant's House . . .6D 4
Medina Chambers
  SO14: South 3B 40
Medina Cl. SO53: Cha F 2G 15
Medina Rd. SO15: South 2F 29
Medlar Cl. SO30: Hed E 5B 34
Medley Pl. SO15: South 4E 29
Medwall Grn. SO19: South . . .6D 32
Medway Dr. SO53: Cha F 5C 8
Megan Rd. SO30: W End 1D 32
Meggeson Av. SO18: South . . .1H 31
Melbourne Gdns.
  SO30: Hed E 5A 34
Melbourne Rd. SO30: Hed E . .5A 34
Melbourne St.
  SO14: South 4H 5 (1D 40)
Melbury Ct. SO17: South 2C 30
Melchet Rd. SO18: South 3C 32
Melick Cl. SO40: March 3D 38
Melrose Cl. SO40: Calm 2C 26
Melrose Rd. SO15: South 1H 29
Melville Cl. SO16: South 4G 21
Melville Gdns. SO31: Sar G . . .1D 48
Mendip Gdns. SO45: Dib P . . .4B 52
Mendip Rd. SO16: South 3D 28
Menzies Cl. SO16: South 4D 20
MEON 5H 51
Meon Cl. SO51: Rom 5F 7
  SO18: South 3D 32
Meon Cres. SO53: Cha F 1F 15
Meon Rd. PO14: Titch 5H 51
  SO51: Rom 5F 7
Mercator Cl. SO16: South 1D 28
Mercer Way SO51: Rom 4D 6
Merchants Wlk.
  SO14: South 6D 4 (2B 40)
Mercury Cl. SO16: South 5D 20
Mercury Gdns. SO31: Hamb . .3G 47
Mercury Marshes
  Local Nature Reserve . . .3G 47
Merdon Av. SO53: Cha F 5E 9
Merdon Cl. SO53: Cha F 5F 9
Mere Cft. PO15: Seg 4H 49
Meredith Gdns. SO40: Tott . . .5D 26
Meredith Towers
  SO19: South 1E 43
Meridians Cross
  SO14: South 3D 40
Meridian Way SO14: South . . .5E 31
Merlin Gdns. SO30: Hed E . . .4H 33
Merlin Lodge SO19: South . . .2F 41
Merlin Quay SO19: South 1E 41
Merlin Way SO53: Cha F 6B 8
Mermaid Way SO14: South . . .3D 40
Merrick Way SO53: Cha F 5C 8
Merridale Rd. SO19: South . . .1G 41
Merrieleas Cl. SO53: Cha F . . .6E 9
Merrieleas Dr. SO53: Cha F . . .6E 9
Merriemeade Cl. SO45: Dib P . .5C 52
Merriemeade Pde.
  SO45: Dib P 5C 52
Merritt Ct. SO53: Cha F 4F 15
Merrivale Cl. SO45: Hythe . . .3C 52
Merryfield PO14: Titch C 3G 49
Merry Gdns. SO52: N Bad 2E 13
MERRY OAK 6H 31
Merryoak Grn. SO19: South . .6H 31
Merryoak Rd. SO19: South . . .1H 41
Mersea Gdns. SO19: South . . .1A 42
Mersham Gdns. SO18: South . .4H 31
Merton Rd. SO17: South 6D 22
Mescott Mdws. SO30: Hed E . .1H 33
Methuen St. SO14: South 4C 30
Metuchen Way SO30: Hed E . .1A 44
The Mews SO16: Rown 3D 20
  SO45: Blac 3C 54
  SO53: Cha F 4E 15
Mews Ct. SO21: Ott 2B 10
Meynell Cl. SO50: E'leigh 4H 15
Michael's Way SO45: Hythe . .2D 52
Michaels Way SO50: Fair O . . .1G 17

Michelmersh Cl.
  SO16: Rown 4C 20
Michigan Way SO40: Tott 3B 26
MIDANBURY 2H 31
Midanbury B'way.
  SO18: South 2H 31
Midanbury Ct. SO18: South . . .3G 31
Midanbury Cres.
  SO18: South 2H 31
Midanbury La. SO18: South . . .4G 31
Midanbury Wlk.
  SO18: South 3H 31
Middlebridge St.
  SO51: Rom 6B 6
Middle Copse SO31: Loc H . . .2F 49
Middle Rd. SO19: South 2H 41
  SO31: P Ga 2F 49
  SO52: N Bad 2E 13
Middle St. SO14: South 4C 30
Middleton Cl. SO18: South . . .1A 32
Middleton M. SO31: P Ga 2F 49
Midhurst Ct. SO53: Cha F 2E 15
Midlands Est. SO30: W End . . .1C 32
Midway SO45: Hythe 3D 52
Milbury Cres. SO18: South . . .5A 32
Miles Pl. SO31: Wars 6E 49
Milford Gdns. SO53: Cha F . . .1G 15
Milkwood Ct. SO40: Tott 4C 26
Millais Rd. SO19: South 2G 41
MILLBANK 6E 31
Millbank Ho. SO14: South 5E 31
Millbank St. SO14: South 6E 31
Millbank Wharf SO14: South . .6E 31
Millbridge Gdns.
  SO19: South 1B 42
MILLBROOK 4E 29
Millbrook Cl. SO53: Cha F 2D 14
Millbrook Flyover
  SO15: South 4C 28
Millbrook Ho. SO30: Hed E . . .3C 34
Millbrook Point Rd.
  SO15: South 6D 28
      (not continuous)
Millbrook Rd. SO15: South . . .4C 28
Millbrook Rd. E.
  SO15: South 1A 4 (5G 29)
Millbrook Rd. W.
  SO15: South 5F 29
Millbrook Station (Rail) 5F 29
Millbrook Towers
  SO16: South 1C 28
Millbrook Trad. Est.
  SO15: South 5D 28
Mill Cl. SO16: Nur 4B 20
Millcourt SO50: Fair O 1G 17
Miller's Pond Gdns.
  SO19: South 2H 41
Millers Vw. SO31: Burs 3G 43
Millers Way SO45: Dib P 4D 52
Mill Est. Yd. SO16: Nur 4A 20
Mill Gdns. SO30: W End 6B 24
Mill Hill SO30: Botl 5E 35
Mill Ho. Bus. Cen.
  SO19: South 1F 41
Mill Ho. Cen. SO40: Tott 4G 27
Milliken Cl. SO45: F'ley 3F 55
Mill La. SO16: Nur 5E 19
  SO51: Rom 5A 6
The Mill Pond SO45: Holb 2B 54
Mill Rd. SO15: South 4D 28
  SO40: Tott 4G 27
Millstream Ri. SO51: Rom 5A 6
Mill St. SO50: E'leigh 3B 16
Mill Way SO40: Tott 6E 27
Milne Cl. SO45: Dib P 4A 52
Milner Ct. SO15: South 3G 29
Milne St. PO15: White 4G 45
Milton Gro. SO31: Loc H 5F 49
Milton Rd. SO15: South 5A 30
  SO50: E'leigh 2B 16
Milverton Cl. SO40: Elin 6G 27
Milverton Rd. SO18: South . . .4B 32
Milverton Rd. SO40: Elin 5G 27
Mimosa Dr. SO50: Fair O 1H 17
Minchin Acres SO30: Hed E . . .1A 34
Minchin Rd. SO51: Rom 2E 7
Minden Ho. SO51: Rom 5D 6
     (off Chambers Av.)
MINOR INJURIES UNIT
  Royal South Hants Hospital
  .5C 30
Minstead Av. SO18: South 3C 32
Minstead Ct. SO17: South 3C 30
     (off Westwood Rd.)
Minster Ct. SO15: South 5G 29
Mintern Cl. SO50: B'stke 2D 16
Mirabella Cl. SO19: South 3F 41

Mirror Cl. SO31: Wars 6D 48
Misselbrook La. SO52: N Bad . .3H 13
Missenden Acres
  SO30: Hed E 3A 34
Mistletoe Gdns. SO31: Sar G . .1C 48
Mistral SO14: South 6H 5 (2D 40)
Mitchell Cl. PO15: Seg 2H 49
  SO19: South 2F 41
     (off Hazel Rd.)
Mitchell Dr. SO50: Fair O 1F 17
Mitchell Ho. SO19: South 3F 41
     (off John Thornycroft Rd.)
Mitchell Point SO31: Hamb . . .5E 47
Mitchell Rd. SO50: E'leigh 5B 16
Mitchells Cl. SO51: Rom 5C 6
Mitchell Way SO18: S'ton A . . .3H 23
Mitre Copse SO50: B'stke 5F 17
Moat Cl. SO45: Holb 5B 54
Moat Hill SO18: South 6H 23
Mollison Ri. PO15: White 1H 49
Monarch Cl. SO31: Loc H 5E 49
Monarch Way SO30: W End . . .1F 33
Monastery Rd. SO18: South . . .4G 31
Mon Cres. SO18: South 4C 32
Monks Brook Cl.
  SO50: E'leigh 6G 15
Monks Brook Ind. Pk.
  SO53: Cha F 2D 14
Monks Path SO18: S'ing 6G 23
Monks Pl. SO40: Tott 5D 26
Monks Rd. SO31: Net A 1B 46
Monks Wlk. SO45: Dib P 6C 52
Monks Way SO18: S'ing 5G 23
  SO50: E'leigh 6G 15
Monks Wood Cl. SO16: Bass . .3D 22
Monkton La. SO40: Tott 5D 26
Monmouth Cl. SO53: Cha F . . .1D 14
Monmouth Gdns. SO40: Tott . .6D 26
Monnow Gdns. SO18: W End . .2B 32
Montague Av. SO19: South . . .2D 42
Montague Cl. SO19: South 2D 42
Montague Rd. SO45: Dib P 6C 52
Montague Rd. SO50: B'stke . . .4D 16
Montefiore Dr. SO31: Sar G . . .3D 48
Monterey Dr. SO31: Loc H 5E 49
Montfort Cl. SO51: Rom 5F 7
Montfort College SO51: Rom . .5F 7
Montfort Hgts. SO51: Rom 5F 7
Montfort Rd. SO51: Rom 6F 7
Montgomery Av. SO40: Tott . . .3D 26
Montgomery Rd.
  SO18: South 4A 32
Montgomery Way
  SO53: Cha F 4D 14
Montpelier Cl. SO31: P Ga 4G 49
Montrose Cl. SO30: Botl 5C 34
Monument Ct. SO14: South . . .6E 5
Moon Cl. SO40: March 4C 38
Moonscross Av. SO40: Tott . . .1F 37
Moore Cl. SO15: South 3B 30
  SO51: Rom 1E 7
Moore Cres. SO31: Net A 6C 42
MOORGREEN 1F 33
MOORGREEN HOSPITAL 1F 33
Moorgreen Park
  SO30: W End 1F 33
Moorgreen Rd. SO30: W End . .1E 33
Moorhead Ct. SO14: South . . .3E 41
Moorhill Gdns. SO18: South . .4E 33
Moorhill Rd. SO30: W End 3D 32
Moorland Cl. SO31: Loc H 3E 49
  SO45: Dib P 3B 52
Moorlands Cres.
  SO18: South 3B 32
Moors Cl. SO21: Col C 4F 11
Mopley Cl. SO45: Blac 6F 55
Mopley Ct. SO45: Blac 6F 55
Mordaunt Rd. SO14: South . . .4C 30
Morgan Le Fay Dr.
  SO53: Cha F 6B 8
Morgan Rd. SO30: Hed E 6A 34
Morland Rd. SO15: South 2G 29
Morley Cl. SO19: South 5H 31
Morley Gdns. SO53: Cha F 5E 9
Morpeth Av. SO40: Tott 3F 27
Morris Cl. SO45: Dib 2B 52
Morrison Cl. SO19: South 2E 43
Morris Rd.
  SO15: South 1B 4 (6A 30)
Morse Cl. SO31: Net A 1A 46
Mortimer Cl. SO31: Net A 1B 46
Mortimer Rd. SO40: Tott 2D 26
  SO19: South 1G 41
  SO30: Botl 4E 35
Mortimers Dr. SO50: Fair O . . .1G 17
Mortimers La. SO50: Fair O . . .1G 17
Mortimer Way SO52: N Bad . . .4D 12

Mosaic Cl. SO19: South 1F **43**
Mosedale Wlk. SO16: South . . .3C **28**
Moselle Ct. SO15: South 6G **29**
Moss Dr. SO40: March 3D **38**
Mossleigh Av. SO16: Rown 4D **20**
Mottisfont Cl. SO15: South 5E **29**
Mottisfont Lodge SO51: Rom . . .5C **6**
Mottisfont Rd. SO16: S'leigh . . .3A **16**
The Mount SO16: Bass 5B **22**
　　SO16: South 2E **29**
Mountain Ash Cl.
　　SO18: South 4C **32**
Mountbatten Av. SO51: Rom . . .5C **6**
Mountbatten Bldg.
　　SO17: South 5C **22**
Mountbatten Bus. Cen.
　　SO15: South 2A **4** (6H **29**)
Mountbatten Dr.
　　SO31: Sar G 2D **48**
Mountbatten Gallery
　　Romsey 1F **19**
Mountbatten Ho. SO15: South . .1D **4**
Mountbatten Retail Pk.
　　. . . . . .2B **4** (1A **40**)
Mountbatten Rd. SO40: Tott . . .4D **26**
　　SO50: E'leigh 2A **16**
Mountbatten Way
　　SO15: South 2A **4** (6G **29**)
Mount Dr. SO53: Cha F 3G **15**
Mountfield SO45: Hythe 2C **52**
Mount Ho. Cl. SO45: Hythe 1E **53**
Mt. Pleasant SO51: Rom 6B **6**
Mt. Pleasant Ind. Pk.
　　SO14: South 4D **30**
Mt. Pleasant Rd.
　　SO14: South 4D **30**
Mount Temple SO51: Rom 5D **6**
Mount Vw. SO50: E'leigh 3B **16**
Mousehole La. SO18: South 3H **31**
　　SO45: Hythe 3E **53**
Mowbray Rd. SO19: South 1B **42**
Muir Ho. SO45: Dib P 5C **52**
Mulberry Cl. SO45: Blac 5E **55**
Mulberry Cnr. SO53: Cha F 3C **14**
Mulberry Ct. SO30: W End 1E **33**
Mulberry La. SO31: Sar G 2C **48**
Mulberry Rd. SO40: March 4D **38**
Mulberry Wlk. SO15: South 3G **29**
Mullen Cl. SO19: South 1G **41**
Multisports Swimming 1H **23**
Munro Cres. SO15: South 4D **28**
Muria Est. SO14: South 6E **31**
Murray Cl. SO19: South 5E **33**
Mursell Way SO31: Hou 1E **47**
Mussett Cl. SO40: Tott 4E **27**
Mustang Av. PO15: White 6F **45**
Myrtle Av. SO40: Tott 5D **26**
Myrtle Rd. SO16: South 5F **21**
Myvern Cl. SO45: Holb 5D **54**

N

Napier Rd. SO19: South 6E **33**
Narrow La. SO51: Rom 5B **6**
Nash Cl. SO45: Dib P 5B **52**
Nash Rd. SO45: Dib P 5B **52**
Nathaniel Cl. SO31: Sar G 3D **48**
Navigators Way SO30: Hed E . . .2A **34**
Neath Way SO53: Cha F 2C **14**
Needlespar Ct. SO31: Wars 5D **48**
Neilson Cl. SO53: Cha F 6E **9**
Nelson Cl. SO45: Holb 5C **54**
　　SO51: Rom 4C **6**
Nelson Ct. SO45: Hythe 5F **53**
Nelson Gate
　　SO15: South 1B **4** (6A **30**)
Nelson Hill
　　SO15: South 2A **4** (6A **30**)
Nelson Ind. Pk. SO30: Hed E . . .2H **33**
Nelson Rd. SO15: South 5G **29**
　　SO50: B'stke 3D **16**
Nelsons Gdns. SO30: Hed E . . .6H **25**
Nelson St.
　　SO14: South 5H **5** (1D **30**)
Neptune Cl. SO16: South 5D **20**
Neptune Ho. SO14: South 6G **5**
Neptune Way SO14: South 3D **40**
Nerquis Cl. SO51: Rom 4E **7**
Netherhill La. SO32: Botl 2F **35**
NETLEY ABBEY 2B **46**
Netley Abbey 1A **46**
Netley Castle SO31: Net A 1A **46**
Netley Cliff SO31: Net A 2B **46**
Netley Cliff Sailing Club 2B **46**
Netley Cl. SO53: Cha F 4D **14**
Netley Firs Cl. SO19: South 1F **43**

Netley Firs Rd. SO30: Hed E . . .6G **33**
NETLEY HILL 6F **33**
Netley Hill Est. SO19: South 1F **43**
Netley Lodge Cl.
　　SO31: Net A 2C **46**
NETLEY MARSH 4A **26**
Netley Marsh Workshops
　　SO40: Net M 4A **26**
Netley Rd. PO14: Titch C 6G **49**
Netley Sailing Club 4C **46**
Netley Station (Rail) 1C **46**
Nettlestone SO31: Net A 6C **42**
Neva Rd. SO18: South 3H **31**
Neville Dr. SO51: Rom 3C **6**
Newbridge SO31: Net A 1C **46**
Newbury Cl. SO50: B'stke 5H **17**
Newbury Pl. SO31: Wars 5D **48**
Newbury Rd. SO15: South 2G **29**
Newcliffe Rd.
　　SO30: Hed E 6H **33**
New Cliff Ho. SO19: South 4G **41**
Newcombe Rd. SO15: South 5A **30**
New Cotts. SO16: South 1A **28**
New Ct. PO15: Seg 2H **49**
New Forest Ent. Cen.
　　SO40: Tott 6E **27**
New Forest Pk. 6E **55**
New Forest Wildlife Pk. 5E **37**
New Inn Cl. SO31: Sar G 1C **48**
Newitt Pl. SO16: Bass 3B **22**
Newlands Av. SO15: South 4G **29**
Newlands Cl. SO45: Blac 4E **55**
　　SO53: Cha F 2A **14**
Newlands Copse SO45: Blac 4F **55**
Newlands Rd. SO45: F'ley 3E **55**
Newlyn Wlk. SO51: Rom 3D **6**
Newmans Copse Rd.
　　SO40: Tott 1G **37**
Newman St. SO16: South 3F **29**
Newport Cl. SO53: Cha F 3C **14**
New Rd. SO14: South 2E **5** (6C **30**)
　　SO21: Col C 4F **11**
　　SO31: Net A 1A **46**
　　SO31: Swanw 5D **44**
　　SO31: Wars 1B **50**
　　SO40: A'hst 2B **36**
　　SO45: Blac 4E **55**
　　SO45: Hard 6G **53**
　　　　　　(not continuous)
　　SO45: Hythe 2E **53**
　　SO50: B'stke 5H **17**
　　SO51: Rom 4D **6**
New Ter. SO16: Bass 4C **22**
Newton La. SO51: Rom 5B **6**
Newton Rd. SO18: South 2G **31**
NEWTOWN
　　SO14 . . . . .5D **30**
　　SO19 . . . . .4B **42**
　　SO31 . . . . .2A **50**
Newtown Ct. SO31: Wars 6A **48**
Newtown Rd. SO19: South 3A **42**
　　SO31: Wars 2A **50**
　　SO50: E'leigh 3A **16**
Nicholas Rd. SO45: Blac 6E **55**
Nichol Rd. SO31: Cha F 4F **9**
Nicholson Wlk. SO16: Rown 3B **20**
Nichols Rd.
　　SO14: South 1G **5** (6D **30**)
NICHOLS TOWN 1F **5** (6C **30**)
Nickleby Gdns. SO40: Tott 4B **26**
Nickson Cl. SO53: Cha F 5D **8**
Nightingale Av. SO50: E'leigh . . .6E **15**
Nightingale Cl. SO31: Burs 5F **43**
　　SO51: Rom 4D **6**
Nightingale Ct. SO15: South 5G **29**
　　SO40: Tott 3C **26**
Nightingale Gro.
　　SO15: South 4G **29**
Nightingale Ho. SO31: Net A 3C **46**
　　SO51: Rom 4D **6**
Nightingale M. SO31: Loc H 4F **49**
　　SO31: Net A 3C **46**
Nightingale Rd.
　　SO15: South 4G **29**
Nightingale Wlk.
　　SO31: Net A 3C **46**
Nile Rd. SO17: South 1C **30**
Nine Elms M. SO50: B'stke 5F **17**
Ninian Cl. SO50: Fair O 2F **17**
Noads Cl. SO45: Dib P 4D **52**
Noads Way SO45: Dib P 5C **52**
Noble Rd. PO14: Titch C 1H **51**
　　SO30: Hed E 5B **34**
NOB'S CROOK 6G **11**
Nob's Crook SO21: Col C 5G **11**
Nomad Cl. SO18: South 2B **32**
The Nook SO50: E'leigh 2B **16**

The Nook Cvn. Pk. 3F **49**
Norbury Cl. SO53: Cha F 6D **8**
Norbury Gdns. SO31: Hamb 5E **47**
Norcliffe Rd. SO17: South 3C **30**
Norcroft Ct. SO16: South 1G **29**
Nordik Gdns. SO30: Hed E 6A **34**
Norfolk Ct. SO53: Cha F 4E **15**
Norfolk Rd. SO15: South 3H **29**
Norham Av. SO16: South 1G **29**
Norham Cl. SO16: South 1G **29**
Norlands Dr. SO21: Ott 1C **10**
Normandy Cl. SO16: Rown 3C **20**
Normandy Ct. SO31: Wars 6A **48**
Normandy Ho. SO51: Rom 5D **6**
　　　　　　(off Chambers Av.)
Normandy Way SO40: March . . .2D **38**
Norman Gdns. SO30: Hed E 6G **33**
Norman Ho.
　　SO14: South 1H **5** (5E **31**)
Norman Rd. SO15: South 6H **29**
　　SO45: Blac 5F **55**
Norris Cl. SO51: Rom 2F **7**
Norris Hill SO18: South 2G **31**
NORTHAM 5E **31**
Northam Bri. SO14: South 5E **31**
　　SO18: South 5E **31**
Northam Bus. Cen.
　　SO14: South 5E **31**
Northampton La. SO45: Blac 5E **55**
Northam Rd.
　　SO14: South 2F **5** (6D **30**)
　　　　　　(not continuous)
NORTH BADDESLEY 2E **13**
Northbourne Cl. SO45: Dib P . . .5E **53**
Northbrook Ind. Est.
　　SO16: South 1G **29**
Northbrook Rd.
　　SO14: South 1G **5** (6D **30**)
Northcliffe Ho. SO16: Nur 3H **19**
North Cl. SO51: Rom 3F **7**
Northcote Rd. SO17: South 1E **31**
North Ct. SO15: South 3F **29**
Northdene Rd. SO53: Cha F 2E **15**
North East Cl. SO19: South 6C **32**
North East Rd. SO19: South 1A **42**
North End Cl. SO53: Cha F 3E **15**
Northern Anchorage
　　SO14: South 2E **5** (6C **30**)
　　　　　　(not continuous)
Northerwood Cl.
　　SO52: N Bad 3D **12**
Northfield Rd. SO18: South 6H **23**
North Front
　　SO14: South 2E **5** (6C **30**)
　　　　　　(not continuous)
Northlands Cl. SO40: Tott 3D **26**
Northlands Gdns.
　　SO15: South 4A **30**
Northlands Rd. SO15: South 4A **30**
　　SO40: Tott 3E **27**
　　SO50: E'leigh 4A **16**
Northleigh Cnr. SO18: S'ing 4G **23**
Nth. Millers Dale SO53: Cha F . . .4C **8**
Northmore Cl. SO31: Loc H 2F **49**
Northmore Rd. SO31: Loc H 2F **49**
Northolt Gdns. SO16: South 4E **21**
North Rd. SO17: South 2E **31**
　　SO40: March 3E **39**
　　SO45: Dib P 4B **52**
North Solent Nature Reserve . .6H **55**
NORTH STONEHAM 2F **23**
Nth. Stoneham Pk. Development
　　SO50: E'leigh 1F **23**
Northumberland Rd.
　　SO14: South 1H **5** (6D **30**)
　　　　　　(not continuous)
Northwood Cl. SO16: Bass 3C **22**
Norton Cl. SO19: South 2G **41**
Norton Welch Cl.
　　SO52: N Bad 3F **13**
Norwich Cl. SO31: Sar G 3C **48**
Norwich Rd. SO18: South 1H **31**
Noyce Cl. SO30: W End 2E **33**
Noyce Dr. SO50: Fair O 2G **17**
NST Campus
　　Southampton 6C **22**
NST City 1D **4** (6B **30**)
Nursery Gdns. SO19: South 5B **32**
　　SO51: Rom 4C **6**
　　SO53: Cha F 4E **15**
Nursery Gro. SO30: Hed E 6A **34**
Nursery Ho. SO31: Net A 3C **46**
Nursery Rd. SO18: South 2F **31**
NURSLING 4B **20**
Nursling Ind. Est. SO16: Nur . . .5H **19**
Nursling St. SO16: Nur 4A **20**
Nutash PO14: Titch C 3G **49**

Nutbeem Rd. SO50: E'leigh 5A **16**
NUTBURN 2F **13**
Nutburn Rd. SO52: N Bad 2F **13**
Nutfield Ct. SO16: South 6C **20**
Nutfield Pl. SO16: Rown 3B **20**
Nutsea Rd. SO16: Nur 5B **20**
Nutsey Av. SO40: Tott 1D **26**
Nutsey Cl. SO40: Tott 6E **19**
Nutsey La. SO40: Tott 1E **27**
Nutshalling Av. SO16: Rown 4B **20**
Nutshalling Cl. SO40: Calm 1C **26**
Nutwood Way SO40: Tott 1E **27**

O

O2 Guildhall Southampton
　　. . . . . .2D **4** (6B **30**)
Oakbank Rd. SO19: South 2F **41**
　　SO50: B'stke 3C **16**
Oak Cl. SO15: South 3A **28**
　　SO45: Dib P 5C **52**
Oak Coppice Cl.
　　SO50: B'stke 5G **17**
Oak Coppice Rd.
　　PO15: White 5H **45**
Oakdene SO17: South 1D **30**
　　SO40: Tott 4C **26**
Oakdene Ct. SO50: Fair O 1F **17**
Oak Dr. SO50: Fair O 1F **17**
Oakenbrow SO45: Dib P 4B **52**
Oakfield Gdns. SO16: South 2F **29**
Oakfield Rd. SO40: Tott 4F **27**
Oakfields SO50: E'leigh 6A **10**
Oak Grn. Way SO18: South 3A **32**
Oakgrove Gdns. SO50: B'stke . . .5E **17**
Oakgrove Rd. SO50: B'stke 5E **17**
Oakhill SO31: Burs 4H **43**
Oakhill Cl. SO31: Burs 4H **43**
　　SO53: Cha F 2G **15**
Oakhill Ct. SO53: Cha F 2G **15**
Oakhill Ter. SO31: Burs 4H **43**
Oakhurst Cl. SO31: Net A 1C **46**
Oakhurst Rd. SO17: South 6C **22**
Oakhurst Way SO31: Net A 1C **46**
Oakland Dr. SO40: March 4D **38**
The Oaklands SO53: Cha F 4E **15**
Oaklands Av. SO40: Tott 4F **27**
Oaklands Gdns.
　　PO14: Titch C 6G **49**
Oaklands Mead SO40: Tott 3F **27**
Oaklands Swimming Pool 4D **20**
Oaklands Way PO14: Titch C 6G **49**
　　SO16: Bass 5B **22**
　　SO45: Dib P 4A **52**
Oak Leaf Cl. SO40: March 5C **38**
Oakleaf Pl. SO53: Cha F 1E **15**
Oakleigh Cres. SO40: Tott 5E **27**
Oakleigh Gdns. SO51: Rom 5D **6**
Oakleigh Sq. SO50: B'stke 2D **16**
Oakley Cl. SO45: Holb 4C **54**
Oakley Ho. SO15: South 4B **30**
Oakley John Wlk.
　　SO19: South 5H **31**
Oakley Rd. SO16: South 2D **28**
Oakmount Av. SO17: South 2B **30**
　　SO40: Tott 3F **27**
　　SO53: Cha F 3F **15**
Oakmount Mans.
　　SO17: South 2B **30**
Oakridge Rd. SO53: Cha F 6G **9**
Oakridge Rd. SO15: South 3B **28**
Oak Rd. SO19: South 3F **41**
　　SO31: Burs 5F **43**
　　SO45: Dib P 5B **52**
The Oaks SO19: South 6H **31**
　　SO31: Burs 5F **43**
Oak Tree Cl. SO21: Col C 5F **11**
Oaktree Ct. SO16: Bass 6A **22**
Oaktree Gdns. SO30: Hed E 5H **33**
Oaktree Pk. SO30: W End 5D **24**
Oak Tree Rd. SO18: South 2F **31**
Oak Tree Way SO50: E'leigh 2A **16**
Oak Va. SO30: W End 6B **24**
Oakville Mans. SO15: South 1C **4**
Oak Wlk. SO50: Fair O 1F **17**
Oakwood Av. SO21: Ott 2C **10**
Oakwood Cl. SO21: Ott 1C **10**
　　SO31: Wars 1B **50**
　　SO51: Rom 3E **7**
　　SO53: Cha F 4F **9**
Oakwood Ct. SO30: W End 6E **25**
　　SO53: Cha F 4F **9**
Oakwood Dr. SO16: South 4G **21**
Oakwood Rd. SO53: Cha F 5F **9**
Oakwood Way SO31: Hamb 4G **47**

Oatfield Gdns.—Pinegrove Rd.

Oatfield Gdns. SO40: Calm 2C 26
Oatlands SO51: Rom 4C 6
Oatlands Cl. SO32: Botl 2D 34
Oatlands Rd. SO32: Botl 2D 34
Oatley Wlk. SO45: F'ley 3F 55
Obelisk Rd. SO19: South 3F 41
Occupation La. PO14: Titch 1H 51
Oceana Blvd.
SO14: South 6E 5 (2C 40)
Ocean Cruise Terminal 3C 40
Ocean Ga. SO14: South 3C 40
Oceanic Way SO40: March 2F 39
Ocean Quay SO14: South 6E 31
Ocean Rd. SO14: South 4C 40
OCEAN VILLAGE 6G 5 (3D 40)
Ocean Village Innovation Cen.
SO14: South 3D 40
(off Ocean Way)
Ocean Way
SO14: South 6H 5 (3D 40)
Ocknell Gro. SO45: Dib 3A 52
O'Connell Rd. SO50: E'leigh 5G 15
Octavia Gdns. SO53: Cha F 6H 9
Octavia Rd. SO18: S'ing 5G 23
Odeon Cinema
Southampton 4B 4 (1A 40)
Odiham Cl. SO16: South 5D 20
SO53: Cha F 4D 14
Ogle Rd. SO14: South . . .3D 4 (1B 40)
Okement Cl. SO18: W End 1B 32
Oldbarn Cl. SO40: Calm 1C 26
Old Bitumen Rd. SO45: F'ley . . .1H 55
Old Bri. Cl. SO31: Burs 4H 43
Old Bridge Ho. Rd.
SO31: Burs 4H 43
Oldbury Ct. SO16: South 1B 28
Old Common SO31: Loc H 3E 49
Old Common Gdns.
SO31: Loc H 3E 49
Old Cracknore Cl.
SO40: March 3D 38
Old Cricket M. SO15: South 3B 30
Old Dairy Cl. SO40: Tott 2E 27
Oldenburg PO15: White 5F 45
Old Farm Dr. SO18: South 6H 23
Old Garden Cl. SO31: Loc H . . .5G 49
Old Ivy La. SO18: W End 1B 32
Old Magazine Cl.
SO40: March 3D 38
Old Mill Way SO16: South 2E 29
OLD NETLEY 4E 43
Old Parsonage Ct. SO21: Ott . . .2C 10
Old Priory Cl. SO31: Hamb 5G 47
Old Rectory Ct. SO40: Elin 6H 27
Old Redbridge Rd.
SO15: South 3A 28
Old Rd. SO14: South 3D 40
SO51: Rom 3D 6
Old Salisbury La. SO51: Rom . . .2A 6
Old School Cl. SO19: South 1A 42
SO31: Net A 6C 42
SO45: Hard 2B 54
Old School Gdns.
SO30: W End 1E 33
Old Shamblehurst La.
SO30: Hed E 1A 34
OLD SHIRLEY 2E 29
Old Swanwick La.
SO31: Lwr Swan 5B 44
Old Ter. SO16: Bass 4C 22
The Old Well Close
SO19: South 2C 42
Oleander Cl. SO31: Loc H 2E 49
Oleander Dr. SO40: Tott 3B 26
Olive Rd. SO16: South 5E 21
Oliver Rd. SO18: S'ing 6F 23
Olivers Cl. SO40: Tott 4B 26
Olympic Way SO50: Fair O 4G 17
Omdurman Rd. SO17: South . . .1C 30
Omega Enterprise Pk.
SO53: Cha F 1E 15
Onibury Cl. SO18: South 2A 32
Onibury Rd. SO18: South 2A 32
Onslow Rd. SO14: South 5C 30
The Orchard SO16: Bass 4D 22
SO16: Chil 6A 14
SO45: Dib P 3B 52
SO50: E'leigh 5A 16
Orchard Av. SO50: B'stke 6F 17
Orchard Cl. SO21: Col C 4F 11
SO32: Botl 1D 34
SO40: Tott 6F 27
SO45: F'ley 2H 55
SO52: N Bad 2D 12
Orchard Ct. SO30: Botl 4C 34
Orchard Ho.
SO14: South 5E 5 (2C 40)
Orchard La.
SO14: South 5F 5 (2C 40)
SO51: Rom 5B 6
Orchard Pl.
SO14: South 6E 5 (2C 40)
Orchard Rd. SO31: Loc H 5D 48
SO50: Fair O 1F 17
Orchards Way SO17: South 1C 30
SO30: W End 2D 32
Orchard Way SO45: Dib P 4C 52
Ordnance Rd. SO15: South 5C 30
Ordnance Survey Head Office
. . . . .5A 20
Ordnance Way SO40: March 2E 39
Oregon Cl. SO19: South 1A 42
Oriana Way SO16: Nur 5H 19
Oriel Dr. PO14: Titch C 6G 49
Oriental Ter.
SO14: South 6E 5 (2C 40)
Orion Cl. SO16: South 5D 20
Orion Ind. Cen. SO18: S'ing 4H 23
Orion's Point SO14: South 5C 30
Orkney Cl. SO16: South 5C 20
Ormesby Dr. SO53: Cha F 4D 8
Ormond Cl. SO50: Fair O 4H 17
Orpen Rd. SO19: South 2C 42
Orwell Cl. SO16: South 2C 28
Orwell Cres. PO14: Titch C 5G 49
Osborne Cl. SO31: Net A 2D 46
Osborne Dr. SO53: Cha F 2G 15
Osborne Gdns. SO17: South 2E 31
SO50: Fair O 1H 17
Osborne Ho. SO14: South 6G 5
Osborne M. SO50: E'leigh 6C 10
Osborne Rd. SO31: Wars 1A 50
SO40: Tott 4G 27
Osborne Rd. Nth.
SO17: South 2E 31
Osborne Rd. Sth.
SO17: South 3D 30
Oslands La. SO31: Lwr Swan . . .6B 44
Oslo Towers SO19: South 5G 41
Osprey Cl. SO16: South 4F 21
SO40: March 4C 38
Osterley Cl. SO30: Botl 5C 34
Osterley Rd. SO19: South 6G 31
Oswald Rd. SO19: South 3F 41
OTTERBOURNE 3B 10
Otterbourne Golf Course 1H 9
Otterbourne Hill SO21: Ott 4A 10
Otterbourne Ho. SO21: Ott 2B 10
Otterbourne Ho. Gdns.
SO21: Ott 3B 10
Otterbourne Park Wood &
Nature Reserve 4B 10
Otterbourne Rd.
SO21: Comp, Ott, Shaw . . .1C 10
Otter Cl. SO50: B'stke 5G 17
Ouse Cl. SO53: Cha F 5C 8
Outer Circ. SO16: South 5E 21
Outlands La. SO30: Curd 5H 35
Overbrook SO45: Hythe 4D 52
Overbrook Way SO52: N Bad . . .2C 12
Overcliff Ri. SO16: Bass 5A 22
Overdell Ct. SO15: South 4A 30
Oviat Cl. SO40: Tott 4B 26
Ovington Ct. SO18: South 3D 32
Ovington Gdns.
SO50: E'leigh 1A 24
Owen Rd. SO50: E'leigh 5H 15
OWER SERVICE AREA 1A 18
Oxburgh Cl. SO50: E'leigh 2H 15
Oxford Av.
SO14: South 1F 5 (5C 30)
Oxford M.
SO14: South 6F 5 (2C 40)
Oxford Rd. SO14: South 4C 30
Oxford St.
SO14: South 6F 5 (2C 40)
Oxlease Cl. SO51: Rom 3D 6
Oxlease Mdws. SO51: Rom 2D 6
Oyster Quay SO31: Hamb 5G 47
Ozier Rd. SO18: South 1A 32

P

Pacific Cl. SO14: South 3D 40
Packridge La. SO51: Toot 6C 12
The Paddock SO40: Calm 1C 26
SO50: E'leigh 1B 16
The Paddocks SO45: F'ley 2H 55
Padwell Rd. SO14: South 4C 30
Page Cl. SO45: Holb 6D 54
Paget Ho. SO16: Nur 3H 19
Paget St.
SO14: South 5H 5 (2D 40)
Paignton Rd. SO16: South 2D 28
Paimpol Pl. SO51: Rom 6B 6
Painswick Cl. SO31: Sar G 1D 48
Paling Bus. Pk. SO30: Hed E . . .1H 43
Pallet Cl. SO21: Col C 5F 11
Pallot Cl. SO31: Burs 4F 43
Palmers Cl. SO50: Fair O 1G 17
Palmerston Ho. SO14: South 5E 5
SO51: Rom 5D 6
(off Fryers Cl.)
Palmerston Rd.
SO14: South 2E 5 (6C 30)
Palmerston St. SO51: Rom 5B 6
Palm Rd. SO16: South 6E 21
Palomino Dr. PO15: White 6F 45
Pandora Cl. SO31: Loc H 4C 48
Pangbourne Cl. SO19: South . . .1A 42
Pansy Rd. SO16: Bass 5C 22
Pantheon Rd. SO53: Cha F 6H 9
Panwell Rd. SO18: South 4A 32
Pardoe Cl. SO30: Hed E 6A 34
Parham Dr. SO50: E'leigh 3H 15
Park Cl. SO40: March 4B 38
SO45: Hythe 2F 53
Park Ct. SO15: South 5G 29
SO51: Rom 2A 12
Parker Ho. SO19: South 3E 41
PARK GATE 2F 49
Park Ga. Bus. Cen.
SO31: P Ga 1F 49
Park Glen SO31: P Ga 3G 49
Parkhill Cl. SO45: Holb 5C 54
Parkland Pl. *SO17: South 3C 30*
(off Westwood Rd.)
Parklands SO18: South 2G 31
SO31: Sar G 3E 49
SO40: Tott 3G 27
Parklands Cl. SO53: Cha F 6E 9
Park La. SO15: South . . .1C 4 (6B 30)
SO21: Ott 6B 10
SO40: March 3A 38
SO45: Holb 4B 54
SO50: E'leigh 4B 10
Park M. SO31: P Ga 2F 49
Park Rd. SO15: South 5G 29
SO53: Cha F 5E 9
Parkside SO40: Tott 6F 27
Parkside Av. SO16: South 3B 28
Park St. SO16: South 3F 29
Park Vw. SO14: South 2F 5
SO30: Botl 4E 35
SO30: Hed E 4H 33
SO50: E'leigh 4A 16
(off Newtown Rd.)
Parkville Rd. SO16: S'ing 5F 23
Park Wlk.
SO14: South 2E 5 (6C 30)
Park Way SO50: Fair O 1H 17
Parkway PO15: White 1H 49
The Parkway SO16: Bass 4C 22
Parkway Ct. SO53: Cha F 6F 9
Parkway Gdns. SO53: Cha F 6E 9
Parkwood Cl. SO30: Hed E 4B 34
Parnell Rd. SO50: E'leigh 5H 15
Parry Rd. SO19: South 1D 42
Parsonage Rd. SO14: South 5D 30
Partridge Rd. SO45: Dib P 5D 52
Partry Cl. SO53: Cha F 5C 8
Passage La. SO31: Wars 6H 47
Passfield Av. SO50: E'leigh 6G 15
Passfield Cl. SO50: E'leigh 5G 15
The Pastures PO14: Titch C 3G 49
SO50: E'leigh 5A 16
(off Cranbury Rd.)
Pat Bear Cl. SO15: South 3A 28
Patricia Cl. SO30: W End 1D 32
Patricia Dr. SO30: Hed E 4B 34
Paulet Cl. SO18: South 2A 32
Paulet Lacave Av. SO16: Nur . . .3B 20
Pauletts La. SO40: Calm 1B 26
Paulson Cl. SO53: Cha F 5E 9
Pavilion Ct. SO15: South 4A 30
Pavilion Gdns. SO45: Blac 4E 55
Pavilion Rd.
SO30: Botl, Hed E 3B 34
Paxton Cl. SO30: Hed E 6B 34
Paxton Ct. SO31: Loc H 5E 49
Paynes La. SO50: Fair O 1F 17
Paynes Pl. SO30: Hed E 1A 34
Payne's Rd. SO15: South 5G 29
(not continuous)
Peach Rd. SO16: South 5E 21
Peacock Trad. Est.
SO50: E'leigh 3G 15
Peak Cl. SO16: South 3D 28
Peartree Av. SO19: South 1G 41
Pear Tree Cl. SO32: Botl 1D 34
Peartree Cl. SO19: South 1F 41
Peartree Gdns. SO19: South . . .5A 32
PEARTREE GREEN 1G 41
Peartree Rd. SO19: South 1F 41
SO45: Dib P 4C 52
Pebble Ct. SO40: March 3D 38
Peckham Cl. PO14: Titch C 5G 49
Peel Cl. SO51: Rom 3F 7
Peel St. SO14: South 1H 5 (6E 31)
Peewit Hill SO31: Burs 2G 43
Peewit Hill Cl. SO31: Burs 2G 43
Pegasus Cl. SO16: South 5D 20
SO31: Hamb 5F 47
Pembers Cl. SO50: Fair O 1G 17
Pembers Hill Dr.
SO50: Hor H 1H 17
Pembrey Cl. SO16: South 4D 20
Pembroke Cl. SO40: Tott 3G 27
SO50: E'leigh 2H 15
SO51: Rom 5C 6
Pembroke Ct. SO17: South 2C 30
Pembroke Rd. SO19: South 1B 42
Penarth Cl. SO19: South 5C 32
Pendle Cl. SO16: South 3D 28
Pendleton Gdns. SO45: Blac 4E 55
Pendula Way SO50: B'stke 2E 17
Penelope Gdns. SO31: Burs 4F 43
Penhale Gdns. PO14: Titch C . . .6F 49
Penhale Way SO40: Tott 6E 27
Penistone Cl. SO19: South 3A 42
Pennard Way SO53: Cha F 3C 14
Pennine Gdns. SO45: Dib P 4B 52
Pennine Ho. SO16: South 4D 28
Pennine Rd. SO16: South 4C 28
Pennine Way SO53: Cha F 3F 15
Pennington Cl. SO21: Col C 5F 11
Pennycress SO31: Loc H 5C 48
Penrhyn Cl. SO50: E'leigh 2H 15
Penshurst Way SO50: E'leigh . . .1A 16
The Pentagon SO45: F'ley 3G 55
Pentire Av. SO15: South 2H 29
Pentire Way SO15: South 1H 29
Pentland Cl. SO45: Dib P 4B 52
Pentridge Way SO40: Tott 6D 26
Peppard Cl. SO18: South 4A 32
Peppercorn Way
SO30: Hed E 6H 25
Pepys Av. SO19: South 6D 32
Percivale Rd. SO53: Cha F 3B 14
Percy Cl. SO45: Hythe 1D 52
Percy Rd. SO16: South 3E 29
Peregrine Cl. SO40: Tott 5C 26
Pern Dr. SO30: Botl 4E 35
Perran Rd. SO16: South 2B 28
Perrywood Cl. SO45: Holb 5C 54
Perrywood Gdns. SO40: Tott . . .3B 26
Pershore Cl. SO31: Loc H 5E 49
Persian Dr. PO15: White 6F 45
Peterborough Rd.
SO14: South 4C 30
Peters Cl. SO31: Loc H 4C 48
Peterscroft Av. SO40: A'hst 4A 36
Peters Rd. SO31: Loc H 4C 48
Pettinger Gdns. SO17: South . . .3F 31
Petty Cl. SO51: Rom 5D 6
Petworth Gdns. SO16: South . . .4F 21
SO50: E'leigh 2A 16
Pevensey Cl. SO16: South 2B 28
Peverells Rd. SO53: Cha F 6G 9
Peverells Wood Av.
SO53: Cha F 6G 9
Peverells Wood Cl.
SO53: Cha F 6H 9
Peveril Rd. SO19: South 1G 41
Pewsey Pl. SO15: South 1H 29
Phi Ho. SO16: Chil 6G 13
Phillimore Rd. SO16: S'ing 5F 23
Phillips Cl. SO16: Rown 3C 20
Philpott Dr. SO40: March 4D 38
Phoenix Cl. SO31: Burs 4G 43
The Phoenix Film Theatre 6C 22
Phoenix Ho. SO30: Hed E 3C 34
Phoenix Ind. Pk.
SO50: E'leigh 5C 16
Pickwick Cl. SO40: Tott 4B 26
Pilchards Av. SO50: Fair O 4H 17
Pilgrim Pl. SO18: S'ing 5G 23
Pilgrims Cl. SO53: Cha F 2B 14
Pimpernel Cl. SO31: Loc H 5C 48
Pine Cl. SO40: A'hst 2C 36
SO45: Dib P 4D 52
SO52: N Bad 2D 12
Pine Cres. SO53: Cha F 4E 9
Pine Dr. SO18: South 4D 32
Pine Dr. E. SO18: South 4E 33
Pinefield Rd. SO18: South 1H 31
Pinegrove Rd. SO19: South 2H 41

72 A-Z Southampton

Pinehurst SO17: South 2C **30**
Pinehurst Rd. SO16: Bass 2B **22**
Pinelands Ct. SO16: South 5G **21**
Pinelands Rd. SO16: Chil 1B **22**
Pine Rd. SO51: Rom 6F **7**
  SO53: Cha F 4D **8**
The Pines SO16: South 6F **21**
Pineview Cl. SO31: Burs 4G **43**
Pine Wlk. SO16: Chil 2A **22**
  SO31: Sar G 2E **49**
Pine Way SO16: Bass 2B **22**
Pinewood SO16: Bass 3B **22**
Pinewood Cl. SO51: Rom 3F **7**
Pinewood Cres. SO45: Hythe . .4F **53**
Pinewood Dr. SO45: Hythe 4F **53**
Pinewood Pk. SO19: South 6F **33**
Pinto Cl. PO15: White 6G **45**
Pipers Cl. SO40: Tott 5D **26**
Piping Cl. SO21: Col C 5F **11**
Piping Grn. SO21: Col C 5F **11**
Piping Rd. SO21: Col C 5F **11**
Pirelli St.
  SO14: South 3C **4** (1B **40**)
Pirelli Way SO50: E'leigh 5A **16**
Pirrie Cl. SO15: South 2H **29**
Pitchpond Rd. SO31: Wars 1A **50**
Pitmore Cl. SO50: E'leigh 5B **10**
Pitmore Rd. SO50: E'leigh 5B **10**
Pitt Rd. SO15: South 5G **29**
Places Leisure Eastleigh 4G **15**
Plaitford Wlk. SO16: South . . .2D **28**
Plantation Dr. SO40: March . . .4C **38**
Platform Rd.
  SO14: South 6E **5** (3C **40**)
Players Cres. SO40: Tott 6E **27**
Plaza M. SO51: Rom 5C **6**
Plaza Theatre 5C **6**
PLEASANT VIEW 2B **42**
Plover Cl. SO16: South 4F **21**
Ploverfield SO31: Burs 5H **43**
Plover Rd. SO40: Tott 4C **26**
Pluto Rd. SO50: E'leigh 4H **15**
The Point
  Eastleigh 4A **16**
Pointout Cl. SO16: Bass 6A **22**
Pointout Rd. SO16: Bass 6A **22**
Polesden Cl. SO53: Cha F 5D **8**
Poles La. SO21: Hurs, Ott 1A **10**
POLYGON 1B **4** (5A **30**)
The Polygon
  SO15: South 1B **4** (6B **30**)
Polygon Ct.
  SO15: South 1B **4** (6A **30**)
Polymond Ho. SO14: South 6D **4**
Pomeroy Cres.
  SO30: Hed E 1H **33**
Pond Cl. SO40: March 3D **38**
Pondhead Cl. SO45: Holb 5C **54**
Pond Rd. SO31: Sar G 1D **48**
Pond Vw. SO18: South 1A **32**
POOKSGREEN 3A **38**
Pooksgreen SO40: March 3A **38**
Poole Rd. SO19: South 1G **41**
Popes Ct. SO40: Tott 4F **27**
Popes La. SO40: Tott 4F **27**
Poplar Dr. SO40: March 4B **38**
Poplar Rd. SO19: South 5H **31**
Poplar Way SO30: Hed E 5B **34**
  SO52: N Bad 2D **12**
Poppy Cl. SO31: Loc H 5D **48**
Poppyfields SO53: Cha F 1C **14**
Poppy Rd. SO16: S'ing 4E **23**
Porchester Rd.
  SO19: South 2G **41**
Porlock Rd. SO16: South 2A **28**
Portal Rd. SO19: South 1B **42**
  SO40: Tott 4D **26**
  SO50: B'stke 4D **16**
Portchester Ri. SO50: E'leigh . .6A **10**
Portcullis Ho.
  SO14: South 6F **5** (3C **40**)
Portelet Ho. SO16: South 6B **20**
Portelet Pl. SO30: Hed E 6A **34**
Porteous Cres. SO53: Cha F . . .1H **15**
Portersbridge M. SO51: Rom . .5B **6**
Portersbridge St. SO51: Rom . .5B **6**
Porter's La.
  SO14: South 6D **4** (2B **40**)
Port Hamble SO31: Hamb 4G **47**
Portland St.
  SO14: South 3D **4** (1B **40**)
Portland Ter.
  SO14: South 2D **4** (1B **40**)
Portside Cl. SO40: March 2E **39**
Portsmouth Rd. SO19: South . . .2F **41**
  SO31: Burs 4G **43**
  SO50: Fis P 6H **11**

PORTSWOOD 2D **30**
Portswood Av. SO17: South . . .3D **30**
Portswood Cen.
  SO17: South 2D **30**
PORTSWOOD PARK 3D **30**
Portswood Pk. SO17: South . . .3D **30**
Portswood Rd. SO17: South . . .3D **30**
Portview Rd. SO18: South 1H **31**
Portway Cl. SO18: South 4B **32**
Postern Ct.
  SO14: South 5D **4** (2B **40**)
Potters Heron Cl.
  SO51: Ampf 2A **8**
Potters Heron La.
  SO51: Ampf 2A **8**
Poulner Cl. SO19: South 4A **42**
Poundbury Ct. SO31: Sar G . . .1E **49**
Pound Ga. Dr. PO14: Titch C . .6G **49**
Pound La. SO40: Tott 2E **37**
  SO51: Ampf 1G **13**
Pound Rd. SO31: Old N 4E **43**
Pound St. SO18: South 4A **32**
Pound Tree Rd.
  SO14: South 3E **5** (1C **40**)
Powell Cres. SO40: Tott 6F **27**
The Precinct SO30: Hed E 5A **34**
  SO45: Holb 4C **54**
Precosa Rd. SO30: Botl 1A **44**
Prelate Way PO14: Titch C 5G **49**
The Premier Cen. SO51: Rom . .6G **7**
Premier Gym 2D **30**
Premier Rd. SO18: South 6H **23**
Premier Way SO51: Rom 2B **12**
Preshaw Cl. SO16: South 5G **21**
Prestwood Rd. SO30: Hed E . . .5A **34**
Pretoria Rd. SO30: Hed E 6H **33**
Priest Cft. SO45: Blac 3E **55**
Priest Cft. Dr. SO45: Blac 3E **55**
Priestfields PO14: Titch C 5G **49**
Priestlands SO51: Rom 4B **6**
Priestlands Cl. SO40: Net M . . .5A **26**
Priestley Cl. SO40: Tott 4D **26**
Primate Rd. PO14: Titch C 4H **49**
Primrose Cl. SO30: Hed E 6A **34**
  SO53: Cha F 3B **14**
Primrose Rd. SO16: Bass 5C **22**
Primrose Way SO31: Loc H . . .5D **48**
  SO51: Rom 4F **7**
Prince of Wales Av.
  SO15: South 4E **29**
Prince Rd. SO16: Rown 3C **20**
Princes Ct. SO14: South 5E **31**
Princes Ho. SO14: South 4E **31**
  (off Graham St.)
Prince's Rd. SO51: Rom 4B **6**
Princes Rd. SO14: South 5H **29**
PRINCESS ANNE HOSPITAL . . .6F **21**
Princess Cl. SO30: W End 1H **33**
Princess Rd. SO40: A'hst 3B **36**
Prince's St. SO14: South 5E **31**
Prince William Ct.
  SO50: B'stke 5F **17**
Priors Hill La. SO31: Old N 5E **43**
Priory Av. SO17: South 2F **31**
Priory Cl. SO17: South 2F **31**
THE PRIORY HOSPITAL
  SOUTHAMPTON 6E **39**
Priory Ho.
  SO14: South 2F **5** (6C **30**)
Priory Rd. SO17: South 2E **31**
  SO31: Net A 1B **46**
  SO50: E'leigh 6H **15**
Proctor Cl. SO19: South 6D **32**
Proctor Dr. SO52: N Bad 4D **12**
The Promenade
  SO45: Hythe 1E **53**
Prospect Pl. SO45: Hythe 1E **53**
  SO53: Cha F 1E **15**
Prospect Rd. SO19: South 6H **31**
Providence Hill SO31: Burs . . .3G **43**
Providence Pk. SO16: Bass . . .4B **22**
Prunus Cl. SO16: South 4G **21**
Pudbrooke Gdns.
  SO30: Hed E 3H **33**
Pudbrook Ho. SO30: Botl 5D **34**
Puffin Cl. SO16: South 5F **21**
Purbrook Cl. SO16: South 5G **21**
Purcell Rd. SO19: South 2D **42**
PureGym
  Southampton 1G **29**
  Southampton Bitterne 5A **32**
  Southampton Central
  . . . . .2B **4** (6A **30**)
Purkess Cl. SO53: Cha F 6F **9**
Purlieu Dr. SO45: Dib P 4B **52**
Purvis Gdns. SO19: South 3B **42**

Pycroft Cl. SO19: South 6A **32**
Pyland's La. SO31: Burs 2H **43**
Pylewell Rd. SO45: Hythe 1E **53**

Q

QE2 Activity Cen. 2B **44**
QEII Cruise Terminal 5D **40**
The Quadrangle
  SO50: E'leigh 3A **16**
  SO51: Rom 6G **7**
Quantock Rd. SO16: South 3C **28**
The Quantocks SO45: Dib P . .4B **52**
The Quay SO31: Hamb 5G **47**
Quay 2000 SO17: South 3E **31**
Quay Haven SO31: Lwr Swan . .6B **44**
Quay La. SO31: Lwr Swan 6B **44**
Quayside SO30: Botl 5E **35**
Quayside Rd. SO18: South 4E **31**
Quayside Wlk. SO40: March . . .2D **38**
The Quays Swimming &
  Diving Complex 5C **4** (2B **40**)
Quebec Gdns. SO31: Burs 4F **43**
Queen Elizabeth Ct.
  SO17: South 6E **23**
Queens Bldgs.
  SO14: South 4F **5** (1C **40**)
Queen's Cl. SO51: Rom 5D **6**
Queens Cl. SO45: Hythe 3F **53**
Queen's Ct.
  SO15: South 1B **4** (6A **30**)
Queens Ho.
  SO14: South 5F **5** (2C **40**)
Queens Ride SO52: N Bad 3C **12**
Queen's Rd. SO15: South 1G **29**
Queens Rd. SO31: Wars 1A **50**
  SO53: Cha F 4F **9**
Queens Ter.
  SO14: South 6F **5** (2C **40**)
Queenstown Rd.
  SO15: South 5H **29**
Queens Vw. SO31: Net A 1B **46**
Queen's Way
  SO14: South 5E **5** (2C **40**)
Querida Cl. SO31: Lwr Swan . . .5B **44**
Quilter Cl. SO19: South 1D **42**
Quintilis M. SO31: South 5G **21**
Quob Farm Cl. SO30: W End . .6E **25**
Quob La. SO30: W End 6E **25**

R

Rachel Cl. SO50: B'stke 5H **17**
Radcliffe Ct.
  SO14: South 1H **5** (5D **30**)
Radcliffe Rd.
  SO14: South 1H **5** (6D **30**)
Radleigh Gdns. SO40: Tott 3B **26**
Radley Cl. SO30: Hed E 2A **34**
Radstock Rd. SO19: South 2F **41**
Radway Cres. SO15: South 3H **29**
Radway Rd. SO15: South 3H **29**
Raeburn Dr. SO30: Hed E 4A **34**
Raglan Cl. SO53: Cha F 3B **14**
Raglan St. SO31: P Ga 2F **49**
  SO50: E'leigh 1A **16**
Railway Cotts. SO15: South . . .3A **28**
Railway Vw. Rd.
  SO17: South 3E **31**
Rainbow Pl. SO15: South 5G **29**
Raleigh Ho. SO14: South 4G **5**
Raley Rd. SO31: Loc H 5E **49**
Ralph La. SO51: Rom 3D **6**
RAMALLEY 5D **8**
Ramalley La. SO53: Cha F 5D **8**
Rampart Rd. SO18: South 4F **31**
Ramsden Rd. SO16: South 1D **28**
Randall Cl. SO40: Calm 1C **26**
Randall Rd. SO53: Cha F 3F **9**
Randolph St. SO15: South 4G **29**
  (not continuous)
Ranelagh Ct. SO17: South 3C **30**
  (off Westwood Rd.)
Ranelagh Gdns.
  SO15: South 4A **30**
Ranfurly Gdns. SO45: Dib P . . .5C **52**
Range Gdns. SO18: South 2B **42**
Ranger Ct.
  SO14: South 6H **5** (3D **40**)
Ranmore Ct. SO45: Dib 3A **52**
  (off Rowhill Dr.)
Rapide Cl. SO50: E'leigh 1A **24**
Ratcliffe Rd. SO30: Hed E 4A **34**
  SO45: Dib P 5D **52**
Rathdora M. SO31: South 5F **43**

RATLAKE 2B **8**
Ratlake La. SO21: Hurs 1B **8**
Rattigan Gdns. PO15: White . .5G **45**
Raven Rd. SO14: South 5D **30**
Ravenscroft Cl. SO31: Burs . . .4F **43**
Ravenscroft Way SO32: Botl . .2D **34**
Raven Sq. SO50: E'leigh 5F **15**
Ravenswood PO14: Titch C . . .4G **49**
Rayleigh Wlk. SO31: Sar G . . .2D **48**
Raymond Cl. SO30: W End 6F **25**
  SO45: Holb 5D **54**
Raymond Rd. SO15: South 3H **29**
Rayners Gdns. SO16: S'ing 5F **23**
Reading Room La.
  SO32: Curd 3H **35**
The Recess SO50: E'leigh 2B **16**
Rectory Cl. SO30: Botl 4D **34**
REDBRIDGE 3A **28**
Redbridge C'way.
  SO15: South 3H **27**
  SO40: South 3H **27**
Redbridge Flyover
  SO15: South 3A **28**
Redbridge Hill SO16: South . . .2D **28**
Redbridge La. SO16: Nur 6A **20**
  SO16: South 1A **28**
Redbridge Rd. SO15: South . . .3A **28**
Redbridge Station App.
  SO15: South 3A **28**
Redbridge Station (Rail) 3A **28**
Redbridge Towers
  SO16: South 3A **28**
Redcar St. SO15: South 3F **29**
Redcote Cl. SO18: South 4B **32**
Redcourt SO16: Bass 5B **22**
Redcroft La. SO31: Burs 4G **43**
The Redfords SO40: Tott 2E **27**
Redhill SO16: Bass 5A **22**
Redhill Cl. SO16: Bass 5A **22**
Redhill Cres. SO16: Bass 5A **22**
Redhill Way SO16: Bass 5A **22**
The Red Ho. SO51: Rom 4C **6**
Redlands Dr. SO19: South 5H **31**
Red Lodge SO53: Cha F 4D **14**
Red Lodge Community Pool . . .5A **22**
Redmoor Cl. SO19: South 5H **31**
Red Oaks Dr. SO31: P Ga 2F **49**
Redrise Cl. SO45: Holb 5B **54**
Redward Rd. SO16: Rown 4D **20**
Redwing Gdns. SO40: Tott 3C **26**
Redwood Dr. SO30: W End 1C **32**
Redwood Gdns. SO40: Tott . . .5C **26**
Redwood Way SO16: Bass 3C **22**
Reed Dr. SO40: March 3D **38**
Reeves Way SO31: Burs 4F **43**
Regal Wlk. SO50: E'leigh 4B **16**
Regent Cl. SO21: Ott 1C **10**
Regent Ct. SO17: South 2C **30**
Regent Ho. SO30: Hed E 1A **34**
Regent Rd. SO53: Cha F 1F **15**
Regents Cl. SO16: South 3F **29**
Regents Ga. SO31: Sar G 2C **48**
Regents Gro. SO15: South 2F **29**
Regent's Pk. Gdns.
  SO15: South 4F **29**
Regent's Pk. Rd.
  SO15: South 5E **29**
Regent St.
  SO14: South 3D **4** (1B **40**)
Reginald Mitchell Ct.
  SO50: E'leigh 3H **15**
Reliant Cl. SO53: Cha F 2D **14**
Renda Rd. SO45: Holb 4C **54**
Renown Cl. SO53: Cha F 2D **14**
Repton Gdns. SO30: Hed E . . .1B **34**
  (not continuous)
Reservoir La. SO30: Hed E 5G **33**
The Retreat SO40: Tott 6G **27**
  SO50: E'leigh 3B **16**
Rex Ind. Est. SO53: Cha F 2F **15**
Reynolds Ct. SO51: Rom 6D **6**
Reynolds Dale SO40: Tott 6D **26**
Reynolds Rd. SO15: South 3G **29**
  SO50: Fair O 2G **17**
Rhinefield Cl. SO50: B'stke 5F **17**
Rhyme Hall M. SO45: F'ley 2H **55**
Ribble Cl. SO53: Cha F 2F **15**
Ribble Ct. SO16: South 2C **28**
Richard Newitt Courts
  SO16: Bass 4C **22**
Richards Cl. SO31: Loc H 4E **49**
  SO45: F'ley 3F **55**
Richards Ct. SO15: South 3F **29**
  SO30: W End 1C **32**
Richard Taunton Pl.
  SO17: South 1C **30**

Richlans Rd. SO30: Hed E 5A 34
Richmond Cl. SO40: Calm ...2B 26
SO53: Cha F 4E 9
Richmond Gdns.
SO17: South 2D 30
Richmond La. SO51: Rom 3D 6
Richmond Pk. SO21: Ott 1D 10
Richmond Rd. SO15: South ...5G 29
Richmond St.
SO14: South 5F 5 (2C 40)
Richville Rd. SO16: South ...3E 29
Ridding Cl. SO15: South 2F 29
RIDGE 1C 18
Ridge La. SO30: Botl 2H 45
SO51: Rom 1B 18
Ridgemount Av. SO16: Bass ..4B 22
Ridgemount La. SO16: Bass ..4B 22
Ridgeway Cl. SO50: Fair O ..4H 17
SO53: Cha F 2G 15
Ridgeway Wlk. SO53: Cha F ..2G 15
Ridgewood Cl. SO45: Dib 2A 52
The Ridings SO50: B'stke 5G 17
Ridley Cl. SO15: Holb 4C 54
Rigby Rd. SO17: South 3D 30
Rimington Gdns. SO51: Rom ...2E 7
The Ring SO16: Chil 2A 22
Ringwood Dr. SO52: N Bad ...2C 12
Ringwood Rd.
SO40: Net M, Tott 4A 26
Ripplewood SO40: March 4E 39
Ripstone Gdns. SO17: South ...6D 22
Ritchie Cl. SO19: South 1B 42
Rivendale SO15: South 5G 29
(off Payne's Rd.)
Rivendale Cl. SO31: Sar G 2D 48
Riverdene Pl. SO18: South 3F 31
River Grn. SO31: Hamb 5G 47
Rivermead Cl. SO51: Rom 5A 6
Rivermead Ho. SO51: Rom 5A 6
River M. SO50: B'stke 4D 16
Riversdale Cl. SO19: South ...5G 41
Riversfield Ct. SO15: South ...4G 29
(off Selby Pl.)
Riverside SO50: B'stke 4D 16
(Harcourt Rd.)
Riverside Ct. SO18: South 3F 31
(Manor Wharf)
Riverside Gdns. SO51: Rom 6A 6
Riverside Holidays 2G 47
Riverview SO40: Tott 6F 27
River Vw. Ho. SO19: South ...2F 41
River Vw. Rd. SO18: South ...1F 31
Riverview Ter.
SO31: Lwr Swan 5B 44
River Wlk. SO18: South 6G 23
The RJ Mitchell Cen.
SO19: South 1F 41
Robard Ho. SO31: Burs 4F 43
Robere Ho. SO19: South 2G 41
Robert Cecil Av. SO18: S'ing ..5G 23
Roberts Rd.
SO15: South 1A 4 (6H 29)
SO40: Tott 6F 27
SO45: Hythe 2D 52
Robert Whitworth Dr.
SO51: Rom 3C 6
Robin Gdns. SO40: Tott 3C 26
Robinia Grn. SO16: South ...4G 21
Robin Pl. SO31: Net A 1B 46
Robin's Mdw. PO14: Titch C ..6G 49
Robin Sq. SO50: E'leigh 5E 15
Rochester St.
SO14: South 2H 5 (6E 31)
Rockall Cl. SO16: South 4C 20
Rockery Cl. SO45: Dib 2A 52
Rockford Ho. SO50: Fair O ...1H 25
Rockleigh Dr. SO40: Tott 1D 36
Rockleigh Rd. SO16: South ...6H 21
Rockram Gdns. SO45: Dib 3A 52
Rockstone Ct. SO14: South ...5C 30
Rockstone La. SO14: South ...5C 30
Rockstone Pl. SO15: South 5B 30
Rodney Cl. SO19: South 1C 42
Roewood Cl. SO45: Holb 5C 54
Roewood Rd. SO45: Holb 5C 54
Rogers Cl. SO50: B'stke 3E 17
Rogers Rd. SO50: B'stke 3E 17
Roker Way SO50: Fair O 6H 17
Roll Ct. SO16: Bass 4C 22
Rollesbrook Gdns.
SO15: South 5A 30
Rollestone Rd. SO45: Holb 5B 54
Rolling Mill Mews
SO50: E'leigh 5H 15
Roman Cl. SO53: Cha F 6G 9
Roman Dr. SO16: Chil 2A 22

Roman Gdns. SO45: Dib P 5B 52
Roman Rd. SO16: Bass, Chil ..1B 22
SO45: Dib P 3A 52
SO45: Hard 2B 54
Roman Way SO45: Dib P 5B 52
Romero Hall SO15: South 4B 30
Romford Rd. SO31: Wars 1B 50
Romill Cl. SO18: W End 6B 24
ROMSEY 5B 6
Romsey Bus Station 5B 6
Romsey By-Pass SO51: Rom ..6A 6
Romsey Cl. SO50: E'leigh 4A 16
Romsey Ct. SO15: South 5H 29
Romsey Golf Course 2A 20
ROMSEY HOSPITAL 4E 7
Romsey Ind. Est. SO51: Rom ...4B 6
Romsey Rapids
Sports Complex 6C 6
Romsey Rd.
SO16: Nur, South 2A 20
SO50: E'leigh 4A 16
SO51: Ower 2A 18
Romsey Sports Cen. 6C 6
Romsey Station (Rail) 4C 6
Romsey Tourist Information Centre
.....................5B 6
Ronald Pugh Ct. SO18: S'ing ..5G 23
Rookery Av. PO15: White 6F 45
(not continuous)
Rookery Grange
SO31: Swanw 6F 45
Rookley SO31: Net A 6C 42
Rooksbridge SO45: Dib 3A 52
Rookwood Cl. SO50: E'leigh ..1B 16
Rope Wlk. SO31: Hamb 5G 47
Ropley Cl. SO19: South 5A 42
Rosebank Cl. SO16: Rown 4C 20
SO31: Sar G 1C 48
Rosebank Lodge
SO16: Rown 4C 20
Roseberry Av. SO45: Hythe ...4E 53
Rosebery Cres.
SO50: E'leigh 1B 16
Rosebrook Ct. SO18: South ...4G 31
Rose Cl. SO30: Hed E 3A 34
SO45: Hythe 4E 53
Rosedale Av. SO51: Rom 5D 6
Roseleigh Cl. SO50: Fair O ...6G 17
Roselands SO30: W End 3D 32
Roselands Cl. SO50: Fair O ...4H 17
Roselands Gdns.
SO17: South 1C 30
Roseleigh Dr. SO40: Tott 5E 27
Rosemary Ct. SO40: Tott 4B 26
(off Alkman La.)
Rosemary Gdns.
PO15: White 5H 45
SO30: Hed E 6A 34
Rosemary Price Ct.
SO30: Hed E 3A 34
Rosemerry Pl. SO45: Blac 6F 55
Rosemoor Gro. SO53: Cha F ..4D 8
Rosemount Cl. SO30: W End ..1C 32
Rosendale Rd. SO53: Cha F ..3F 15
Rose Rd. SO14: South 3C 30
SO40: Elin 5G 27
Rosewall Rd. SO16: South 6D 20
Rosewood Gdns.
SO40: March 4E 39
Rosida Gdns.
SO15: South 1A 4 (5A 30)
Rosman Cl. SO19: South 1H 41
Rosman Rd. SO19: South 1H 41
Rossan Av. SO31: Wars 1B 50
Ross Gdns. SO16: South 1E 29
Rossington Av. SO18: South ..4H 31
Rossington Way
SO18: South 4H 31
Rosslyn Cl. SO52: N Bad 3E 13
Ross Mews SO31: Net A 2A 46
Roston Cl. SO18: W End 6A 24
Rostron Cl. SO18: W End 1C 32
Rosyth Rd. SO18: South 4H 31
Rotary Ho. SO15: South 2H 29
Rothbury Cl. SO19: South 1A 42
SO40: Tott 2D 26
Rother Cl. SO18: W End 2B 32
Rother Dale SO19: South 2E 43
Rothsbury Dr. SO53: Cha F ...1D 14
Rothschild Cl. SO19: South ...4G 41
Rothschild Dr. SO31: Sar G ...3D 48
Rotterdam Towers
SO19: South 4H 41
ROUGHDOWN 6C 54
Roughdown La.
SO45: Blac, Holb 6C 54

Round Copse SO45: Dib 3A 52
Roundhill Cl. SO18: South ...2A 32
Roundhouse Dr. SO40: Tott ...5B 26
Routs Way SO16: Rown 2C 20
Rowan Cl. PO15: White 5H 45
SO16: South 6E 21
SO31: Burs 5F 43
SO40: Tott 5D 26
SO51: Rom 6F 7
Rowan Ct. SO16: South 1G 29
SO19: South 2H 41
SO53: Cha F 1G 15
Rowan Gdns. SO30: Hed E ...5B 34
The Rowans SO40: March ...4D 38
Rowborough Rd.
SO18: South 3H 31
Rowe Ashe Way
SO31: Loc H 4D 48
Rowhill Dr. SO45: Dib 3A 52
Rowlands Cl. SO53: Cha F ...3C 14
Rowlands Wlk. SO18: South ..1A 32
Rowley Cl. SO30: Botl 3D 34
Rowley Ct. SO30: Botl 3D 34
Rowley Dr. SO30: Botl 3D 34
ROWNHAMS 2C 20
Rownhams Cl. SO16: Rown ...3C 20
Rownhams Ct. SO16: South ...6D 20
Rownhams Ho. SO16: Rown ...3C 20
Rownhams La. SO16: Rown ...1D 20
SO16: South 3C 20
(not continuous)
SO52: N Bad 2D 12
Rownhams Pk. SO16: Rown ...3C 20
Rownhams Rd. SO16: Rown ...1D 28
SO52: N Bad 4E 13
Rownhams Rd. Nth.
SO16: Rown 1D 20
ROWNHAMS SERVICE AREA ..1D 20
Rownhams Way SO16: Rown ..3C 20
Rowse Cl. SO51: Rom 3C 6
Roxan M. SO17: South 1E 31
Roxburgh Ho. SO31: Loc H ...4E 49
Royal Air Force Yacht Club ..5G 47
Royal Ct. SO17: South 1D 30
Royal Cres. Rd.
SO14: South 6G 5 (2D 40)
Royal Gdns. SO15: South 4D 28
Royal London Pk.
SO30: Hed E 3H 33
Royal Southampton Yacht Club
Channel Way 6H 5 (3E 41)
Royal Southern Yacht Club ..5G 47
ROYAL SOUTH HANTS
.....................5C 30
Royal Victoria Country Pk.
.....................3C 46
Royal Victoria Country Pk.
Heritage Cen. 3C 46
Royal Victoria Country Pk.
Vis. Cen. 3C 46
Roy's Copse SO45: Dib 2A 52
Royston Cl. SO50: E'leigh 2A 16
Royston Cl. SO17: South 1D 30
Royston Ct. SO40: Tott 2E 27
Rozel Ct. SO16: South 6C 20
Ruby Cl. SO40: Tott 2D 26
Ruby Rd. SO19: South 5A 32
Rudd Way
SO14: South 5G 5 (2D 40)
Rufford Cl. SO50: E'leigh 1A 16
Rufus Cl. SO16: Rown 3B 20
SO53: Cha F 5G 9
Rufus Gdns. SO40: Tott 4G 27
Rumbridge Gdns. SO40: Tott ..4G 27
Rumbridge St. SO40: Tott 5F 27
Runnymede SO30: W End ...2D 32
Runnymede Cl.
SO30: W End 2D 32
The Rushes SO40: March 3D 38
Rushington Av. SO40: Tott 5F 27
Rushington Bus. Pk.
SO40: Tott 6E 27
Rushington Cl. SO40: Tott 6E 27
Rushington La. SO40: Tott 6E 27
Rushpole Ct. SO45: Dib 3A 52
Ruskin Rd. SO50: E'leigh 3A 16
Rusland Cl. SO53: Cha F 6D 8
Russell Cl. SO40: March 3D 38
Russell Equestrian Cen. 5C 24
Russell Pl. SO17: South 2D 30
SO40: Tott 4G 27
Russell St.
SO14: South 5F 5 (2C 40)
Russet Ho. SO30: Hed E 5H 33
Rustan Cl. SO30: Hed E 5A 34
SO50: Fair O 1G 17
Rutland Ct. SO18: South 4A 32
Rutland Gdns. SO31: Burs 4G 43

Rutland Way SO18: South ...2A 32
Ruxley Cl. SO45: Holb 4C 54
Ryde Ter.
SO14: South 5H 5 (2D 40)
Rye Cl. SO53: Cha F 1B 14
Ryecroft PO14: Titch C 5G 49
Ryedale SO40: A'hst 2C 36
Rye Paddock La. SO45: F'ley ..1H 55
Rylandes Ct. SO16: South 6D 20

S

Sable Cl. SO31: Sar G 4C 48
Saddlers Cl. SO50: E'leigh ...1A 16
Sadlers La. SO45: Dib P 5E 53
Saffron Cl. SO31: Loc H 5C 48
Saffron Way PO15: White 5H 45
St Agathas Rd. SO31: Hamb ..3G 47
St Alban's Rd.
SO14: South 1G 5 (6D 30)
St Andrews Bldgs.
SO31: Hamb 5F 47
St Andrews Cl. SO52: N Bad ..2C 12
St Andrews Rd.
SO14: South 1F 5 (6C 30)
St Anne's Gdns.
SO19: South 3G 41
St Anne's Ho. SO51: Rom 6B 6
(off Banning St.)
St Annes M. SO14: South 3C 30
St Anne's Rd. SO19: South ...3G 41
St Aubin's Av. SO19: South ...6A 32
St Augustine Gdns.
SO17: South 2F 31
St Austell Cl. SO50: B'stke ...4E 17
St Barbe Cl. SO51: Rom 6D 6
St Bernard Ho. SO14: South ...5F 5
St Blaize Rd. SO51: Rom 4E 7
St Boniface Ct. SO52: N Bad ..4E 13
St Brelade Pl. SO16: South ...6B 20
St Catherine's Rd.
SO18: South 2F 31
SO50: E'leigh 2A 16
St Catherines Vw.
SO30: Hed E 5G 33
St Christophers Cl.
SO52: N Bad 3D 12
St Clements Cl. SO51: Rom 4B 6
St Contest Way SO40: March ..5D 38
St Cuthbert's Cl.
SO31: Loc H 3F 49
St Cuthbert's La.
SO31: Loc H 3F 49
St Davids Cl. SO40: Calm 2C 26
St David's Ct. SO52: N Bad ...4E 13
St Davids Rd. SO31: Loc H ...4D 48
ST DENYS 3E 31
St Denys Rd. SO17: South 2D 30
St Denys Station (Rail) 3E 31
St Edmund Cl.
PO14: Titch C 6F 49
St Edmunds Rd.
SO15: South 3F 29
SO16: South 3F 29
(not continuous)
St Edwards Rd. SO31: Net A ...6B 42
St Elizabeths Av.
SO18: South 4B 32
St Evox Cl. SO16: Rown 4D 20
St Francis Av. SO18: South ...3B 32
St Francis Cl. SO45: Blac 6E 55
St Francis Rd. SO45: Blac 6E 55
St Gabriel's Rd.
SO18: South 4B 32
St George Cl. SO31: Burs 4F 43
St George's Ct. SO52: N Bad ..4E 13
St Georges Cl. SO45: Blac 5F 55
St Georges Rd. SO31: Loc H ...4D 48
St George's St.
SO14: South 4F 5 (1C 40)
St Helena Gdns.
SO18: South 6H 23
St Helens M. SO50: Fair O 1G 17
(off Stubbington Way)
St Helens Rd. SO15: South ...2G 29
St Helier Pl. SO16: South 6E 21
St James Cl. SO15: South 2G 29
St James Ho.
SO14: South 5F 5 (2C 40)
St James Pk. SO52: N Bad 4C 8
St James Pk. Rd.
SO16: South 1G 29
St James Rd. SO15: South 2G 29
SO30: W End 2E 33
St John's Cen. SO30: Hed E ...5H 33
SO52: N Bad 2E 13
St Johns Cl. SO16: Rown 2C 20

St John's Ct. SO52: N Bad 4F 13
St Johns Ct. SO40: March 4D 38
St Johns Dr. SO40: March 4C 38
St John's Gdns. SO51: Rom 4C 6
St John's M. SO31: Loc H 4G 49
St John's Glebe SO16: Rown .3C 20
St John's Rd. SO30: Hed E ..1G 43
  SO31: Loc H 5F 49
  SO50: E'leigh 3B 16
St John St. SO31: Wars 2E 53
St Joseph Cl. SO31: Loc H 4F 49
St Julien's Hospital Almshouses
  SO14: South 6E 5
St Lawrence Cl. SO30: Hed E ..1B 34
St Lawrence Rd.
  SO14: South 6G 5 (2D 40)
  SO50: E'leigh 3A 16
St Lukes Cl. SO30: Hed E ...2A 34
St Margarets Cl.
  SO18: South 4B 32
St Margarets Ho.
  SO15: South 3B 30
                    (off Hulse Rd.)
St Margaret's Rd.
  SO50: B'stke 3C 16
St Mark's Cl. SO53: Cha F ...4H 9
St Marks Rd.
  SO14: South 1G 5 (6D 30)
St Martin's Cl. SO50: B'stke ..3D 16
St Martins Cl. SO16: South ...6C 20
ST MARY'S 1F 5 (5C 30)
St Mary's SO51: Rom 6B 6
                  (off Banning St.)
St Mary's Church Cl.
  SO18: S'ing 5G 23
St Mary's Leisure Cen.
  ....1F 5 (5C 30)
St Mary's Pl.
  SO14: South 4F 5 (1C 40)
St Mary's Rd.
  SO14: South 1F 5 (5C 30)
  SO31: Net A 1C 46
  SO50: B'stke 3D 16
St Mary's Stadium ...3H 5 (1D 40)
St Mary St.
  SO14: South 2G 5 (6D 30)
St Matthews Cl.
  SO14: South 1F 5 (6D 30)
St Michaels Cl. SO45: Blac ...4F 55
St Michael's Rd.
  SO31: Loc H 5D 48
St Michaels Rd. SO40: Tott ...2F 27
St Michael's Sq. SO14: South ..5D 4
St Michael's St.
  SO14: South 5D 4 (2B 40)
St Monica Rd. SO19: South ...2A 42
St Patrick's Ct. SO52: N Bad ..4E 13
St Pauls Rd. SO31: Sar G ...1C 46
St Peters Cl. SO32: Curd 3H 35
St Philip's Way SO18: South ..4B 32
St Simon Cl. SO14: South 1F 49
St Swithun's Cl. SO51: Cram ..3G 7
St Swithuns Ct. SO14: South ..5C 30
                  (off Cranbury Pl.)
St Thomas Ct. SO50: Fair O ..1G 17
St Tristan Cl. SO31: Loc H ...5F 49
St Vigor Way SO21: Col C 4F 11
St Winifred's Rd.
  SO16: South 1G 29
Salcombe Cl. SO53: Cha F ...3D 14
Salcombe Cres. SO40: Tott ...5E 27
Salcombe Rd. SO15: South ...4G 29
  SO40: Tott 5E 27
Salem St. SO15: South 2G 29
Salerno Ho. SO51: Rom 5E 7
                  (off Chambers Av.)
Salerno Rd. SO16: South 5G 21
Salisbury Cl. SO50: E'leigh ...3B 16
Salisbury Ct. SO50: E'leigh ...3B 16
Salisbury Rd. SO17: South ...6C 22
  SO40: Calm, Tott 5A 18
  SO51: Ower 5A 18
  SO51: Rom 6A 6
Salisbury Rd. Arc.
  SO40: Tott 4F 27
Salisbury St. SO15: South 5B 30
Salmon Dr. SO50: B'stke 5F 17
Salona Cl. SO53: Cha F 6H 9
Salterns La. SO31: Burs 1G 47
  SO45: F'ley 1H 55
Saltmarsh Rd.
  SO14: South 6H 5 (2D 40)
Saltmead SO17: South 1E 31
Salwey Rd. SO30: Botl 6B 34
Sam Ford Pl. SO50: E'leigh ..5A 16
Sampan Cl. SO31: Wars 6C 48
Sanctuary Cl. SO19: South ...5B 32

Sandell Ct. SO16: Bass 4D 22
Sandhurst Rd. SO15: South ...5A 30
Sandilands Way
  SO45: Hythe 5E 53
Sandlewood Cl. SO40: Calm ..3C 26
Sand Martin Cl.
  SO50: E'leigh 6F 15
Sandown Ho. SO19: South 3F 41
                  (off John Thornycroft Rd.)
Sandown Rd. SO15: South 2F 29
Sandpiper Cl. SO40: March ...4C 38
Sandpiper Rd. SO16: South ...4E 21
Sandringham Cl.
Sandringham Ct.
  SO15: South 5E 29
                  (off Regent's Pk. Rd.)
  SO17: South 2C 30
                    (off Winn Rd.)
Sandringham Rd.
  SO18: South 2G 31
Sandycroft Rd. SO31: Wars ...6B 48
Sandy La. SO31: Loc H 5H 17
  SO51: Brai, Ower, Rom 1D 6
  SO52: N Bad 2F 13
                    (not continuous)
Sapphire Cl. SO14: South 3B 14
Sapphire Way SO31: Loc H ...4C 48
Saracens Rd. SO53: Cha F ...6H 9
Sarisbury Ga. SO31: P Ga 2F 49
SARISBURY GREEN 1C 48
Sarnia Ct. SO16: South 5C 20
Sartoris Cl. SO31: Wars 6B 48
Sarum Ho. SO40: Tott 2D 26
Sarum Rd. SO53: Cha F 1G 15
Satchell La.
  SO31: Hamb, Hou 1E 47
Saturn Cl. SO16: South 5D 20
Savernake Cl. SO51: Rom 3E 7
Savernake Rd.
  SO50: Fair O 4H 17
Saville Cl. SO50: B'stke 2D 16
Saxholm Cl. SO16: Bass 3B 22
Saxholm Dale SO16: Bass 3B 22
Saxholm Way SO16: Bass 3B 22
Saxon Cl. SO31: Wars 6C 48
Saxon Gdns. SO30: Hed E ...6G 33
Saxon Ho.
  SO14: South 1H 5 (5E 31)
Saxon Rd. SO15: South 6H 29
  SO45: Blac 4F 55
Saxon Wlk. SO53: Cha F 2G 15
Saxon Way SO51: Rom 5E 7
Sayers Rd. SO50: B'stke 5D 16
Scantabout Av. SO53: Cha F ..6G 9
School Cl. SO53: Cha F 2D 14
School La. SO31: Hamb 6G 47
  SO53: Cha F 3C 14
School Pl. SO19: South 1G 41
School Rd. SO31: Burs 4G 43
  SO40: Elin 5G 27
  SO45: F'ley 2G 55
  SO45: Hythe 2E 53
Schooner Way SO31: Wars 6C 48
Scotland Cl. SO50: Fair O 1H 17
Scotter Rd. SO50: B'stke 4D 16
Scotter Sq. SO50: B'stke 4D 16
Scott-Paine Dr. SO45: Hythe ..2F 53
Scott Rd. SO19: South 4H 41
Scotts Cl. SO21: Col C 5G 11
SCRAG HILL 1D 12
Scullards La.
  SO14: South 3D 4 (1B 40)
SeaCity Mus. 2D 4 (6B 30)
Seacole Cl. SO16: South 1G 29
Seacombe Grn.
  SO16: South 2B 28
Seafield Rd. SO16: South 1B 28
Seaford Cl. SO31: Burs 4F 43
Seagarth Cl. SO16: South 6H 21
Seagarth La. SO16: South 6H 21
Sea Rd. SO19: South 2F 41
Seaton Cl. SO18: W End 2C 32
Sea Vw. Est. SO31: Net A 2B 46
Seaward Gdns. SO31: Wars ...1G 41
Seaward Rd. SO19: South 1G 41
Seaweed Cl. SO19: South 5G 41
Second Av. SO15: South 3B 28
  SO45: Hard 6H 53
Second La. SO31: Net A 2B 46
Sedgemead SO31: Net A 2B 46
Sedgemead Ct. SO31: Net A ..2B 46

Sedgwick Ct. SO50: B'stke ...4D 16
Sedgewick Rd.
  SO19: South 6C 32
Sedgwick Rd. SO50: B'stke ...4D 16
SEGENSWORTH 3H 49
Segensworth East Ind. Est.
  PO15: Seg 2H 49
                    (not continuous)
Segensworth Nth. Ind. Est.
  PO15: Seg 2H 49
Segensworth Rd.
  PO15: Seg, Titch 3H 49
                    (not continuous)
Segensworth West Ind. Est.
  PO15: Seg 2G 49
Selborne Av. SO18: South ...3C 32
Selborne Ct. SO16: Bass 4C 22
Selborne Rd. SO51: Rom 3E 7
Selborne Rd. SO40: Tott 3D 26
Selborne Wlk. SO18: South ...3C 32
Selbourne Dr. SO50: E'leigh ..3A 16
Selby Pl. SO15: South 4G 29
Selhurst Way SO50: Fair O ...2F 17
Sellwood Rd. SO31: Net A 1C 46
Selman Cl. SO45: Hythe 2F 53
Selsdon Av. SO51: Rom 4E 7
Selsey Cl. SO16: South 6C 20
Selwood Pl. SO45: Blac 4E 55
Selwyn Gdns. SO50: E'leigh ..2A 16
Sembal Ho.
  SO15: South 1B 4 (5A 30)
Sengana Ct. SO30: Botl 5C 34
Seniac Rd. SO51: South 5E 7
September Cl. SO30: W End ..2D 42
Serle Cl. SO40: Tott 4B 26
Serle Gdns. SO40: Tott 5D 26
Settlers Cl. SO21: Col C 5F 11
Settle Cl. SO16: South 3F 29
Severn Rd. SO16: South 3C 28
Severn Way SO30: W End 1D 32
Sewall Dr. SO50: B'stke 3E 17
Seward Grn. SO45: Hythe 3F 53
Seward Ri. SO51: Rom 4F 7
Seward Rd. SO45: Hythe 3F 53
Seymour Cl. SO16: South 6G 21
  SO40: Calm 2C 26
  SO53: Cha F 2G 15
Seymour Ho. SO16: South 6H 21
Seymour La. SO52: N Bad 3D 12
Seymour Rd. SO16: South 6G 21
Shafford Mdws. SO30: Hed E ..4G 33
Shaftesbury Av. SO17: South ..2D 30
  SO53: Cha F 3E 15
Shakespeare Av.
  SO17: South 3D 30
Shakespeare Bus. Cen.
  SO50: E'leigh 3B 16
Shakespeare Dr. SO40: Tott ..1D 26
Shakespeare Rd.
  SO50: E'leigh 2H 15
Shalcombe SO31: Net A 6C 42
Shalden Cl. SO16: South 5G 21
Shales Rd. SO18: South 4B 32
Shamblehurst La.
  SO30: Hed E 1A 34
Shamblehurst La. Nth.
  SO32: Hed E 1B 34
Shamblehurst La. Sth.
  SO30: Hed E 3A 34
Shamrock Quay SO14: South ..6F 31
Shamrock Rd. SO19: South ...2F 41
Shamrock Vs. SO17: South ...2E 31
Shamrock Way SO45: Hythe ..1E 53
Shanklin Cres. SO15: South ..2A 30
Shanklin Rd. SO15: South ...1H 29
Shannon Ho. SO14: South 4D 4
                    (off Kent St.)
Shannon Way SO53: Cha F ...1C 14
Shapton Cl. SO45: Holb 4B 54
Sharon Rd. SO30: W End 1C 32
                    (not continuous)
Shaw Cl. SO18: W End 1A 32
  SO40: Tott 4D 26
Shawford Cl. SO16: Bass 5A 22
  SO40: Tott 4B 26
Shayer Rd. SO15: South 2G 29
Shears Rd. SO50: B'stke 4E 17
Sheffield Cl. SO50: B'stke 2D 16
Sheldrake Gdns.
  SO16: South 4F 21
Shell Ct. SO40: March 3D 38
Shellcroft SO31: Wars 1B 50
Shelley Ct.
  SO15: South 1B 4 (6A 30)
Shelley Rd. SO19: South 5D 32
  SO40: Tott 1D 26
  SO50: E'leigh 6H 15

Shepherds Hey Rd.
  SO40: Calm 2B 26
Shepherds Purse Cl.
  SO31: Loc H 5C 48
Shepherds Way SO16: Nur ...4A 20
Sherborne Ct. SO17: South ...1D 30
Sherborne Cl. SO31: Loc H ...1H 15
Sherborne Way SO30: Hed E ..5A 34
Sherecroft Gdns. SO30: Botl ..4F 35
Sherfield Ho. SO15: South 3A 30
                    (off Burton Rd.)
Sheridan Cl. SO19: South 6D 32
Sheridan Gdns.
  PO15: White 5G 45
  SO40: Tott 4D 26
Sherley Grn. SO31: Burs 4G 43
Sherringham Cl. SO45: F'ley ..2H 55
Sherwood Av. SO30: Hed E ...1A 44
Sherwood Cl. SO16: Bass 6A 22
Sherwood Gdns.
  SO31: Sar G 3C 48
Sherwood Rd. SO53: Cha F ...4G 9
Sherwood Way SO45: Blac ...6E 55
Shetland Cl. SO40: Tott 3B 26
Shetland Ri. PO15: White 6F 45
Shinewell Gdns.
  SO16: South 3C 28
Shires Wlk. SO15: South 2F 29
Shire Cl. PO15: White 6F 45
The Shires SO30: Hed E 5G 33
Shires Wlk. SO40: Tott 3B 26
SHIRLEY 3G 29
Shirley Av. SO15: South 3G 29
Shirley Bus. Pk.
  SO15: South 5G 29
Shirley High St. SO15: South ..3F 29
  SO16: South 3F 29
Shirley Pk. Rd. SO16: South ..3F 29
Shirley Retail Pk.
  ....1H 29
Shirley Rd.
  SO15: South 1A 4 (3G 29)
Shirley Swimming Pool 4G 29
Shirley Towers SO15: South ..3G 29
SHIRLEY WARREN 1F 29
Shoblands Way SO45: Hythe ..5E 53
                  (off Rosebery Av.)
SHOLING 3H 41
SHOLING COMMON 6C 32
Sholing Rd. SO19: South 1G 41
Sholing Station (Rail) 3H 41
Shooters Hill Cl.
  SO30: W End 2D 32
Showcase Cinema
  Southampton 4D 4 (1B 40)
Shravenhill Cl. SO40: Tott ...2D 26
Shrubland Cl. SO18: South ...3B 32
The Siblings SO19: South 5E 33
The Sidings SO31: Net A 2C 42
Siddal Cl. SO19: South 2C 42
The Sidings SO31: Net A 2D 46
Sidings Ind. Est.
  SO31: Net A 2D 46
Silkin Gdns. SO40: Tott 5D 26
Silver Birch Cl. SO19: South ..1C 42
Silver Birches SO31: Burs 5F 43
Silver Birch Way
  PO15: White 5H 45
Silverdale Cl. SO15: South ...4A 30
Silverdale Rd. SO15: South ...4A 30
Silverlake Stadium 2G 23
Silvers End SO45: Dib P 5E 53
Silvers Wood SO40: Calm ...2C 26
Silvertrees PO15: White 1H 49
  SO31: Sar G 1C 48
Silverweed Cl. SO53: Cha F ...6B 8
Silverweed Ct. SO31: Loc H ...5C 48
Silverwood Ri. SO51: Rom 3F 7
Simmonds Cl. SO30: Hed E ...3A 34
Simnel St.
  SO14: South 5D 4 (2B 40)
Simon Ct. SO18: South 4E 33
Simon Way SO18: South 5E 33
Sinclair Rd. SO16: South 4E 21
Singleton Way SO40: Tott 3B 26
Sir Christopher Ct.
  SO45: Hythe 2F 53

Sirdar Ho.—Suffolk Grn.

Sirdar Ho. SO17: South 6E **23**
Sirdar M. SO17: South 6E **23**
Sirdar Rd. SO17: South 6E **23**
Sir Galahad Rd. SO53: Cha F ...1B **14**
Sir George's Rd.
SO15: South 5H **29**
Sir Lancelot Cl.
SO53: Cha F 1B **14**
Sirocco SO14: South 6H **5** (2D **40**)
Siskin Cl. SO16: South 4E **21**
Sissinghurst Cl.
SO19: South 4A **42**
Six Dials SO14: South ...2F **5** (6C **30**)
Six Oaks Rd. SO52: N Bad 3E **13**
Sixpenny Cl. PO14: Titch C 6E **49**
Sizer Way SO45: Dib 3A **52**
Skintle Grn. SO21: Col C 5F **11**
Skipper Cl. SO40: March 2E **39**
Skipton Rd. SO53: Cha F 3F **15**
Skylark Wlk. SO40: Tott 3B **26**
Skys Wood Rd. SO53: Cha F 1B **14**
Slades Hill SO45: F'ley 3F **55**
Slater Cl. SO40: Tott 3B **26**
Sloane Av. SO45: Holb 4D **54**
Sloane Ct. SO45: Holb 4D **54**
Sloe Tree Cl. SO31: Loc H 5G **49**
Slowhill Copse
SO40: March 2C **38**
Smith Cl. SO45: F'ley 3F **55**
Smith Gro. SO30: Hed E 6A **34**
Smiths Fld. SO51: Rom 3D **6**
Smiths Quay SO19: South 1E **41**
Smythe Rd. SO19: South 2D **42**
Snapdragon Cl. SO31: Loc H 5D **48**
Snellgrove Cl. SO40: Calm 1C **26**
Snellgrove Pl. SO40: Calm 1C **26**
Snowdrop Cl. SO31: Loc H 5D **48**
Soberton Ho. SO17: South 3C **30**
Solent Av. SO19: South 5E **33**
SOLENT BREEZES 4D **50**
Solent Breezes Holiday Village
......................4C **50**
Solent Bus. Cen.
SO15: South 5F **29**
Solent Bus. Pk. PO15: White ...6H **45**
Solent Cl. SO53: Cha F 1G **15**
Solent Dr. SO31: Wars 3B **50**
SO45: Hythe 2D **52**
Solent Homes SO19: South 5E **33**
Solent Ind. Cen.
SO15: South 5G **29**
Solent Ind. Est.
SO30: Hed E 2H **33**
Solent Mdws. SO31: Hamb 6G **47**
Solent Rd.
SO15: South 4A **4** (1A **40**)
SO45: Dib P 6C **52**
Solent Sky Mus. 6H **5** (2D **40**)
Solent Way PO15: White 1G **49**
Solutions Sports Cen. ...2E **5** (6C **30**)
Solway Ho. *SO14: South 5E 31*
(off Kent St.)
Somborne Ct. *SO17: South 2C 30*
(off Westwood Rd.)
Somerford Cl. SO19: South 5A **32**
Somerset Av. SO18: South 4C **32**
Somerset Ct. SO15: South 5G **29**
Somerset Cres.
SO53: Cha F 4F **15**
Somerset Rd. SO17: South 1E **31**
Somerset Ter. SO15: South 5G **29**
Somers Way SO50: E'leigh 1H **23**
Somerton Av. SO18: South 4B **32**
Sommers Ct. SO19: South 2F **41**
Sopwith Rd. SO50: E'leigh 4H **15**
Sopwith Way SO31: Swanw 5C **44**
Sorrel Cl. SO31: Loc H 5D **48**
SO51: Rom 3F **7**
Sorrel Dr. PO15: White 6H **45**
SOUTHAMPTON 2D **4** (6B **30**)
Southampton Airport 3A **24**
Southampton Airport Parkway Station
(Rail) 3H **23**
Southampton Central Station
(Rail) 2B **4** (6A **30**)
SOUTHAMPTON CHILDREN'S
HOSPITAL *1F 29*
(within General Hospital)
Southampton City Art Gallery
..................1D **4** (6B **30**)
Southampton Crematorium 3D **22**
Southampton FC 2H **5** (6D **30**)
SOUTHAMPTON GENERAL
HOSPITAL 1F **29**
Southampton Golf Course 3A **22**
Southampton Outdoor Sports Cen.
...................5H **21**
Southampton Rd.
PO14: Titch 3G **49**
PO15: Seg 2F **49**
SO31: P Ga, Titch C 2F **49**
(not continuous)
SO45: Dib, Hythe 2C **52**
SO50: E'leigh 1A **24**
SO51: Rom 5C **6**
Southampton St Michael's Church
.....................5D **4**
Southampton Solent University
East Park Terace Campus
.................2E **5** (6C **30**)
Sir James Matthews Building
.................1D **4** (6B **30**)
Warsash Maritime Cen. 2A **50**
Southampton St.
SO15: South 5B **30**
Southampton Town Walls 5D **4**
Southampton Water Activities Cen.
...................2E **41**
South Av. SO45: F'ley 2E **55**
Southbourne Av. SO45: Holb ...4C **54**
Southbrook Rd.
SO15: South 2A **4** (6A **30**)
Southcliff Rd. SO14: South 4C **30**
South Cl. SO51: Rom 3F **7**
South Ct. SO15: South 3F **29**
SO31: Hamb 5E **47**
Southdale Ct. SO53: Cha F 1E **15**
Southdene Rd. SO53: Cha F 2E **15**
Southdown Rd. SO21: Shaw ...1D **10**
South East Cres.
SO19: South 1A **42**
South East Rd. SO19: South 1A **42**
Southern Gdns. SO40: Tott 4E **27**
Southern Rd.
SO15: South 3A **4** (1A **40**)
SO30: W End 3D **32**
South Front
SO14: South 3F **5** (1C **40**)
SO51: Rom 5C **6**
Sth. Hampshire Ind. Pk.
SO40: Tott 1D **26**
SOUTH HILL 3G **15**
South Hill SO16: Bass 5C **22**
Sth. Millers Dale SO53: Cha F ...6D **8**
South Mill Rd. SO15: South 4D **28**
South Pde. SO40: Tott 4F **27**
South Point SO31: Hamb 5E **47**
South Rd. SO17: South 3E **31**
SO40: March 3E **39**
Sth. Stoneham Ho.
SO18: S'ing 6F **23**
South St. SO45: Hythe 3E **53**
SO50: E'leigh 1A **24**
South Vw. Rd. SO15: South 3H **29**
Sth. Western Ho.
SO14: South 6G **5** (2D **40**)
Southwinds Ct. SO31: Sar G 2B **48**
Southwold Ho. SO31: P Ga 1F **49**
Southwood Gdns.
SO31: Loc H 4D **48**
Sovereign Cl. SO40: Tott 3C **26**
Sovereign Ct. SO17: South 2B **30**
SO50: E'leigh 5A **16**
Sovereign Cres.
PO14: Titch C 6E **49**
Sovereign Dr. SO30: Hed E 5B **34**
Sovereign Way SO50: E'leigh ...1H **15**
Sowden Cl. SO30: Hed E 4H **33**
Spalding Rd. SO19: South 6E **33**
Spa Rd. SO14: South ...4D **4** (1B **40**)
Sparrowgrove SO21: Ott 1C **10**
Sparrow Sq. SO50: E'leigh 5F **15**
Sparsholt Rd. SO19: South 5H **41**
Spear Rd. SO14: South 3C **30**
Speedwell Cl. SO31: Loc H 5D **48**
SO53: Cha F 2D **14**
Speggs Wlk. SO30: Hed E 5A **34**
Spence Cl. SO50: B'stke 2D **16**
Spencer Gdns. SO52: N Bad 2E **13**
Spencer Rd. SO19: South 5D **32**
SO50: E'leigh 5G **15**
Spenser Cl. SO31: Wars 1B **50**
Spicers Hill SO40: Tott 6E **27**
Spicers Way SO40: Tott 5E **27**
Spindlewood Cl. SO16: Bass ...3C **22**
Spindlewood Way
SO40: March 5D **38**
Spinnaker Ct. SO31: Net A 1B **46**
Spinnaker M. SO31: Wars 6B **48**
The Spinney SO16: Bass 3B **22**
SO40: Calm 2C **26**
SO50: B'stke 5G **17**
SO50: E'leigh 5A 16
(off Desborough Rd.)
Spinney Dale SO45: Hythe 4F **53**
Spinney Gdns. SO45: Hythe 4F **53**
Spinney Wlk. SO18: South 6H **23**
Spire Cl. PO14: Titch C 4G **49**
SPIRE SOUTHAMPTON
HOSPITAL 1G **29**
Spirit Health Club
Eastleigh 4G **15**
Southampton 5C **4** (2B **40**)
Spitfire Ct. SO19: South 2F **41**
Spitfire Loop SO18: S'ton A 2H **23**
Spitfire Quay SO19: South 1E **41**
Spitfire Way SO31: Hamb 5F **47**
Sportsman Pl. SO30: W End 2E **33**
Spring Cl. SO19: South 1H **41**
SO50: Fair O 1F **17**
Spring Ct.
SO15: South 1A **4** (6A **30**)
Spring Cres. SO17: South 3D **30**
Springdale Ct. SO40: Tott 4F **27**
Springfield SO31: Sar G 4B **48**
Springfield Av. SO45: Holb 4D **54**
Springfield Ct. SO19: South 3H **41**
Springfield Dr. SO40: Tott 5E **27**
Springfield Gro. SO45: Holb ...4D **54**
Springfields Cl. SO21: Col C 4F **11**
Spring Firs SO19: South 2H **41**
Springford Cl. SO16: South 5F **21**
Springford Cres.
SO16: South 6F **21**
Springford Gdns.
SO16: South 5F **21**
Springford Rd. SO16: South 6F **21**
Spring Gdns. SO30: Hed E 5B **34**
SO52: N Bad 2D **12**
Spring Gro. SO31: Burs 4G **43**
Springhill Rd. SO53: Cha F 1E **15**
Spring Hills SO19: South 6C **32**
Spring Ho. Cl. SO21: Col C 4G **11**
Spring La. SO21: Col C 4F **11**
SO50: B'stke 3D **16**
Spring Pl. SO51: Rom 5B **6**
Spring Rd. SO19: South 5H **31**
SO31: Sar G 1D **48**
SO45: Hythe 2E **53**
Spruce Cl. SO31: Wars 1B **50**
Spruce Dr. SO19: South 6E **33**
SO40: Tott 3B **26**
The Square SO31: Hamb 5G **47**
SO45: F'ley 2H **55**
SO50: Fair O 1F **17**
Squires Wlk. SO19: South 4G **41**
Squirrel Cl. SO31: P Ga 2G **49**
SO50: B'stke 5F **17**
Squirrel Dr. SO19: South 2A **42**
Squirrels Wlk. SO45: Dib P 4D **52**
Stable Cl. PO14: Titch C 5H **49**
Stableyard M. SO31: Sar G 2D **48**
Stafford Rd. SO15: South 4H **29**
Stagbrake Cl. SO45: Holb 5B **54**
Stag Cl. SO50: B'stke 5F **17**
Stag Dr. SO30: Hed E 3B **34**
Stag Gates SO45: Blac 4E **55**
Stainer Cl. SO19: South 2D **42**
Staith Cl. SO19: South 6C **32**
Stalybridge Cl. SO31: P Ga 1E **49**
Stamford Way SO50: Fair O 2F **17**
Stanbridge La. SO51: Rom 1A **6**
Standen Rd. SO16: Nur 4A **20**
Standford St.
SO14: South 4H **5** (1D **40**)
Stanford Ct. SO19: South 2D **42**
Stanier Way SO30: Hed E 6H **25**
Stanley Rd. SO17: South 2E **31**
SO40: Tott 2D **26**
SO45: Holb 4D **54**
Stannington Cres. SO40: Tott ...3F **27**
Stannington Way SO40: Tott 3F **27**
Stanstead Rd. SO50: E'leigh ...3H **15**
Stanton Rd. SO15: South 4D **28**
Stanton Rd. Ind. Est.
SO15: South 4E **29**
Stapleford Cl. SO51: Rom 3E **7**
Staplehurst Cl. SO19: South ...4B **42**
Staplewood La.
SO40: March 6H **37**
(not continuous)
Starling Sq. SO50: E'leigh 5F **15**
Station App. SO51: Rom 4C **6**
Station Hill SO30: Curd 4G **35**
SO31: Burs 6H **43**
SO32: Curd 4G **35**
Station La. SO53: Cha F 1E **15**
Station M. SO51: Rom 4C **6**
Station Rd.
SO15: South 3A **28**
SO16: Nur 4G **19**
Station Rd. SO19: South 3H **41**
SO31: Burs 5H **43**
SO31: Net A 2B **46**
SO31: P Ga 2E **49**
SO51: Rom 5B **6**
Station Rd. Nth. SO40: Tott 4H **27**
Station Rd. Sth. SO40: Tott 4H **27**
Steele Cl. SO53: Cha F 3F **15**
Steep Cl. SO18: South 3C **32**
Steeple Way PO14: Titch C 4H **49**
Steinbeck Cl. PO15: White 5G **45**
Stenbury Way SO31: Net A 6C **42**
Stephen Ct. SO45: Holb 5D **54**
Stephens Ct. SO51: Rom 6B **6**
Stephenson Rd. SO40: Tott 6D **18**
Stephenson Way
SO30: Hed E 6H **25**
Steuart Rd. SO18: South 4F **31**
Steventon Rd. SO18: South 4C **32**
Stewart Ho. SO53: Cha F 4E **9**
Stillmeadows SO31: Loc H 5E **49**
Stinchar Dr. SO53: Cha F 2C **14**
Stirling Cl. SO40: Tott 3G **27**
Stirling Cres. SO30: Hed E 2A **34**
SO40: Tott 3G **27**
Stirling Wlk. SO51: Rom 5B **6**
Stockbridge Rd. SO51: Tims 1B **6**
Stockholm Dr. SO30: Hed E 6A **34**
Stocklands SO40: Calm 1C **26**
Stockley Cl. SO45: Holb 5C **54**
Stockton Cl. SO30: Hed E 4B **34**
Stoddart Av. SO19: South 5H **31**
STOKE COMMON 2E **17**
Stoke Comn. Rd.
SO50: B'stke 2E **17**
Stoke Hgts. SO50: Fair O 4H **17**
STOKE PARK 5F **17**
Stoke Pk. Dr. SO50: B'stke 3D **16**
Stoke Pk. Rd. SO50: B'stke 3D **16**
Stoke Rd. SO16: South 2E **29**
Stokesay Cl. SO45: Hythe 6E **53**
Stokes Ct. *SO15: South 5A 30*
(off Archers Rd.)
Stoke Wood Cl. SO50: Fair O ...5H **17**
Stonechat Dr. SO40: Tott 3B **26**
Stonecrop Cl. SO31: Loc H 5D **48**
Stoneham Cemetery Rd.
SO18: S'ing 5H **23**
Stoneham Cl. SO16: S'ing 4F **23**
Stoneham Ct. SO16: Bass 4D **22**
Stoneham Gdns. SO31: Burs 4F **43**
Stoneham Golf Course 3D **22**
Stoneham La. SO16: S'ing 4F **23**
SO50: E'leigh 6G **15**
Stoneham Way SO16: S'ing 5F **23**
STONEHILLS 2H **55**
Stone Ter. SO21: Ott 4A **10**
Stoney Croft Rise
SO53: Cha F 5E **15**
Stonymoor Cl. SO45: Holb 5C **54**
Stour Cl. SO18: W End 6B **24**
Stourvale Gdns.
SO53: Cha F 2F **15**
Stowe Cl. SO30: Hed E 2B **34**
Stragwyne Cl. SO52: N Bad 2D **12**
Straight Mile SO51: Ampf 3G **7**
Stranding St. SO50: E'leigh 4H **15**
Strategic Pk. SO30: Hed E 4F **33**
Stratfield Dr. SO53: Cha F 4D **8**
Stratford Ct. SO16: Bass 4C **22**
Stratford Pl. SO50: E'leigh 3B **16**
Stratton Rd. SO15: South 2G **29**
Strawberry Flds.
SO30: Hed E 5G **33**
Strawberry Hill SO31: Loc H ...4D **48**
Strawberry Mead
SO50: Fair O 6G **17**
Streamleaze PO14: Titch C 5G **49**
Street End SO52: N Bad 2F **13**
Strides Way SO40: Tott 4B **26**
Strongs Cl. SO51: Rom 4E **7**
Stroudley Way SO30: Hed E 1B **34**
Stuart Bridgewater Ho.
SO18: South 4A **32**
Stubbington Way
SO50: Fair O 1G **17**
Stubbs Drove SO30: Hed E 4B **34**
Stubbs Rd. SO19: South 3C **42**
Studland Cl. SO16: South 2B **28**
Studland Rd. SO16: South 3B **28**
Studley Av. SO45: Holb 4C **54**
Sturminster Ho. SO16: South ...2E **29**
Suffolk Av. SO15: South 4H **29**
Suffolk Cl. SO53: Cha F 5E **15**
Suffolk Dr. PO15: White 6F **45**
SO53: Cha F 4E **15**
Suffolk Grn. SO53: Cha F 5E **15**

76 A-Z Southampton

Sullivan Rd. SO19: South 1D 42
Summerfield Gdns.
 SO16: S'ing 4F 23
Summerfields SO31: Loc H ...6F 49
Summerlands Rd.
 SO50: Fair O 1F 17
Summers St. SO14: South ...5E 31
Summit Way SO18: South ...2H 31
Sundowner
 SO14: South 6H 5 (2D 40)
Sunningdale SO45: Hythe ...3D 52
Sunningdale Cl. SO50: B'stke ..5F 17
Sunningdale Gdns.
 SO18: South 4B 32
Sunningdale Mobile Home Pk.
 SO21: Col C 4F 11
Sunnydale Farm Camping &
 Cvn. Site 5C 42
Sunnyfield Ri. SO31: Burs ...4G 43
Sunnyside SO31: Loc H 4G 49
Sunny Way SO40: Tott 4F 27
Sunset Av. SO40: Tott 3E 27
Sunset Rd. SO40: Tott 3E 27
Sunvale Cl. SO19: South 2B 42
Surbiton Rd. SO50: E'leigh ..2B 16
Surrey Cl. SO40: Tott 6D 26
Surrey Ct. SO15: South 5G 29
 SO53: Cha F 4F 15
Surrey Point SO16: Bass 6A 22
Surrey Rd. SO19: South 3F 41
 SO53: Cha F 4E 15
SUSSEX PLACE 3D 4 (1C 40)
Sussex Rd.
 SO14: South 3E 5 (6C 30)
 SO53: Cha F 4F 15
Sutherland Cl. SO51: Rom 3E 7
Sutherland Rd. SO16: South ..4D 20
Sutherlands Ct. SO53: Cha F ..1E 15
Sutherlands Way
 SO53: Cha F 6D 8
Suttones Pl. SO15: South ...4B 30
Sutton Rd. SO40: Tott 2E 27
Swale Dr. SO53: Cha F 6C 8
Swallow Cl. SO40: Tott 5C 26
Swallow Sq. SO50: E'leigh ..5F 15
Swanage Cl. SO19: South 1G 41
The Swan Cen. SO50: E'leigh ..5B 16
Swan Cl. SO31: Lwr Swan ...6B 44
Swanley Cl. SO50: E'leigh ...2A 16
Swanmore Av. SO19: South ..2B 42
Swan Quay SO18: South 3F 31
Swanton Gdns. SO53: Cha F ..6D 8
SWANWICK 6F 45
Swanwick Bus. Cen.
 SO31: Lwr Swan 6B 44
SWANWICK HILL 1G 49
Swanwick Lakes Nature Reserve
 ....4D 44
Swanwick La.
 SO31: Lwr Swan, Swanw
 ....5A 44
Swanwick Shore
 SO31: Lwr Swan 6A 44
Swanwick Shore Rd.
 SO31: Lwr Swan 6B 44
Swanwick Station (Rail) 1F 49
SWAYTHLING 5F 23
Swaythling Rd. SO18: W End ..6B 24
 SO30: W End 1C 32
Swaythling Station (Rail) 5F 23
Sweethills Cres.
 PO15: White 5F 45
Swift Cl. SO50: E'leigh 5F 15
Swift Gdns. SO19: South 4F 41
Swift Hollow SO19: South ...4F 41
Swift Rd. SO19: South 4F 41
 (not continuous)
Swincombe Ri. SO18: W End ..2B 32
Swithuns Ct. SO16: Nur 3H 19
Sycamore Av. SO53: Cha F ...4E 9
Sycamore Cl. PO14: Titch C ..6G 49
 SO31: Burs 5F 43
 SO51: Rom 6F 7
 SO52: N Bad 2D 12
Sycamore Ct. SO16: South ...1F 29
Sycamore Dr. SO45: Holb 3B 54
Sycamore Rd. SO16: South ...1E 29
 SO45: Hythe 3D 52
The Sycamores SO45: Hythe ..2E 53
Sycamore Wlk. SO30: Botl ...4E 35
Sydmanton Cl. SO51: Rom ...6D 6
Sydney Av. SO31: Hamb 4E 47
Sydney Rd. SO15: South 2F 29
 SO50: B'stke 3D 16
Sylvan Av. SO19: South 5C 32
Sylvan Ct. SO31: Sar G 3E 49
Sylvan Dr. SO52: N Bad 3D 12

Sylvan La. SO31: Hamb 6G 47
The Sylvans SO45: Dib P 3B 52
Sylvia Cres. SO40: Tott 2E 27
Symes Rd. SO51: Rom 5E 7
Symonds Cl. SO53: Cha F ...3F 15
Symphony Cl. SO31: Loc H ...4C 48

T

Tadburn Cl. SO51: Rom 5D 6
 SO53: Cha F 2F 15
Tadburn Grn. SO51: Rom 6B 6
Tadburn Meadows
 Local Nature Reserve 4E 7
Tadburn Rd. SO51: Rom 5D 6
Tadfield Cres. SO51: Rom 5D 6
Tadfield Rd. SO51: Rom 5D 6
Talbot Cl. SO16: Bass 5B 22
Talbot Ct.
 SO14: South 6E 5 (2C 40)
Talbot Rd. SO45: Dib P 5B 52
Talisman Bus. Cen.
 SO31: P Ga 1F 49
Talland Rd. PO14: Titch C ...6F 49
Tamar Cl. SO31: W End 1B 32
Tamar Gro. SO45: Hythe 3C 52
Tamarisk Gdns. SO18: South ..3G 31
Tamarisk Rd. SO30: Hed E ...4H 33
Tamella Rd. SO30: Botl 5C 34
Tamorisk Dr. SO40: Tott 5C 26
Tanglewood SO40: March 4E 39
Tangmere Dr. SO16: South ...5D 20
Tangmere Ri. SO53: Cha F ...3F 15
Tanhouse Cl. SO30: Hed E ...6B 34
Tanhouse La.
 SO30: Botl, Hed E 6B 34
 (not continuous)
Tankerville Rd. SO19: South ..2F 41
The Tanners PO14: Titch C ...1G 51
Tanner's Brook Way
 SO15: South 5D 28
Tanner's Cl. SO16: South 5F 21
Tanners Rd. SO52: N Bad 4E 13
Tansy Mdw. SO53: Cha F 3B 14
The Tanyards SO14: South 4D 8
Taplin Dr. SO30: Hed E 3A 34
Taranto Rd. SO16: South 5G 21
Tarver Cl. SO51: Rom 2E 7
Tasman Cl. SO14: South 3D 40
Tasman Ct. SO14: South 3D 40
Tatchbury La. SO40: Wins ...3A 26
Tatchbury Mount Hill Fort ...2A 26
TATCHBURY MOUNT HOSPITAL
 ....1A 26
Tate Cl. SO51: Rom 1E 7
Tate Ct. SO15: South 3A 28
Tate M. SO15: South 3A 28
Tate Rd. SO15: South 3A 28
Tates Rd. SO45: Hythe 3F 53
 (not continuous)
Tatwin Cl. SO19: South 6D 32
Tatwin Cres. SO19: South ...6D 32
Taunton Dr. SO18: South 4B 32
Tavells Cl. SO40: March 4C 38
Tavells La. SO40: March 4B 38
Taverner Cl. SO19: South ...2D 42
Tavistock Cl. SO51: Rom 3E 7
Tavistock Rd. SO16: South ...1D 28
Tavy Cl. SO53: Cha F 1D 14
Taylor Cl. SO19: South 4F 41
Teachers Way SO45: Holb 4B 54
Teal Cl. SO40: Tott 4C 26
TeamSport Indoor Karting
 Eastleigh 4B 16
Tebourba Way SO16: South ..4C 28
 SO30: Curd 4H 35
Ted Bates Ct. SO15: South ...5A 30
Ted Bates Rd.
 SO14: South 5H 5 (2D 40)
Tedder Rd. SO18: South 3A 32
Tedder Way SO40: Tott 4D 26
Tees Cl. SO53: Cha F 6C 8
Tees Farm Rd. SO21: Col C ..5F 11
Tees Grn. SO21: Col C 5F 11
Telegraph Rd. SO30: W End ..3E 33
Telegraphy Hgts.
 SO30: W End 2E 33
Telford Gdns. SO30: Hed E ...1B 34
Telford Way PO15: Seg 2G 49
Teme Cres. SO16: South 2C 28
Teme Rd. SO16: South 2C 28
Templars Mede SO53: Cha F ..4D 14
Templars Way SO53: Cha F ...3B 14
Templecombe Rd.
 SO50: B'stke 6F 17

Temple Gdns. SO19: South ...3H 41
Temple Rd. SO19: South 3H 41
Tenby Cl. SO18: South 3A 32
Tenby Ct. SO14: South 3C 14
Tench Way SO51: Rom 4C 6
Tennyson Cl. SO45: Holb 3B 54
Tennyson Ct. SO17: South ...2C 30
Tennyson Rd. SO17: South ...3D 30
 SO40: Tott 1D 26
 SO50: E'leigh 6H 15
Tenpin Bowling
 Southampton 4D 28
Tenterton Av. SO19: South ...4B 42
Terminus Ter.
 SO14: South 6F 5 (2D 40)
 (not continuous)
Tern Cl. SO45: Hythe 4F 53
The Terrace SO21: Ott 1B 10
Terrier Cl. SO30: Hed E 6H 25
Terriote Cl. SO53: Cha F 6E 9
Testbourne Av. SO40: Tott ...4D 26
Testbourne Cl. SO40: Tott ...4D 26
Testbourne Rd. SO40: Tott ...4D 26
Testlands Av. SO16: Nur 3B 20
Test La. SO16: South 6H 19
Test Mill SO51: Rom 4A 6
Test Rd. SO14: South 4C 40
Test Valley Bus. Cen.
 SO16: South 1H 27
Test Valley Bus. Pk.
 SO52: N Bad 2E 13
TESTWOOD 2E 27
Testwood Av. SO40: Tott 2E 27
Testwood Cres. SO40: Tott ...1D 26
Testwood La. SO40: Tott 3F 27
Testwood Pl. SO40: Tott 3G 27
Testwood Rd. SO15: South ...5F 29
Testwood Stadium 6D 18
Tetney Cl. SO16: South 6C 20
Teviot Ho. SO14: South 5E 31
 (off York Cl.)
Teviot Rd. SO53: Cha F 2C 14
Thackeray Rd. SO17: South ...3D 30
Thacking Grn. SO21: Col C ...5F 11
Thames Cl. SO18: W End 6B 24
Theo Ho. SO31: P Ga 2F 49
Thetford Gdns. SO53: Cha F ..5C 8
The Thicket SO51: Rom 6F 7
Third Av. SO15: South 4C 28
Thirlmere SO50: E'leigh 5H 15
Thirlmere Rd. SO16: South ...1C 28
Thirlstane Firs SO53: Cha F ...3D 14
Thistle Rd. SO30: Hed E 5H 33
 SO53: Cha F 2B 14
Thomas Cl. SO40: Tott 5D 26
Thomas Lewis Way
 SO14: South 3D 30
 SO16: S'ing 2E 31
 SO17: South 2E 31
Thomas Rd. SO52: N Bad ...3E 13
Thornbury Av. SO15: South ..4A 30
 SO45: Blac 5E 55
Thornbury Hgts. SO53: Cha F ..4H 9
Thornbury Wood
 SO53: Cha F 4H 9
Thorn Cl. SO50: E'leigh 2A 16
Thorndike Cl. SO16: South ...1E 29
Thorndike Rd. SO16: South ...1D 28
Thorners Ct. SO15: South 5B 30
Thorner's Homes
 SO15: South 3F 29
Thorness Cl. SO16: South 6D 32
THORNHILL 6D 32
Thornhill Av. SO19: South ...5D 32
Thornhill Cl. SO45: F'ley 3F 55
Thornhill Homes
 SO19: South 6D 32
 (off Tatwin Cl.)
THORNHILL PARK 4D 32
Thornhill Pk. Rd.
 SO18: South 4D 32
Thornhill Rd. SO16: South ...5H 21
 SO45: F'ley 3F 55
Thornleigh Rd. SO19: South ..3G 41
Thornton Av. SO31: Wars 6A 48
Thornycroft Av. SO19: South ..3F 41
Thorold Cl. SO18: South 2G 31
Thorold Rd. SO18: South 3G 31
 SO53: Cha F 4G 9
Threefield La.
 SO14: South 5F 5 (2C 40)
Three Oaks SO19: South 6E 33
Thruxton Cl. SO19: South 6G 31
Thurmell Cl. SO30: Hed E ...1A 44
Thurmell Wlk. SO30: Hed E ...1A 44
Thurston Cl. SO53: Cha F 6F 9
Thyme Av. PO15: White 5H 45

Tichborne Rd. SO18: South ...3D 32
 SO50: E'leigh 1H 23
Tickleford Dr. SO19: South ...5A 42
Tickner Cl. SO30: Botl 6C 34
Ticonderoga Gdns.
 SO19: South 4G 41
Tides Reach SO18: South 3F 31
Tilbrook Rd. SO15: South 3E 29
Tillingbourn PO14: Titch C ...4G 49
Timberley Cl. SO45: Holb 4C 54
Timor Cl. PO15: White 5F 45
Timsbury Dr. SO16: South ...2D 28
Timson Cl. SO40: Tott 5C 26
Tindale Rd. SO16: South 1C 28
Tinker All. SO18: S'ton A 2A 24
Tinning Way SO50: E'leigh ...4G 15
Tintagel Cl. SO16: South 3G 21
Tintern Gro.
 SO15: South 1A 4 (6A 30)
Tiptree Cl. SO50: E'leigh 2A 16
Titanic Engineers Memorial
 ....1D 4 (6C 30)
Titchbourne Ho.
 SO30: Hed E 4A 34
TITCHFIELD COMMON 6G 49
TITCHFIELD PARK 4H 49
Titchfield Pk. Rd.
 PO15: Seg 4H 49
Tithe Mead SO51: Rom 3C 6
Tithewood Cl. SO53: Cha F ...3D 8
Tivoli Cl. SO31: Sar G 6H 9
Tolefrey Gdns. SO53: Cha F ..1B 14
Tollbar Way SO30: Hed E 2G 33
Tollgate SO53: Cha F 5E 15
Tollgate Rd.
 SO31: Lwr Swan 5B 44
Tomkyns Cl. SO53: Cha F 1B 14
Tommy Grn. Wlk.
 SO50: E'leigh 4H 15
Toogoods Way SO16: Nur 4B 20
Toomer Cl. SO45: F'ley 3F 55
Toothill Rd. SO51: Toot 6A 12
Topiary Gdns. SO31: Loc H ...3F 49
Torch Cl. SO50: B'stke 5H 17
Torcross Cl. SO19: South 3G 41
Tormead SO45: Hythe 3D 52
Tornay Gro. SO52: N Bad 3D 12
Toronto Ct. SO16: South 3D 28
Torquay Av. SO15: South 3H 29
Torque Cl. SO19: South 1E 43
Torre Cl. SO50: E'leigh 1A 16
Torridge Gdns. SO18: W End ..6B 24
Torrington Cl. SO19: South ...1A 42
Torwood Gdns. SO50: B'stke ..5F 17
Tosson Cl. SO16: South 3C 28
Totland Cl. SO16: South 3C 28
Totnes Cl. SO50: E'leigh 2H 15
Tottehale Cl. SO52: N Bad ...4D 12
TOTTON 4F 27
Totton & Eling Bowls Cen. ...4B 26
Totton & Eling Heritage Cen.
 ....5H 27
Totton & Eling Tennis Cen. ..4B 26
Totton By-Pass SO40: Tott ...5F 27
Totton Health & Leisure Cen.
 ....3D 26
Totton Station (Rail) 4G 27
Totton Western By-Pass
 SO51: Ower 4A 18
Tourist Info. Cen.
 Southampton 1D 4 (6B 30)
Tower Ct. SO31: Wars 6A 48
Tower Gdns. SO16: Bass 5B 22
Tower Ho. SO19: South 3G 41
Tower La. SO50: E'leigh 5C 16
Tower La. Ind. Est.
 SO50: E'leigh 6C 16
Tower Pl. SO30: W End 2D 32
Tower Rd. SO19: South 2A 46
Townhill Farm District Cen.
 SO18: W End 1B 32
TOWNHILL PARK 1B 32
Townhill Way SO18: W End ...6B 24
Town Quay
 SO14: South 6D 4 (2B 40)
Town Wall
 Southampton 5D 4
Toynbee Cl. SO50: E'leigh ...4A 16
Toynbee Rd. SO50: E'leigh ...4A 16
Trafalgar Cl. SO53: Cha F ...2D 14
Trafalgar Rd. SO15: South ...5G 29
Trafalgar Way SO15: South ...5F 53
Trafford Rd. SO50: Fair O ...6H 17
Tranby Rd. SO19: South 1G 41
Treagore Rd. SO40: Calm ...2C 26

Trearnan Cl. SO16: South 3D 28
Treeside Av. SO40: Tott 4G 27
Treeside Rd. SO15: South 3G 29
Treloyhan Cl. SO53: Cha F 3F 15
Tremona Cl. SO16: South 1F 29
Tremona Rd. SO16: South 6F 21
Trenley Cl. SO45: Holb 5C 54
Trent Ho. SO14: South 6E 31
Trent Rd. SO18: South 2H 31
Trent Way SO30: W End 1D 32
Tresillian Gdns.
　　SO18: W End 1B 32
Trevone Cl. SO16: South 6E 27
Trevose Cl. SO53: Cha F 3F 15
Trevose Cres. SO53: Cha F 2F 15
Trevose Way PO14: Titch C 6F 49
The Triangle SO18: South 2F 31
Triangle Gdns. SO16: Nur 6B 20
Triangle La. PO14: Titch 5H 51
Trident Bus. Pk.
　　SO45: Hythe 2F 53
Trimaran Rd. SO31: Wars 6C 48
Trinity Cl. SO15: South 5G 29
　　SO21: Col C 5H 11
　　SO40: March 3D 38
　　SO40: Tott 1E 27
　　SO53: Cha F 1F 15
Trinity Ind. Est. SO15: South 4D 28
Trinity Rd.
　　SO14: South 1F 5 (6C 30)
Tripps End Cvn. Site 4B 34
Tristram Cl. SO53: Cha F 3B 14
The Triton Cen. SO51: Rom 2B 12
TROTTS 2H 37
Trotts La. SO40: March 1A 38
Trowbridge Cl. SO16: Rown 4C 20
Truro Ri. SO50: B'stke 4E 17
Tudor Cl. SO40: Calm 3C 26
Tudor Gdns. SO30: Hed E 6G 33
Tudor House & Gardens
　　. . . . . .5D 4 (2B 40)
Tudor Wood Cl. SO16: Bass 5B 22
Tuffin Cl. SO16: Nur 4A 20
Tulip Gdns. SO31: Loc H 4D 48
Tulip Rd. SO16: Bass 5E 23
Tumulus Cl. SO19: South 1E 43
Tunstall Rd. SO19: South 1E 43
Tunstall Rd. SO19: South 1E 43
Turner Sims Concert Hall 6C 22
Turners Oak Ct. SO15: South 2G 29
Turnpike Way SO30: Hed E 3H 33
Turnstone Gdns. SO16: South 4F 21
Tuscan Wlk. SO53: Cha F 1G 15
The Tussocks SO40: March 3D 38
Tutland Rd. SO52: N Bad 3D 12
Tutor Cl. SO31: Hamb 4F 47
Tweed Cl. SO53: Cha F 6C 8
Twiggs End Cl. SO31: Loc H 3D 48
Twiggs La. SO40: March 6B 38
Twin Oaks SO30: Botl 4E 35
Twyford Av. SO15: South 2G 29
Twyford Ho. SO15: South 4B 30
Twyford Rd. SO50: E'leigh 4B 16
Twynham Way SO50: B'stke 3D 16
The Tyleshades SO51: Rom 6D 6
Tyne Cl. SO53: Cha F 2C 14
Tyne Way SO30: W End 1E 33
Tyrrel Rd. SO53: Cha F 6E 9
Tytherley Rd. SO18: South 3C 32

U

Ullswater SO50: E'leigh 6A 16
Ullswater Av. SO18: W End 2B 32
Ullswater Rd. SO16: South 2C 28
Undercliff Gdns. SO16: Bass 5A 22
Underwood Cl. SO16: Bass 5A 22
Underwood Rd. SO16: Bass 5A 22
　　SO50: B'stke 3D 16
Union Pl. SO15: South 5H 29
Union Rd. SO14: South 5E 31
Unity Ct. SO50: E'leigh 5B 16
Universal Marina
　　SO31: Sar G 1A 48
University Cres.
　　SO17: South 6D 22
University of Southampton
　　Avenue Campus 1C 30
　　Highfield Campus 6C 22
　　Maritime Centre of Excellence
　　 . . . . .5B 22
　　National Oceanography Cen.
　　 . . . . .4D 40

University of Southampton
　　Sports Ground 2H 23
University Parkway
　　SO16: Chil 6G 13
University Rd. SO17: South 5D 22
Unwin Cl. SO19: South 4F 41
Uplands Way SO17: South 1C 30
Upmill Cl. SO30: W End 6B 24
Up. Banister St.
　　SO15: South 5B 30
Up. Barn Copse
　　SO50: Fair O 4H 17
Up. Brook Dr. SO31: Loc H 5C 48
Up. Brownhill Rd.
　　SO16: South 6D 20
Up. Bugle St.
　　SO14: South 5D 4 (2B 40)
Up. Crescent Rd.
　　SO52: N Bad 2D 12
Up. Deacon Rd.
　　SO18: South 5B 32
Upper Mkt. St. SO14: South 4B 16
Up. Mead Cl. SO50: Fair O 1G 17
Up. Moors Rd. SO50: B'dge 5F 11
Up. Mullins La.
　　SO45: Hythe 3C 52
Up. New Rd. SO30: W End 2D 32
Up. Northam Cl.
　　SO30: Hed E 5G 33
Up. Northam Dr.
　　SO30: Hed E 5E 33
Up. Northam Rd.
　　SO30: Hed E 4G 33
Up. St Helens Rd.
　　SO30: Hed E 1H 43
Up. Shaftesbury Av.
　　SO17: South 1D 30
UPPER SHIRLEY 1H 29
Up. Shirley Av. SO15: South 2G 29
Upper Spinney SO31: Wars 1A 50
Up. Toothill Rd. SO16: Rown 6C 12
Up. Weston La. SO19: South 3A 42
UPTON 3A 20
Upton Cres. SO16: Nur 2B 20
Upton Ho. SO16: South 2D 28
Upton La. SO16: Nur 4G 19
Uxbridge Cl. SO31: Sar G 1D 48

V

The Vale SO31: Loc H 5F 49
　　SO45: Hythe 3D 52
Vale Dr. SO18: South 2H 31
Valentine Av. SO19: South 2C 42
Valentine Ct. SO19: South 2C 42
Valerian Rd. SO30: Hed E 5A 34
Valley Cl. SO21: Col C 5F 11
　　SO45: Blac 4F 55
Valleydene SO45: Dib P 4D 52
Valley Ri. SO31: Sar G 3C 48
Valley Rd. SO40: Tott 6F 27
　　SO53: Cha F 6E 9
Vanburgh Ho. SO30: Hed E 3B 34
Vanburgh Way SO53: Cha F 4D 8
Vanguard Rd. SO18: South 3A 32
Vardy Cl. SO19: South 2D 42
Varna Rd. SO15: South 6G 29
Vaudrey Cl. SO15: South 2G 29
Vaughan Cl. SO19: South 6E 33
Vaughan Rd. SO45: Dib 2A 52
Veals La. SO40: March 6E 39
Vear's La. SO21: Col C 5G 11
Vectis Ct. SO16: Bass 5B 22
Vellan Ct. SO16: South 2B 28
Velmore Rd. SO53: Cha F 3D 14
Velsheda Ct. SO45: Hythe 1E 53
Ventnor Ct. SO16: Bass 4E 23
Venture Rd. SO16: Chil 6H 13
Verbena Way SO30: Hed E 5B 34
Verdon Av. SO31: Hamb 4E 47
Verger Cl. PO14: Titch C 4G 49
Vermont Cl. SO16: Bass 5B 22
Verne Cl. PO15: White 4F 45
Vernon Wlk. *SO15: South* 4D 30
　　　　　　　 (off Winchester St.)
Verona Rd. SO53: Cha F 6G 9
Verulam Rd. SO14: South 4D 30
Vespasian Ct. SO18: South 4E 31
Vespasian Quay
　　SO18: South 3E 31
Vespasian Rd. SO18: South 4F 31
Vespasian Way SO53: Cha F . . .1G 15
Vesta Way SO53: Cha F 6G 9
Vicarage Dr. SO30: Hed E 6H 33

Vicarage La. SO32: Curd 4G 35
Vicarage Rd. SO40: March 4D 38
Viceroy Rd. SO19: South 2A 42
Victena Rd. SO50: Fair O 1F 17
Victor Ct. SO18: South 5D 32
Victoria Cl. SO31: Loc H 6E 49
Victoria Glade SO31: Net A 2C 46
Victoria Lodge SO17: South 2D 30
Victoria M. SO31: Net A 2B 46
Victoria Pl. *SO51: Rom* 5B 6
　　　　　　　　 (off Love La.)
Victoria Rd. SO19: South 4F 41
　　SO31: Net A 1A 46
　　SO50: E'leigh 2B 16
Victoria St.
　　SO14: South 2H 5 (6E 31)
Victoria Wlk. SO30: W End 1E 33
Victor St. SO15: South 2F 29
Victory Cl. SO53: Cha F 2D 14
Victory Cres. SO15: South 4F 29
Victory Rd. SO15: South 5F 29
Victory Sq. SO15: South 5F 29
Victory Way SO16: Rown 2C 20
Viking Cl. SO16: South 5C 20
　　SO45: Blac 4F 55
The Vikings *SO51: Rom* 5F 7
Village M. SO40: March 4D 38
Villeneuve St.
　　SO50: E'leigh 4G 15
Villiers Rd. SO15: South 4G 29
　　SO45: Dib P 6D 52
Vincent Av. SO15: South 3G 29
Vincent's Gro. SO15: South 3F 29
Vincent St. SO15: South 3G 29
Vincent's Wlk.
　　SO14: South 4E 5 (1C 40)
Vine Bank SO18: South 3C 32
Vine Cl. SO31: Sar G 4B 48
Vine Rd. SO16: South 6E 21
Vinery Gdns. SO16: South 1G 29
Vinery Rd. SO16: South 1G 29
Vineyard Cl. SO19: South 2F 41
The Vineyards *SO52: N Bad* . . .3E 13
Viney Av. SO51: Rom 4E 7
Violet Cl. SO53: Cha F 1C 14
Violet Rd. SO16: Bass 5C 22
Viscount Gdns.
　　SO50: E'leigh 1H 23
Vixen Cl. SO40: A'hst 1C 36
Vokes Cl. SO19: South 6B 32
The Vokes Memorial Gdns. 3C 40
Vosper Rd. SO19: South 3F 41
VT House SO30: Hed E 3B 34
Vue Cinema
　　Eastleigh 5B 16
Vulcan Cl. SO53: Cha F 4D 28
Vulcan Rd. SO15: South 4D 28
Vyse La.
　　SO14: South 6D 4 (2B 40)

W

Wade Hill Drove SO40: Calm 5A 18
　　　　　　　　 (not continuous)
Wades Cres. SO16: Nur 5B 20
Wadham Cl. SO51: Rom 1E 7
Wadhurst Gdns.
　　SO19: South 5A 42
Wadhurst Rd. SO30: Hed E 5A 34
Wadmore Cl. SO45: Hythe 2F 53
Wagtail Cl. SO50: E'leigh 5F 15
Wainwright Gdns.
　　SO30: Hed E 6H 25
Wakefield Ct. SO18: South 2A 32
Wakefield Rd. SO18: South 2A 32
Wakeford Cl. SO51: Rom 5C 6
Wakeford Pl. SO31: Wars 6E 49
Waldegrave Cl.
　　SO19: South 5A 42
Waldon Gdns. SO18: W End 1B 32
Walker Gdns. SO30: Hed E 2A 34
Walker Pl. SO31: Hamb 5F 47
Walker Rd. SO50: Fair O 1G 17
Walker's La. Nth.
　　SO45: Blac 4E 55
Walker's La. Sth.
　　SO45: Blac 6F 55
Wallace Rd. SO19: South 4H 41
Wallington Dr. SO53: Cha F 5D 8
Walmer Cl. SO50: E'leigh 6A 10
Walnut Av. SO18: S'ing 4G 23
Walnut Cl. SO16: South 2D 28
　　SO53: Cha F 3E 9

Walnut Gro. SO16: South 3D 28
Walnut Way SO16: Nur 4B 20
Walpole La.
　　SO31: Lwr Swan 5C 44
Walsingham Gdns.
　　SO18: South 6H 23
Waltham Cres. SO16: South 5F 21
Walton Rd. SO19: South 1D 42
Waltons Av. SO45: Holb 4C 54
Wangfield La. SO32: Curd 2F 35
Wansbeck Cl. SO53: Cha F 2D 14
Warbler Cl. SO16: South 3F 21
Warblington Cl.
　　SO53: Cha F 4C 14
Warburton Cl. SO19: South 1E 43
Warburton Rd. SO19: South 6E 33
Warden Cl. SO30: W End 2D 32
Wardle Rd. SO50: Highb 6D 10
Warlock Cl. SO31: Hamb 2D 42
Warner Cl. SO30: Hed E 1A 34
Warner M. SO30: Botl 4E 35
Warnford Ct. SO15: South 4B 30
The Warren SO45: Holb 3B 54
Warren Av. SO16: South 1E 29
　　SO53: Cha F 2G 15
Warren Cl. SO16: South 1E 29
　　SO53: Cha F 2G 15
Warren Cres. SO16: South 1E 29
Warren Gdns. SO51: Rom 3E 7
Warren Pl. SO40: Calm 1C 26
Warrior Cl. SO53: Cha F 3D 14
Warrior Pk. Ind. Est.
　　SO53: Cha F 3D 14
Warrys Cl. SO45: Hythe 6E 53
WARSASH 6B 48
Warsash Ct. SO31: Wars 6A 48
Warsash Rd.
　　PO14: Titch, Titch C 1H 51
　　SO31: Loc H, Wars 6B 48
　　　　　　　　 (not continuous)
Warwick Cl. SO53: Cha F 3C 14
Warwick Ho. *SO14: South* 5E 31
　　　　　　　　 (off Kent St.)
Warwick Rd. SO15: South 1H 29
　　SO40: Tott 3F 27
Waterbeech Dr. SO30: Hed E . . .3A 34
Waterhouse La. SO15: South 4F 29
Waterhouse Way
　　SO15: South 4F 29
Water La.
　　SO15: South 1C 4 (6B 30)
　　SO40: Tott 3D 26
　　SO45: Dib P 4C 52
　　SO53: B'stke 2C 16
Waterloo Ind. Est.
　　SO30: Hed E 2H 33
Waterloo Rd.
　　SO15: South 1A 4 (5G 29)
Waterloo Ter. SO15: South 5B 30
Watermans La. SO45: Dib P 5C 52
Watermark SO45: Hythe 2D 52
Waters Edge SO30: Hed E 5H 33
Waterside SO45: Hythe 1D 52
The Waterside Heritage Cen.
　　 . . . . .2F 53
Waterside Rd. SO51: Rom 3D 6
Waterside Sq. SO45: Hythe 1D 52
Waterside Theatre & Club 3C 54
Waterworks Rd. SO21: Ott 1C 10
Watkin Rd. SO30: Hed E 1B 34
Watley Cl. SO16: Nur 4B 20
Watley La. SO21: Twy 1H 11
Watson Cl. SO30: Hed E 6A 34
　　SO31: Net A 6C 42
Watson Wlk. SO14: South 4C 26
Watton Rd. SO45: Holb 4C 54
Watts Cl. SO15: South 1C 40
Watt's Monument 1D 4 (6B 30)
Watts Rd. SO30: Hed E 4A 34
Wavecrest Cl. SO40: March 2E 39
Wavell Rd. SO18: South 4A 32
Waveney Grn. SO16: South 2C 28
Waverley Av. SO31: Net A 2C 46
Waverley Ct. SO31: Net A 2C 46
Waverley Rd. SO15: South 6H 29
Wayfarer Cl. SO31: Wars 6D 48
Waylands Pl. SO30: Hed E 1H 43
Wayside SO31: Lwr Swan 5B 44
Weald Cl. SO31: Loc H 3E 49
Weardale Rd. SO53: Cha F 3F 15
Weavers Pl. SO53: Cha F 4D 8
Weavills Rd. SO50: B'stke 5G 17
Webburn Gdns.
　　SO18: W End 6A 24

Wedgewood Cl. SO45: Holb 4C 54
Welbeck Av. SO17: South 1D 30
Welch Way SO16: Rown 4D 20
Welland Gdns.
 SO18: W End 1B 32
Welland Grn. SO16: South 3C 28
Wellbrooke Gdns.
 SO53: Cha F 6D 8
Wellers Cl. SO40: Tott 4B 26
Welles Rd. SO53: Cha F 1F 15
Wellington Av. SO18: South . . .4B 32
Wellington Cl. SO45: Dib P . . .5B 52
Wellington Ct. SO15: South . . .5H 29
 SO30: W End 1C 32
Wellington Pk. SO30: Hed E . . .2G 33
Wellington Rd. SO18: South . . .1F 31
Well La. SO31: Hamb 5G 47
Wellowbrook Cl.
 SO53: Cha F 1C 14
Wellow Cl. SO18: South 4C 32
Wellow Ct. SO18: South 3G 31
Wellow Gdns.
 PO14: Titch C 5G 49
Wells Cl. PO15: White 5G 45
Wellsmoor PO14: Titch C 5G 49
Wells Rd. SO50: E'leigh 5B 16
Wellstead Way
 SO30: Hed E 1H 33
Wembley Way SO50: Fair O . . .2F 17
Wendleholme
 Nature Reserve 3A 48
Wentworth Gdns.
 SO19: South 4B 42
 SO45: Holb 6D 54
Wentworth Gro. SO45: Holb . . .5D 54
Wesley Cl. SO19: South 1D 42
Wessex Bus. Pk.
 SO21: Col C 5G 11
Wessex Cl. SO45: Blac 5F 55
Wessex Ct. SO17: South 3C 30
 SO19: South 1A 42
Wessex Gdns. SO51: Rom 5E 7
Wessex Ga. SO15: South 4A 30
Wessex La. SO18: S'ing 6F 23
WESSEX NUFFIELD HEALTH
 HOSPITAL 4A 10
Wessex Rd. SO18: W End 6B 24
Wessex Vale Crematorium . . .5H 25
Wessex Way SO21: Col C 5G 11
West Bargate
 SO14: South 4D 4 (1B 40)
West Bay Rd.
 SO15: South 3A 4 (5E 29)
Westbourne Av. SO45: Holb . . .4C 54
Westbourne Cres.
 SO17: South 2C 30
Westbourne Mans.
 SO17: South 2C 30
Westbroke Gdns. SO51: Rom 3C 6
Westbrook Cl. SO31: P Ga 1E 49
Westbrook Way SO18: S'ing . . .5G 23
Westbury Cl. SO30: Hed E 6H 33
Westbury Rd. SO15: South 4D 28
Westcliff Pl. SO17: South 2F 41
Westcliff Wlk. SO45: Hythe . . .1D 52
 (off Waterside)
WEST COMMON 6E 55
West Comn. SO45: Blac 6E 55
Westcot Rd. SO45: Holb 5B 54
West Ct. SO15: South 3F 29
West Dr. SO50: B'stke 3D 16
WEST END 2D 32
West End Local History Mus.
 . . . . .2D 32
W. End Rd.
 SO18: South, W End 4H 31
 SO19: South 1F 43
 SO30: W End 2D 32
 SO31: Burs 1F 43
Westering SO51: Rom 3F 7
Westerley Cl. SO31: Wars 6C 48
Western Av. SO15: South 6D 28
WESTERN COMMUNITY HOSPITAL
 . . . . .2E 29
Western District Cut
 SO15: South 4H 29
Western Esplanade
 SO14: South 2B 4 (6A 30)
 (Central Sta. Bri.)
 SO14: South 6D 4 (2B 40)
 (Town Quay)
 SO15: South 4B 4 (1A 40)
Western Rd. SO30: W End 2D 32
 SO53: Cha F 4G 9

Westfield Cl. SO31: Hamb 5E 47
Westfield Comn.
 SO31: Hamb 5D 46
Westfield Cnr. SO18: S'ing 4G 23
Westfield Cres. SO53: Cha F . . .3E 15
Westfield Rd. SO15: South 4E 29
 SO40: Tott 3F 27
 SO53: Cha F 4E 15
Westgate Hall 6D 4
Westgate M. SO30: W End 2E 33
Westgate St.
 SO14: South 6D 4 (2B 40)
W. Hill Ct.
 SO15: South 1B 4 (6A 30)
W. Hill Dr. SO45: Hythe 1D 52
W. Horton Cl. SO50: B'stke 5F 17
W. Horton La. SO50: B'stke 6F 17
West La. SO52: N Bad 2C 12
Westmarch St. SO17: South . . .1E 31
W. Marlands Rd.
 SO14: South 2D 4 (6B 30)
Westminster Gdns.
 PO14: Titch C 4G 49
Westmorland Way
 SO53: Cha F 1G 15
WESTON 4H 41
Weston Cl. SO19: South 4H 41
WESTON COMMON 1C 42
Weston Ct. SO19: South 5H 41
Weston Cres. SO18: South 4C 32
Weston Gro. Rd.
 SO19: South 3F 41
Weston La. SO16: Nur 5G 19
 SO19: South 5G 41
Weston Pde. SO19: South 5G 41
Weston Rd. SO50: E'leigh 4A 16
Weston Sailing Club 6H 41
West Pk. Lodge SO17: South . .2C 30
 (off Westwood Rd.)
West Pk. Rd.
 SO15: South 2C 4 (6B 30)
West Quay Retail Pk. . . .3B 4 (1A 40)
W. Quay Rd.
 SO15: South 2A 4 (1A 40)
 (Southern Rd.)
 SO15: South 2C 30
 (W. Quay Rd. Ind. Est.)
W. Quay Rd. Ind. Est.
 SO15: South 5B 4 (2A 40)
Westquay Shop. Cen. . . .3D 4 (1B 40)
Westquay South 4D 4 (1B 40)
Westridge Ct. SO17: South . . .2D 30
Westridge Rd. SO17: South . . .2D 30
West Rd. SO19: South 3G 41
 SO30: Hed E 5F 33
 SO45: Dib P 5B 52
 SO45: Hard 5H 53
Westrow Gdns. SO15: South . . .4A 30
Westrow Rd. SO15: South 4A 30
West St. SO14: South 5D 4 (2B 40)
 SO45: Hythe 1D 52
Westward Rd. SO30: Hed E . . .3A 34
Westways Cl. SO16: Nur 4B 20
Westwood Bus. Pk.
 SO40: Tott 6D 18
Westwood Ct. SO17: South . . .2C 30
 SO30: W End 2D 32
 SO40: Tott 1E 27
Westwood Gdns. SO53: Cha F . .5G 9
Westwood Mans.
 SO17: South 2C 30
WESTWOOD PARK 2C 30
Westwood Rd. SO17: South . . .3B 30
 SO31: Net A 6B 42
Westwood Woodland Pk. 5A 42
Wetherby Cl. SO40: Tott 3C 26
Wetherby Gdns. SO40: Tott . . .3C 26
Wey Cl. SO53: Cha F 1D 48
Whalesmead Cl.
 SO50: B'stke 6F 17
Whalesmead Rd.
 SO50: B'stke 5F 17
Wharf Rd. SO19: South 2F 41
Wharncliffe Ho. SO19: South . .2F 41
Wharncliffe Rd. SO19: South . .2F 41
Whartons Cl. SO40: A'hst 2C 36
Whartons La. SO40: A'hst 1C 36
Wheat Cl. SO53: Cha F 1B 14
Wheatcroft Dr. SO18: South . . .2B 32
Wheatlands PO14: Titch C 3G 49
Wheatsheaf Ct. SO30: Hed E . .5H 33
Wheelers Mdw.
 SO31: Old N 4E 43
Wheelers Wlk. SO45: Blac 5F 55

Wheelhouse Pk. Cvn. Pk. 4C 8
Whernside Cl. SO16: South 3D 28
Whinchat Cl. SO16: South 3F 21
Whinfield Rd. SO45: Dib P 5C 52
Whistler Cl. SO19: South 2C 42
Whistler Rd. SO19: South 2C 42
Whitchurch Ct. SO19: South . . .2H 41
Whitcombe Cl. SO40: Tott 4E 27
Whitebeam Cl. SO21: Col C . . .5G 11
Whitebeam Rd. SO30: Hed E . .5B 34
Whitebeam Way
 SO52: N Bad 2E 13
Whitecroft SO45: Hythe 4E 53
Whitefield Rd. SO45: Holb 5C 54
White Harmony Acres Ind. Est.
 SO30: W End 4E 25
White Hart Rd. SO50: Fair O . . .2F 17
Whitehaven Home Pk.
 SO45: Blac 5E 55
White Heather Ct.
 SO45: Hythe 1E 53
Whitehill Cl. SO18: South 3C 32
Whitehouse Gdns.
 SO15: South 5E 29
Whitelaw Rd. SO15: South 4F 29
White Rd. SO50: B'stke 3D 16
Whites La. SO45: F'ley 2H 55
White's Rd. SO19: South 6A 32
White Star Pl.
 SO14: South 5G 5 (2D 40)
White Star Way
 SO14: South 3C 40
Whitestone Cl. SO16: South . . .3D 28
Whites Way SO30: Hed E 1H 33
Whitewater Ri. SO45: Dib P . . .4D 52
Whitedwood Av.
 SO15: South 3H 29
Whittington Cl. SO45: Hythe . . .4D 52
Whittle Av. PO15: Seg 2G 49
Whitwell SO31: Net A 6C 42
Whitworth Ct. SO18: South 3F 31
Whitworth Cres.
 SO18: South 3F 31
Whitworth Rd. SO18: South . . .3F 31
Whyte Cl. SO45: Holb 5B 54
Whyteways SO50: E'leigh 3A 16
The Wicket SO45: Hythe 4D 52
Wickham Cl. SO40: Tott 4E 27
Wickham Ho. SO17: South 2C 30
Wickham Rd. SO32: Curd 4G 35
Wicklow Dr. SO53: Cha F 2C 14
Widecombe Dr. SO45: Hythe . . .2C 52
Wide La.
 SO18: S'ing, S'ton A 4G 23
 SO50: E'leigh 2H 23
Wide Lane Sports Complex . . .2H 23
Widgeon Cl. SO16: South 3F 21
Wightway M. SO31: Wars 6A 48
Wild Arum Way
 SO53: Cha F 2B 14
Wildburn Cl. SO40: Calm 1C 26
Wild Cherry Way
 SO53: Cha F 1C 14
Wilde Cl. SO40: Tott 4D 26
WILDERN 3A 34
Wildern Cl. SO31: Loc H 4D 48
Wildern Ct. SO30: Hed E 3H 33
Wilderness Hgts.
 SO18: W End 2C 32
Wildern La. SO30: Hed E 3A 34
Wildern Leisure Cen. 4A 34
Wildground La. SO45: Hythe . . .5E 53
Wild Rose Cres.
 SO31: Loc H 5C 48
Wildwood Cl. PO14: Titch C . . .1H 51
Wilkins Rd. SO30: Hed E 4A 34
Wilks Cl. SO16: Nur 4A 20
William Ho. SO16: South 4E 21
William Macleod Way
 SO16: South 2E 29
William Panter Ct.
 SO50: E'leigh 5A 16
Williams Cl. SO45: Holb 5D 54
William St. SO14: South 6E 31
Willis Av. SO52: N Bad 3F 13
Willis Rd. SO16: S'ing 4F 23

Willment Marine & Bus. Pk.
 SO19: South 1F 41
Willments Ind. Est.
 SO19: South 2E 41
Willow Cl. SO30: Hed E 5B 34
 SO30: W End 1E 33
Willow Ct. SO16: South 6E 21
Willow Dr. SO40: March 5D 38
Willow Gdns. SO52: N Bad 2D 12
Willow Grn. SO21: Col C 5G 11
Willow Gro. SO50: Fair O 1G 17
Willow Herb Cl.
 SO31: Loc H 5C 48
Willow Mead SO30: Hed E 3H 33
The Willows PO14: Titch C 3G 49
 SO30: W End 1E 33
 SO53: Cha F 4E 15
Willow Tree Wlk.
 SO19: South 2B 42
Wills Way SO51: Rom 6D 6
Wilmer Rd. SO50: E'leigh 5A 16
Wilmington Cl. SO18: South . . .6H 23
Wilmot Cl. SO50: B'stke 2E 17
Wilroy Gdns. SO16: Southampton .1D 28
Wilson St.
 SO14: South 1H 5 (6E 31)
Wilton Av. SO15: South 5A 30
Wilton Ct. SO15: South 3H 29
Wilton Cres. SO15: South 2H 29
Wilton Gdns. SO15: South 2H 29
Wilton Mnr. SO15: South 5B 30
 (off Wilton Av.)
Wilton Rd. SO15: South 1G 29
Wilshire Rd. SO53: Cha F 4F 15
Wilverley Pl. SO45: Blac 4E 55
Wimborne Ho. SO16: South . . .2D 28
WIMPSON 2D 28
Wimpson Gdns.
 SO16: South 2D 28
Wimpson La. SO16: South 3C 28
Winchester Cl. SO31: Net A . . .1B 46
 SO51: Rom 3E 7
Winchester Hill SO51: Rom 5D 6
Winchester Rd.
 SO16: Bass, South 2E 29
 SO16: Chil 1C 22
 SO32: Botl 1C 34
 SO50: Fair O 1F 17, 3H 17
 SO51: Cram, Rom 3F 7
 SO51: Rom 5C 6
 SO53: Cha F 1E 15
Winchester St. SO15: South . . .5B 30
 SO30: Botl 3D 34
Winchester Way SO40: Tott . . .4C 26
Winchfield Cl. SO19: South 4A 42
Windbury Rd. SO16: South 1C 28
Windermere Av.
 SO16: South 1B 28
Windermere Gdns.
 SO40: Tott 3E 27
Windermere Rd.
 SO18: W End 2B 32
Windfield Dr. SO51: Rom 4E 7
WINDHOVER RDBT. 3F 43
Windmill Copse
 SO45: Dib P 5D 52
Windmill La. SO31: Burs 3G 43
Windover Cl. SO19: South 5C 32
Windrush Cl. SO45: Hythe 3F 53
Windrush Rd. SO16: South 2C 28
Windrush Way SO45: Hythe . . .3E 53
Windsor Ct. SO15: South 5E 29
 (off Regent's Pk. Rd.)
 SO17: South 3C 30
 (Candlemas Pl.)
 SO17: South 3C 30
 (Kinterbury Ct.)
 SO18: South 4G 31
 SO50: B'stke 3D 16
Windsor Ga. SO50: E'leigh 1A 16
Windsor Pl. SO21: Col C 4F 11
Windsor Rd. SO40: Tott 5G 27
Windsor Ter.
 SO14: South 2D 4 (6B 30)
Winfrid Ho. SO40: Tott 4D 26
Winfrith Way SO16: South 4B 20
Wingate Dr. SO19: South 6B 32
Wingate Rd. SO40: Tott 3D 26
Wingrove Rd. SO40: A'hst 2C 36
Winifred Cl. SO50: Fair O 1F 17
Winkle St.
 SO14: South 6E 5 (3C 40)
Winnards Pk. SO31: Sar G 3B 48
Winn Rd. SO17: South 3B 30
Winsford Av. SO50: B'stke 6G 17

Winsford Cl. SO50: B'stke 6G 17
Winsford Gdns. SO50: B'stke ..6G 17
Winstanley Rd. SO16: Nur 4A 20
Winston Cl. SO16: South 1D 28
 SO50: E'leigh 3A 16
Winstone Cres. SO52: N Bad ..4E 13
Winterbourne Rd.
 SO51: Rom 3E 7
Winters Cl. SO45: Holb 5D 54
Winters Pl. SO50: E'leigh 5B 10
Winton Cl. SO30: W End 2D 32
Winton St.
 SO14: South 2F 5 (6C 30)
  (not continuous)
Witham Cl. SO53: Cha F 1C 14
Witherbed La. PO15: Seg 3H 49
  (not continuous)
Withers Rd. SO51: Rom 1E 7
Withewood Mans.
 SO15: South 4G 29
Withy Cl. SO51: Rom 4C 6
Wittering Rd. SO16: South ...4E 21
Witt Rd. SO50: Fair O 1F 17
Witts Hill SO18: South 2H 31
Woburn Cl. SO50: E'leigh 1A 16
Woburn Rd. SO16: South 4F 21
Wodehouse Rd.
 SO19: South 1G 41
Wolseley Rd. SO15: South ...4G 29
Wolverley Ct. SO16: South ...6H 21
Wolverton Rd.
 SO14: South 1G 5 (6D 30)
Wolvesey Pl. SO53: Cha F ...3C 14
Wonston Rd. SO16: South 5F 21
Woodbind Wlk.
 SO31: Loc H 5D 48
Woodcote Rd. SO17: South ...6E 23
Wood Cl. SO19: South 2C 42
Wood End Way SO53: Cha F ...1C 14
Wooderson Cl. SO50: Fair O ..4H 17
Woodglade Cl. SO40: March ..4D 38
Woodgreen Wlk.
 SO40: Calm 2B 26
WOODHAVEN 1A 26
Woodhouse La. SO30: Botl ...4B 34
The Woodland SO53: Cha F 4C 8

Woodland Cl. SO18: South 4D 32
Woodland Drove
 SO21: Col C 2G 11
Woodland Gdns. SO45: Blac ...5E 55
Woodland M. SO30: W End 2D 32
Woodland Pl. SO15: South 4A 30
Woodlands Cl. SO31: Sar G ...1D 48
 SO45: Dib P 5C 52
 SO53: Cha F 3F 9
Woodlands Ct. SO45: Dib P ...5C 52
Woodlands Dr. SO31: Net A ...1D 46
Woodlands Drove
 SO40: A'hst 2A 36
Woodlands Gdns. SO51: Rom ...3E 7
Woodlands Rd.
 SO40: A'hst, Woodl, Net M
  ....6A 26, 3A 36
Woodlands Way
 SO15: South 3B 30
 SO31: Burs 5F 43
 SO52: N Bad 3D 12
Woodland Vale SO19: South ...1B 42
Woodland Vw. SO31: Burs 5F 43
Woodlea Gdns.
 SO30: W End 2E 33
Woodlea Way SO51: Ampf 3B 8
WOODLEY 2F 7
Woodley Cl. SO51: Rom 2F 7
Woodley Cl. Flats
 SO51: Rom 2F 7
Woodley Grange SO51: Rom ...3F 7
Woodley La. SO51: Rom 4D 6
Woodley Rd. SO19: South 2F 41
Woodley Way SO51: Rom 2F 7
Wood Lodge SO40: Calm 2B 26
Woodmill La. SO18: S'ing 6F 23
Woodmill Outdoor Activities Cen.
  ....6F 23
Woodmoor Cl. SO40: March ...4E 39
Woodpecker Copse
 SO31: Loc H 4F 49
Woodpecker Dr.
 SO40: March 4C 38
Woodpecker Way
 SO50: E'leigh 5F 15
Wood Rd. SO40: A'hst 3B 36

Woodrush Cres.
 SO31: Loc H 5C 48
Woodside SO16: Chil 5A 14
Woodside Av. SO50: E'leigh ..4G 15
Woodside Cl. SO40: March ...4C 38
Woodside Ct. SO17: South ...3D 30
Woodside Cres. SO16: Chil ...5H 13
Woodside Gdns.
 SO40: A'hst 2C 36
Woodside Rd. SO17: South ...3D 30
 SO50: E'leigh 3G 15
 SO52: N Bad 3D 12
Woodside Way
 SO30: Hed E 6G 33
Woodstock Cl. SO30: Hed E ...6B 34
Woodstock Dr. SO17: South ...2C 30
Woodthorpe Gdns.
 SO31: Sar G 1D 48
Woodview Cl. SO16: Bass 3C 22
Woodview Pk. Cvn. Pk. 4G 35
Woodville Rd. SO45: F'ley ...2H 55
Woolley Ho. SO14: South 2F 5
WOOLSTON 4F 41
Woolston Rd. SO31: Net A ...5B 42
Woolston Station (Rail) 2F 41
Woolwich Cl. SO31: Burs 3F 43
Wootton SO31: Net A 6C 42
Worcester Pl. SO19: South ...3B 42
Wordsworth Pl. PO15: White ..4G 45
Wordsworth Rd.
 SO15: South 2G 29
Workman's La. SO31: Wars ...3C 50
Wren Rd. SO50: E'leigh 6G 15
Wright's Hill SO19: South 3A 42
Wrights Wlk. SO31: Burs 4F 43
Wryneck Cl. SO16: South 3E 21
Wychwood Dr. SO45: Blac 6E 55
Wychwood Gro. SO53: Cha F ...5G 9
Wycliffe Rd. SO18: South 2A 32
Wykeham Cl. SO16: Bass 5A 22
 SO31: Net A 1B 46
Wykeham Rd. SO31: Net A ...1B 46
Wylye Cl. SO18: W End 6B 24
Wyndham Ct.
 SO15: South 1B 4 (6A 30)
Wyndham Dr. SO51: Rom 1E 7

Wyndham Pl.
 SO15: South 1B 4 (6A 30)
Wynsdale Chase
 SO31: Wars 2A 50
Wynter Rd. SO18: South 3B 32
Wynyards Gap SO52: N Bad ...3D 12
Wyre Cl. SO53: Cha F 1D 14
Wyvern Cl. SO53: Cha F 1F 15
Wyvern Leisure Cen. 2F 17

Y

Yachtsman Cl. SO31: Burs 5A 44
Yardley Rd. SO30: Hed E 6H 33
Yarmouth Gdns.
 SO15: South 2F 29
Yarrow Way SO31: Loc H 5C 48
Yaverland SO31: Net A 1C 46
Yeats Cl. PO15: White 4G 45
Yelverton Av. SO45: Hythe ...5E 53
Yeomans Way SO40: Tott 3F 27
Yeovil Chase SO18: South 3B 32
Yewberry Way SO53: Cha F ...1A 14
Yew Rd. SO18: South 3A 32
Yew Tree Cl. SO30: Hed E 5H 33
 SO45: Hythe 6E 53
 SO50: Fair O 1F 17
Yew Tree Ct. SO30: W End ...2E 33
 SO31: Swanw 6F 45
Yew Tree Dr. PO15: White 6F 45
Yewtree La. SO16: Nur 6A 20
Yonge Cl. SO50: E'leigh 4B 16
York Cl. SO14: South 5E 31
 SO40: Tott 3C 27
 SO53: Cha F 3B 14
Yorkdale SO31: Wars 4A 48
York Drove SO18: South 4B 32
Yorke Way SO31: Hamb 4E 47
York Ga. SO14: South 4E 5 (1C 40)
York Ho. SO14: South 5E 31
York Rd. SO15: South 4G 29
 SO31: Net A 1A 46
 SO50: E'leigh 1A 24
York Wlk.
 SO14: South 4E 5 (1C 40)

SAFETY CAMERA INFORMATION

PocketGPSWorld.com's CamerAlert is a self-contained speed and red light camera warning system for SatNavs and Android or Apple iOS smartphones/tablets. Visit www.cameralert.com to download.

Safety camera locations are publicised by the Safer Roads Partnership which operates them in order to encourage drivers to comply with speed limits at these sites. It is the driver's absolute responsibility to be aware of and to adhere to speed limits at all times.

By showing this safety camera information it is the intention of Geographers' A-Z Map Company Ltd. to encourage safe driving and greater awareness of speed limits and vehicle speed. Data accurate at time of printing.

Printed and bound in the United Kingdom by Gemini Press Ltd., Shoreham-by-Sea, West Sussex
Printed on materials from a sustainable source